John Sampson

The Northern genealogist

John Sampson

The Northern genealogist

ISBN/EAN: 9783743332713

Manufactured in Europe, USA, Canada, Australia, Japa

Cover: Foto ©ninafisch / pixelio.de

Manufactured and distributed by brebook publishing software (www.brebook.com)

John Sampson

The Northern genealogist

JANUARY 1897.

THE
Northern Genealogist.

CONTENTS:

	PAGE		PAGE
Title page and Contents for 1896		Durham, Carlisle, and Allertonshire Marriage Bonds..	39
Notes and Queries	1	Peculiar Jurisdiction of St. Leonard's Hospital, York	42
Papist Returns, 18th Century	4		
Lincoln Marriage Bonds..	9	Act Books of the Prerogative Court of York	44
St. Peter's, York—School Register	13		
The Rebellion of 1745	17	Langton of Langton, co. Lincoln	48
Some Richmond Wills	25	Stonehouse—A Cleveland Catholic Family	50
Clay Coton Parish Register	29	Startforth Parish Register	54
Marriage Bonds of the Dean and Chapter of York	33	Supplement—	
Rokeby Family—Bible Fly-leaves	37	Richmondshire Wills ..	25

Subscription 10s. 6d. per annum.

YORK:

PRINTED BY JOHN SAMPSON, 13, CONEY STREET.

WORKS BY THE SAME EDITOR.

EARLY LINCOLN WILLS; an Abstract of all the Wills and Administrations recorded in the Episcopal Registers at Lincoln, 1280—1547, 8vo. 21/-.

LIBER ANTIQUUS HUGONIS WELLS, Episcopi Lincolniensis; comprising the Endowments of Vicarages in Oxfordshire, Bucks., Beds., Hunts., Herts., Northants., Rutland, and Lincolnshire. 1209—1235, 8vo. 10/6.

LINCOLN MARRIAGE LICENCES; an Abstract of the Allegation Books preserved in the Registry of the Bishop of Lincoln, 1598—1628, 8vo. 15/-.

ELY EPISCOPAL RECORDS; a Calendar and Concise View of the Records preserved in the Muniment Room of the Palace at Ely. Compiled by direction of the Rt. Rev. Alwyne, Lord Bishop of Ely, 8vo. 42/-.

REPORTS on the Registry of the Bishop of Lincoln, and on the Records of the Corporation of Grimsby. Compiled for Her Majesty's Hist. MSS. Commission.

YORK WILLS INDEXES, 1544—1553 and 1554—1568. Compiled for the Yorkshire Archæological Society. (*In Progress.*)

NOTES ON THE HERALDS' VISITATION OF LINCOLNSHIRE in 1634. With Supplements containing Indexes of the Wills in the Consistory Court and the Court of the Dean and Chapter at Lincoln, 8vo. (*In Progress.*)

The Northern Genealogist is issued quarterly, in January, April, July, and October, and is supplied to subscribers only, at 10s. 6d. per annum, payable in advance.

Notes, Articles, or Queries, on Antiquarian subjects, will be gladly received, as also Books or Articles for review.

Terms for Advertisements can be had on application.

The Editor personally undertakes Genealogical and Antiquarian Researches in any part of the Kingdom, and, in questions not involving such research, will be happy to give to Subscribers, free of charge, any advice or assistance in his power.

Transcripts or Abstracts of Wills, &c., in London, or in the York or other Provincial Registries, are supplied according to Scale of Charges to be had on application.

All communications to be addressed to

A. GIBBONS, F.S.A.,

Heworth, York.

The Northern Genealogist.

NOTES AND QUERIES.

A curious, as well as interesting and instructive discussion has lately been going on in the public press—not only in the daily papers, but in weekly journals so far removed from each other as the *Saturday Review* and *Punch*—as to the alleged misdemeanour of using Armorial Bearings without authority from the College of Arms. We say "curious" because, as we are told, those who can read between the lines see more in this apparently frivolous discussion than appears on the surface to the general public.

We have no desire to enter the argumentative arena, but to a disinterested onlooker, many of the arguments and suggestions are very amusing, and savour more of *Punch* than of the *Saturday Review*. For instance, there appears in the *Standard* an amusing, but apparently perfectly serious proposal, by a gentleman of high standing, for the formation of an Armorial Club, one of the qualifications for which shall be the production of a certificate from the Heralds of the candidate's right to Arms.

All mortals are divided into two classes: those authorised by the Heralds to bear Arms, and those not authorised. By the way, it seems to have escaped the notice of the Heralds (or rather of their too officious supporters, for we are sure that the Heralds themselves have no part in this controversy), that the Excise Licence to use Armorial Bearings also emanates from the Crown, the Fountain of Honour, and is *prima facie* as good an article at a guinea as that offered by the Earl Marshal at £76 10s.! Then those mortals who bear Arms, authorised only by the Excise Licence, are further considered under three heads. First, the man who wilfully adopts the Arms belonging to another family, or invents and uses Arms without authority: This man is a common cheat. Secondly, the

A

man who continues to use Arms, to which he knows he is not entitled, on the ground that his father or grandfather used them before him : This man is a swindler, but in a lesser degree. (We hope it is not necessary to remark that these epithets are not ours, but are quotations.) Thirdly, the man who bears the name of an armigerous family, and who conscientiously believes that he is descended from that family, but is unable to furnish conclusive proof sufficient to satisfy the College of Arms. This man, unlike the others, preserves his self-respect, and need only apply to the College for a new grant. This seems at first sight a little hard on a man (and there are many such) whose Arms date back to a time when the College was not in existence ; but on the other hand he would then, no doubt, be eligible for the Armorial Club.

If, however, this Armorial Club proposal is really dictated by a desire to distinguish between families who are entitled to bear Ancestral Arms, and those who have only a new grant from the Heralds, it seems intelligible enough and sensible enough too, but the gist of the whole discussion has been to distinguish between those who are "authorised" to bear Arms, and those who are not ; and in this sense, anyone who cares to spend £76 10s. in Queen Victoria Street on a new grant, can annihilate "that distinction of birth, which, be it remembered, no money can buy, and not even the Fountain of Honour can bestow."

* * * * *

Many antiquaries will be glad to hear that the Dean and Chapter of York are having their inestimable collection of Muniments in York Minster arranged and calendared. Few people are aware of the extent of the ancient jurisdiction of the Liberty of St. Peter, which included places in counties so far south as Devonshire, and, in fact, apparently everywhere where the Dean and Chapter had property. So long as our much-lamented Canon Raine lived, these Muniments seemed to belong peculiarly to his province, and, had he lived and his health permitted, he would, no doubt, have performed this work in a far more able and satisfactory manner than Mr. Gibbons, who has now undertaken it, can ever hope to do. A similar work is also being carried out with regard to the Archbishop's Manuscripts at Bishopthorpe, of which some trifling specimens are printed in the following pages.

* * * * *

By the courtesy of Dr. G. B. Longstaff, we have had an opportunity of seeing the first proof sheets of his forthcoming work on the Longstaff and Langstaff families. He seems to have been at very great pains to collect information as to the various families bearing the name, and the work will, no doubt, be one of considerable value. A curious instance of early migration is found in the prevalence of the name in the neighbourhood of Horncastle in Lincolnshire, where one would little expect to find a Cumberland or Westmoreland family, but it is no doubt explained, by the early Longstaffs having come thither in the train of the Bishops of Carlisle, who held the Manor of Horncastle from the reign of Henry 3 to that of Edward 6, and who, when their See was laid waste by the Scots in the Border Wars, made it for some considerable time their principal residence. It would be interesting to ascertain what other families in the neighbourhood owe their Lincolnshire origin to this cause. Dr. Longstaff, whose address is The Highlands, Putney Heath, London, S.W., would be grateful for any information (especially for references to isolated marriages), and would be glad to enter into correspondence with any person of the name, or allied by marriage, who may be interested.

* * *

Trollope. Copy of entry in parish register required of the marriage of Thomas Trollope, about 1753, probably at or near Louth, Lincolnshire. Also copies of entries of the baptisms of his children Thomas, Frances, and Joseph, in 1754, 1755, and 1756. £2 reward.

Address—C. G. NAPIER TROLLOPE, Esq.,
49, Warwick Gardens,
Kensington, W.

Fairfax. £15 reward will be paid by the Editor for evidence (satisfactory to the College of Arms) of the identity of Joseph Fairfax, bapt. at Saxton, co. York, March 27, 1706, with Joseph Fairfax, buried at Windlesham, co. Surrey, June 22, 1783, aged 77. A reward will also be paid for any information as to the family, which may prove of service as a clue to the above.

PAPIST RETURNS TO THE ARCHBISHOPS OF YORK,

In the 18th Century.

The following specimens are taken at random from the original Returns, in order to show their great value for Genealogical and Historical purposes.

Papists, 1735. Abberford.

In that part of the town of Abberford which is in the parish of Abberford:—
John Bell, a taylor.
The wife of Thomas Smith, labourer.
Thomas Simpson, grocer, and his wife, and Mary his daughter.
Anne Price, a boarder with Thomas Simpson, grocer.
—— Davis, a reputed priest living with Thomas Simpson, grocer.
Hannah Bell, and Anne her daughter.
Elizabeth, wife of Gabriel Thomlinson, shoemaker.
Anthony Saxton, a farmer.
Stephen Bustard, taylor, and his wife.
Richard Pepper, labourer, and his wife.
Mary, the daughter of Elizabeth Chandler, innholder.
Anne Ellison, servant-maid to Thomas Simpson, grocer.
Gertrude Ellison, servant-maid to Anthony Saxton, farmer.

In that part of the town of Abberford which is in the parish of Sherburn. In the town of Parlington in the parish of Abberford, are:—
Sir Edward Gascoign, bart., and his lady.
Jonathan Gladall, butler to Sir Edward Gascoign.
John Pickering, stable-groom.
Nicholas Le Beck, cook.

Nicholas Banes, porter.
Frances Johnson, chamber-maid.
Mary Witherington, house-keeper.
Jane Richardson, the lady's-maid.
Ann Milner, a chamber-maid.
Ann Lassey, cook-maid.
The laundress: could not learn her name.
—— Rogers, supposed chaplain to Sir Edward.
Mr. — Hammond, a boarder with Sir Edward.
John Cheatham, his servant.
Robert Hartley, merchant, and Jane his daughter.
Temperance, the wife of Robert Thorus, farmer.
Eleanor, the wife of John Sparling, carpenter.
Elizabeth Hewit, widdow.
John Hunter, labourer, and Frances his wife, and a daughter.
Paul Gilmore, a reputed priest.
Mary Bywater, widow.
Richard Hastings: uncertain whether 13 years old or not.
George Barker, farmer, and Barbara his wife.

Mass is said to be performed in the house of Sir Edward Gascoign, in Parlington, by Mr. Rogers his chaplain; and in the same town by Mr. Paul Gilmore, a reputed priest, at his own lodgings.

It doth not appear that any popish school is taught in the parish, but there are grounds of suspicion that Paul Gilmore, above mentioned, is guilty of such a practice.

Can hear of none that have been perverted for several years past, but one or two at the point of death about four years since.

Papists, 1735.   Leeds.

Anne Jackson, widow, and her daughter.
John Jackson, a datal cloth dresser.
John Robshaw, and his wife, and Mary their daughter.
John Grocock, a root-seller.

Richard Grocock, a fiddler.
John Northouse, a root-seller, and his wife and daughter.
Peter Railton, a datal cloth dresser, and his wife and daughter.
Wm. Pickering, whitesmith, and his wife.
Thomas Peart, a woolcomber.
Wm. Tolson and his wife.
John, son of Mr. John Wade, a merchant, who was perverted in Flanders two years ago.
Elizabeth Thorp, who teaches a sewing school in this town, her husband living at Middleton in the parish of Rothwell.

We have no popish priest, or any suspected to be such.

No house or place in our parish in which mass is understood to be performed. No popish school.

No Visitation or Confirmation hath been understood to have been held amongst us by any popish bishop.

(Signed) Jos. Cookson, *Vicar*.

EVERINGHAM, 1767.

Name.	Occupation.	Residence.	Age
Wm. H. Constable, esq.	...	12 years	32
Winefrid, his lady	...	8 ,,	...
Catherine Constable	...	...	5
Wm. Fleetwood	Gentleman	12 ,,	63
Charles Pegge	Butler	2 months	...
Mary Goodrick	Housekeeper	4 ,,	43
Mary Smith	Servant	2 years	42
Wm. Lazenby	,,	1 ,,	17
Ann Oakland	,,	3 months	22
Ann Randerson	,,	1 year	20
Mary Bates	,,	1 ,,	22
Catherine Yeoman	,,	3 months	22
Philip Londsbro'	,,	...	...
Thomas Maltas	Farmer	Native	41
Barbara, his wife	...	,,	48
Marmaduke Beal	Labourer	,,	69
Ann, his wife	...	,,	62

In Mr. Constable's family. (bracket covering Charles Pegge through Philip Londsbro')

Name.	Occupation.	Residence.	Age
Matthew Beal	Taylor	Native	33
Dorotha, his wife	...	,,	33
Rebecca	...	,,	10
John	Their children	,,	7
Mary	...	,,	1
Mary Jackson, widow	...	,,	75
John Catton	...	,,	84
William Baxter	Butcher	,,	50
Mary, his wife	...	,,	42
John	...	,,	13
Alice	Their children	,,	11
Mary	...	,,	8
Matthew Bentley	Farmer	30 years	52
Mary, his wife	...	Native	51
John	...	,,	26
Sarah	...	,,	21
Elizabeth	Their children	,,	16
Jane	...	,,	14
Ann	...	,,	15
Agnes	...	,,	11
Francis Whelton	Labourer	28 years	...
Elizabeth, his wife	...	...	...
Ann, their daughter	...	...	2
Richard Marshal	Farmer	9 years	30
Mary, his wife	...	...	28
John		...	2
Richard, an infant	Their children	...	...
John Marshal	...	...	...
Mary Jackson, widow	...	Native	67
John, her son	Grocer	,,	38
Ann Norrey	...	,,	29
Mary, her daughter	...	,,	4
Ann Kemply, widow	Farmer	10 years	48
Thomas	...	...	24
Ursula	Her children	...	20
Henry	...	...	12
Ann	...	...	11

Name.	Occupation.	Residence.	Age
Robert Wilson	Farmer	10 years	57
Elizabeth	...	...	14
Mary	} His children	...	12
Sarah		...	10
Robert Dean	Farmer	Native	64
Prudence, his wife	...	,,	60
Peter	} Their children	...	24
Robert		...	21
Grandchild	...	...	6
Philip Dean	Farmer	Native	21
Joseph Catton	Land Steward	,,	52
Elizabeth, his wife	...	...	45
Mary		...	18
Ann		...	17
Thomas	Their children	...	16
Joseph		...	14
Sarah		...	7
John		...	4
John Holmes	Servant	...	23
Elenor Norris	,,	...	24
Sarah Clark	Farmer	30 years	42
Mary Rudd		...	17
Ann Rudd	Her children	...	14
Sarah Rudd		...	11
John Rudd		...	6
Mary Plowman	...	3 years	31
Ann	} Her children	...	3
Mary		...	1
William Lane	...	14 years	28
Philip Lonsbro'	Servant	6 ,,	35
John How	...	6 ,,	30

LINCOLN MARRIAGE LICENCES.*

1666. Dec. 29. Brownley, Thomas, of Barnsly, co. York, and
Elizth. Lambe, of St. Benedict's, Lincoln, widow. Surety,
Roger Wescom (?) of the City of Lincoln, saddle tree maker.
[St. Benedict or South Carlton.]

1591. May 17. Act Book.—Brownerige, Oswald, of Kirton, and
Alice Purye, of same. [St. Michael on Mount.]

1661. Nov. 11. Brownsword, John, citizen of London, and Margt.
Ashurst, of Grantham, spinster. Surety, Robert White, of
Lincoln, tradesman. [Grantham.]

1604. Feb. 4. C.—Bruce, Bushop, of Goldington, co. Bedford,
yeoman, and Mary Kinge, dau. of Henry Kinge, late vicar
of Steventon, co. Bedford, decd.

1591. Aug. 1. Bucke, Thos., of Billesbie, and Martha Barret, of
Aistrop, in the parish of Willoughby. [St. Peter.]

1585. June 3. Act Book.—Buckminster, Rob., of Frestone, and
Eliz. Burdall, of Butterwick. [St. Michael.]

1665. June 17. Buckminster, Thomas, of the City of Hartford,
tanner, and Mary Saul, of Sleeford, widow. Surety, Wm.
Cooke, of .... carpenter. [Wigtoft or Sutterton.]

1662. July 4. Bucknall, John, of Anderby, husbandman, and
Ffrances Sybrons, of same, spinster. Surety, William
Sybrons, of Mumby, carpenter. [Anderby or Mumbie.]

1663. May 8. Bucknall, John, of East Terrington, husbandman,
and Elizth. Skelton, of same, spinster. Snrety, Thomas
Brightie, of Collowe, in the parish of Leggesbie, yeoman.
[East or West Terrington.]

1663. Feb. 24. Bull, William, of Dunesby, husbandman, æt. 43,
and Bridgett Doncaster, of same, widow, æt. 30. Their
parents are dead. Surety, Wm. Garwell, of Hale Magna,
yeoman. [St. Benedict or St. Peter.]

1633. Feb. 4. Bullimer, Robert, of Gunerby, husbandman, æt. 30,
and Margaret Cant, of Grantham, spinster, æt. 30. Application by Michael Clipsam, of Manthorpe, in the parish of
Grantham, gent. [Grantham.]

* Continued from page 167 of Vol. for 1896.

1631. April 15. Bulson, John, of ...., and Elizth. .... of Eveden, spinster.

1668. Dec. 12. Bunting, Robert, of Asserby, in the parish of Billesby, mercer, and widower, æt. 40, and Ffrances Ffox, of Stallingborrow, widow, æt. 40. Application by Thomas Cooke, of the Close of Lincoln, clerk.
[St. Mark or Stallingborrow.]

1628. Feb. 11. Burbotte, Edward, of Burton Pedwardine, yeoman, æt. 26, and Anne Bell, of Helpringham, spinster, æt. 24.
[Burton Pedwardine.]

1669. May 10. Burchinall, Matthew, of Boston, nauta, æt. 23, and Mary Gannock, of Sibsey, spinster. His parents and her father consent. Surety, Roger Green, of Boston, tapster.
[St. Peter at Arches.]

1637. Aug. 10. Burdis, Peter, of Boston, marriner, æt. 40, and Grace Cooper, of same, widow, æt. 40. Surety, Henry Lonn, of same, gent. [Boston.]

1637. Jan. 18. Burgan, George, of Bonby, æt. 20, and Alice Ffarfoote, of same, spinster, æt. 27. Surety, William Baily, of Worletby. [St. Michael.]

1611. May 16. Burley, Thos., of Gunby, gent. (son of John Burley, of same, clerk, who is bound), and Amy Kirke, *als*. Diccons, of Candlesby, widow, dau. of George Diccons, of Sturton, co. Notts., gent., who is surety.

1599. May 12. C.—Burnebye, William, clerk, (vicar of Helpringham), and Wynifride Browne, of Boston.

1664. April 22. Burnitt, Robert, of Snelland, and Elizth. Laminge, of same, spinster.
[St. Paul in Bail or St. Michael on Mount.]

1634. Dec. 2. Burnitt, Thos., of Boston, ffelmonger, æt. 30, and Anne Creake, of same, widow. [Boston.]

1668. Dec. 7. Burroman, Thomas, of Covenham St. Bartholomew, yeoman, æt. 22, and Ffrances Tompson, of South Elkington, spinster, æt. 22. His parents are dead; her mother consents. [St. Peter at Arches.]

1662. Oct. 15. Burritt, Robert, of Cawkwell, yeoman, and Anne Coa........., *alias* Tomblinson, of Ranbie. Surety, John Chambers, of Cawkwell, sheppard.
[Stan......... Ranby or Cawkwell.]

1668. Nov. 17. Burt, Thomas, of Beckingham, yeoman, and Anne Archer, of same, spinster. Surety, George Archer, of Corringham, yeoman.
[St. Peter at Arches or Beckingham.]

1639. Nov. 1. Burt..., Thomas, of Newarke, co. Notts., gent., and Marie Crosley, of Straglethorp, spinster. Bond by Christr. Crosley, of Haldingham, gent.

1605. Jan. 18. C.—Burton, Brian, rector of Langton juxta Partney, and Elizth. Vaughan, widow of Francis Vaughan, clerk, deceased.

1649. March 1. D.—Burton, John, of Belton, husbandman, and Magdalene Sheacrofte, of Barkston in the Willowes, widow. Witnesses, Leonard Wade (?) and Ben. Sargeint.
[Belton, Gunnerby or Loudonthorpe.]

1661. Dec. 14. Burton, John, of Boston, gent., and Elizth. Hedley, spinster. Surety, Andrew Slee, of Boston, gent. Witness, Thomas Marshall, notary public. (On parchment.)

1664. Feb. 4. Burton, Joseph, of Morton, in the parish of Gainsburgh, cordwainer, æt. 24, and Easter Whittington, of Torksey, spinster, æt. 21. His parents and her father are dead; her mother consents. Surety, William Akes, of Gainsbro', butcher. [St. Paul in Bail or Gainsburgh.]

1665. March 2. Burton, Richard, of Hemswell, yeoman, æt. 36, and Hellen Laming, of Midle Rasin, spinster, æt. 20. Her parents are dead; his mother consents.
[Buslingthorp or Hemswell.]

1585. July 20. Act Book.—Burtonne, Simon, and Eliz. Dimocke.
[Bardney.]

1606. Jan. 26. C.—Burton, Thomas, S.T.B. of ...., chaplain, and Anne Dorrington, of Warboise, co. Hunt., gentlewoman.

1669. June 16. Burton, Thomas, of Great Grymesby, marriner, æt. 32, and Anne Loggon, of same, spinster, æt. 29. His parents are dead; hers consent. Application by William Brass, of same, marriner. [Rothwell or Grimsby.]

1666. June 5. Burton, Thomas, of Saxleby, labourer, æt. 27, and Emme Storr, of Wisby, spinster, æt. 27. Her parents are dead; his consent. Surety, David Storr, of Wisby, labourer.
[St. Peter at Arches or St. Paul in Bail.]

1667. Jan. 2. Burton, William, of Billingborrow, æt. 25, and Helen Jolly, of Spaulding, spinster, æt. 30. His parents consent; hers are dead.
[Pinchbecke, Spauldinge or Wytham.]

1628. Nov. 20. Bushe, Henry, of Claypole, husbandman, æt. 27, and Ann Senyard, of same, widow. [Claipole.]

1668. July 21. Bushie, Samuell, of Ffreshney, yeoman, æt. 32, and Anne Sansom, of Wainfleet, spinster, æt. 20. His parents are dead; hers consent. [St. Paul in Bail.]

1669. May 10. Busk, Richard, of Gunnerby, mason, æt. 23, and Margaret Gold, of same, spinster, æt. 27.
[Marston or Hough on the Hill.]

1669. June 10. Bussy, Ffrancis, of Norton Disney, gent., and Bridgett Disney, of same, spinster. Surety, Hy. Wanless, of the Close of Lincoln, innkeeper. [Norton Disney.]

1634. Oct. 6. Bust, Stephen, of Brant Broughton, labourer, æt. 30, and Rebecca Wetherill, of same, spinster, æt. 30. Surety, Wm. Bust, of same, labourer. [Brant Broughton.]

1663. June 24. Buston, John, of Aisterbie, Ffuller, and Ellen Ffox, widow. Surety, John Rogers, of Benniworth, labourer.
[St. Paul in Baile or St. Margaret.]

1662. Aug. 6. Butler, John, of ...., yeoman, and Alice Rudd, of Ffleet. Surety, George Rudd, of .... husbandman.
[Ffleet or ......ston.]

1640. May 13. Butler, Thomas, of Great Ponton (?), æt. 22, and Ann Gouldinge, of Gunwerby, spinster, æt. 18. Surety, Thomas Darby. [Great Ponton.]

1607. Feb. 8. C.—Butler, Thomas, and ....

1640. March 1. Button, John, of Ffulstowe, yeoman, and Alice Cooke, of same, widow. Surety, Arthur Johnson, of Yarburgh, gent. [Easterrington.]

1669. April 20. Button, Robert, of Stainton in the Hole, yeoman, and Susanna Wilson, of same. Surety, John Mitchinson, of Swinop, yeoman. [Stainton or Would Newton.]

1630. May 18. Buttrie, Richard, of Boothbie, husbandman, and Grace Mapletofte, of same, spinster. Application by Robt. Bagshawe, of Hougham. [Gunerbie.]

ST. PETER'S, YORK.—SCHOOL REGISTER.*

1835. August 18. 200. John William Smyth, aged 10. See 140. From Mr. Bulmer's school. Left at Xmas., 1840.

August 18. 201. George Bell, aged 13. Son of Mr. Bell, tanner, Clifton, near York. From Mr. Stoner's school, Tadcaster. Left at Midsummer, 1837.

August 18. 202. William Walker, aged 12. Son of the Rev. Mr. Walker, Slingsby. From Rev. Mr. Buckle's school, Durham. Left at Xmas., 1839.

August 18. 203. Edward Belcombe, aged 9. Son of Dr. Belcombe. Not at school before. Removed Nov., 1841.

August 19. 204. Robert Duffin, aged 14. Son of Lt.-Col. Duffin, Bengal Army. From Rev. T. Flin's school, Dublin. Left at Midsummer, 1838.

August 19. 205. Joseph William Atkinson, aged 13. Son of Mrs. Atkinson, Knaresbro'. From Mr. Stocken's school, Knaresbro'. Left at Midsummer, 1838.

1835. Oct. 1. 206. Henry Beckwith, aged 11. Son of Rev. Mr. Beckwith, Collingham. Brought up at home. Left at Michaelmas, 1840.

Oct. 1. 207. John Beckwith, aged 10. Son of Rev. Mr. Beckwith, Collingham. Brought up at home. Left at Midsummer, 1836.

Oct. 1. 208. John Campbell, aged 10. Son of Mrs. Campbell, Lord Mayor's Walk. From Mr. Watson's school, Gillygate. Left at Easter, 1837.

Oct. 1. 209. Richard Ibbotson, aged 10. Son of Mr. Ibbotson, of Cambridge, but lives with Mr. Andrew, Stonegate. From Mr. Bulmer's school, College Street. Left at Xmas., 1840.

1836. Feb. 3. 210. Clement Price, aged 10. Son of T. Price, esq., Clementhorpe. From Rev. Mr. Shackley's school, York. Left at Xmas., 1840.

* Continued from page 163 of Vol. for 1896.

1836. Feb. 3. 211. Richard Shepherd, aged 10. Nephew of R. Shepherd, esq., Scarbro'. From Mr. Manner's school, Middleton. Left at Xmas., 1841.

Feb. 3. 212. Charles Comber, aged 9. Son of Rev. Mr. Comber, Oswaldkirk. Not at school before. Left at Xmas., 1841.

Feb. 3. 213. Arthur Wilson, aged 9. See 177. From Mr. Shearman's school, Cockermouth. Left at Midsummer, 1842.

Feb. 8. 214. John Middleton, aged 15. Lives with Mr. Sowerby, Goodramgate. From Mr. Monkman's school, York. Left at Midsummer, 1838.

1836. April 11. 215. John Coopland, aged 10. Son of Rev. Mr. Coopland, Tanner Row. From Mr. Shackley's school. Died Feb. 1844.

April 11. 216. George Coopland, aged 8. Son of Rev. Mr. Coopland, Tanner Row. From Mr. Shackley's school.

April 11. 217. Charles Butterfield, aged 12. Son of Mrs. Butterfield, The Mount. From Mr. Watson's school, Gillygate. Exhibitioner 1841.

April 11. 218. Edward Ellis, aged 11. Nephew to Rev. R. Ellis. From Mr. Fletcher's school, Southwell. Left at Midsummer, 1838.

1836. August 17. 219. Michael William Barstow, aged 12. See 20. From Mr. Charnock's school, Bishopton. Left at Easter, 1839.

August 17. 220. Thomas Wilson, aged 13. Son of Mr. Wilson, Marygate. From Mr. Tabor's school, Monkgate. Not at school in 1838.

August 17. 221. William Richardson, aged 9. Son of Mr. Richardson, solicitor, Micklegate. From Mr. Shackley's school. Left at Xmas., 1840.

August 17. 222. Henry Cowling, aged 12. Son of Mrs. Cowling, Castlegate. From Mr. Watson's school, Gillygate. Left Midsummer, 1840.

August 18. 223. Thomas Taylor, aged 8. Son of Mr. Taylor, Coppergate. Not at school before. Not at school in 1838.

1836. August 22. 224. Robert Johnson, aged 14. Son of Mr. Johnson, printer, Blossom street. From Mr. Gillat's school, Bansdale. Left at Midsummer, 1837.

August 22. 225. Samuel Anderson, aged 12. Son of Mr. Anderson, Robin Hood Inn, Castlegate. From Mr. Potter's school, Spofforth. Left at Midsummer, 1837.

August 22. 226. Richard Cordukes, aged 12. Son of Mr. Cordukes, surgeon, Tockwith. Not at school before. Left at Xmas., 1837.

August 22. 227. Clement Manby, aged 12. Son of Rev. Mr. Manby, Knaresbro'. From Mr. Husband's school, Whixley. Left at Midsummer, 1838.

1836. Oct. 10. 228. Frank Lipscomb, aged 11. Son of Rev. Mr. Lipscomb, Wilbury, near Northallerton. Taught at home. Left at Midsummer, 1837.

1837. Feb. 1. 229. John N. Fowler, aged 17. .... of Robert Nottingham, esq., Latham, near Howden. From Rev. J. Shackley's school, York. Left at Midsummer, 1837.

Feb. 1. 230. James Collins, aged 13. Son of Rev. T. Collins, Knaresbro'. Taught at home. Left at Xmas., 1838.

Feb. 1. 231. George Pearson, aged 11. See 25. From Rev. J. Shackley's school, York. Left at Xmas., 1840.

Feb. 1. 232. William Smithson, aged 12. See 124. From Rev. J. Shackley's school, York. Left at Xmas., 1840.

Feb. 1. 233. George Barstow, aged 11. See 20. From Rev. Mr. Charnock's school, Bishopton. Left at Midsummer, 1838.

Feb. 2. 234. George Carey, aged 14. Son of Mr. Carey, Walmgate. From Mr. Monkman's school, College Street. Left at Easter, 1842.

Feb. 2. 235. Richard Wood, aged 10. Son of Mr. Wood, coroner, St. Saviourgate, York. From Mr. Holmes' school, Wilberfoss. Left at Midsummer, 1841.

Feb. 6. 236. Franceis Belcombe, aged 9. Son of Dr. Belcombe. Not at school before. Left at Xmas., 1841.

1837. April 4. 237. Daniel Thompson, aged 12. Son of Mrs. Thompson, 49, Monkgate. From Mr. Scholefield's school, Thornton, near Pickering. Left at Midsummer, 1838.

1837. August 16. 238. William L. Newman, aged 11. Son of Mr. Newman, St. Helen's Square. Not at school before. Left at Xmas., 1837.

August 16. 239. Arthur Pigou, aged 12. Son of Mr. Pigou, with Mrs. Smith, Bootham. At school in Germany. Left Midsummer, 1838.

August 16. 240. John Langbourne, aged 14. Nephew of Mr. Barwick, Whitby. From Wakefield Prop^y. School. Left Midsummer, 1840.

August 16. 241. Thos. Langbourne, aged 12. Nephew of Mr. Barwick, Whitby. From Mr. Breckon's school, Whitby. Left at Xmas., 1840.

August 16. 242. Charles Hackett, aged 13. Son of Mr. Hackett, St. Leonard's Place. From Rev. Mr. Burnaby's school, Quarndon, Leicestershire. Left Feb. 1842.

August 16. 243. Frederick Hackett, aged 11. Son of Mr. Hackett, St. Leonard's Place. Not at school before. Left at Xmas., 1843.

August 16. 244. Wm. Wyrill, aged 13. Son of Mr. Wyrill, Coney Street. From Mr. Charter's school, Ferrybridge. Left at Midsummer, 1838.

August 16. 245. Lewis Barstow, aged 8. Son of T. Barstow, esq. From Mr. Charnock's school, Ripon. Left Midsummer, 1839.

August 16. 246. Marmaduke Richardson, aged 8. Son of Mr. Richardson, solicitor. Not at school before. Left at Xmas., 1842,

1838. Jan. 31. 247. James Thompson, aged 8. South Parade. Orphan. From Mr. Shackley's school. Left Midsummer, 1842.

Jan. 31. 248. Thomas Walker, aged 11. Son of Rev. Thos. Walker, Slingsby. Not at school before. Left Oct., 1841.

Feb. 7. 249. Thos. Fishburn, aged 12. Whitby (notice of removal on entrance). Not at school before. Left at Easter, 1839.

April 23. 250. Thomas Hughes, aged 13. Son of Mr. Thos. Hughes, chemist, York. From Mr. Wills' school, Oxford Street, London. Left at Xmas., 1838.

THE REBELLION OF 1745.

Accounts, Correspondence, and Muster Rolls of the Yorkshire Association, in the possession of the Archbishop of York.

	£	s.	d.
THE EXPENSES OF A COMPANY OF FOOT—			
50 Private men at 12d. a day	2	10	0
2 Serjeants at 1s. 6d. „	0	3	0
2 Corporals at 1s. 3d. „	0	2	6
1 Drummer	0	1	3
	£2	16	9
One month or 28 days	79	9	0
Cloathing for 55 men at 1s. 10d. per man 82 10 0			
Bounty Money for 55 men at 5s. „ and Trophys 20 0 0			
	102	10	0
Raising, cloathing, and pay for a month	£181	19	0
WEST RIDING—			
25 Companies raising and cloathing	2562	10	0
A month's pay	1986	5	2
	£4548	15	2
NORTH RIDING—			
9 Companies raising and cloathing	922	10	0
A month's pay	715	1	0
	£1637	11	0
EAST RIDING—			
7 Companies raising and cloathing	717	10	0
A month's pay	556	3	0
	£1273	13	0
For 6 Adjutants at 5s. a day each for a month	42	0	0
Total	£7501	19	0

NORTH RIDING— 9 Companies of Foot (55 men each).

John Hutton, esq.	Gregory Elsley, esq.
Sir Reginald Graham.	S. Robinson, esq.
Christopher Crowe, esq.	John Hall, esq.
William Danby, esq.	Thos. Duncombe, esq.

Hugh Cholmley, esq.

Account of Rd. Milnes, of Wakefield, for clothing the 9 Companies:

	£	s.	d.
Cloth materials for 55 men in each Company, at 14s. 3d. ...	39	3	9
55 Hatts ... 2s. 6d.	6	17	6
2 Sheets and cords, at 4s.	0	8	0
Canvas for Hatts	0	0	9
	£46	10	0

CUTHBERT MARLEY'S ACCOUNT:—   £ s. d.

    16, 17, 18, 19, 20, 21 Nov., 1745. By the order of the Lieutenant of the North Riding, Cuthbert Marley's jorney those six days into Westmoreland and Cumberland to watch the motions of the Rebels in their passing those counties, and to give intelligence thereof to the Lieutenant and Deputy Lieutenants at their assemblie at Richmond 3 3 0

    22, 23, 24 Nov. Upon my return on the 21st, at night, my jorney again by the like order into the said countys on the same errand, where I stayed till the whole body of the Rebels' Army had pass'd Cumberland 1 11 6
My horse and self expenses 1 16 0

    15, 16, 17, 18, 19, 20 Dec. My jorney those 6 days into Westmorland and Cumberland to watch the motions of the Rebels on their return into Scotland 3 3 0
My horse and self expenses in the said 6 days jorney 1 16 6

    24 and 25. My jorney to Middleham with a Letter to Sir Reginald Grayham; my horse and self expenses 0 5 0

	£	s.	d.
8 Jan. My jorney to Allerton, and from thence to Greata Bridge, riding all night; my horse and self expenses	0	10	6
	12	5	6

Received of Mr. Ralph Close the sum of £1 1s. which is to be allowed out of the above mentioned sum.

1 Feb. Received of Mr. Hutchinson £1 1s. in part payment.

1 Feb. For a journey to Bishopthorpe with a letter; myself and horse	0	14	0
	£12	19	6

March 14th, 1745-6. Received then of Geo. Hutchinson, servant to the Rt. Hon. Sir Conyers Darcy, the above mentioned sum of £12 19s. 6d., in payment of the above, &c.

CUTH. MARLEY.

CAPTAIN HUTTON's COMPANY. (North Riding).

John Hutton, *Captain.* | Wm. Dodsworth, *Lieut.*
Wm. Brown, *Ensign.*

Inlisted October ye 10th, 1745.

James Francis \ *Serjeants.*   John Coates \ *Corporals.*
Benjamin Dale /   Hy. Goodwill /

Henry Marley, *Drummer.*

1 John Irwin
2 Charles Wensley
3 William Peacock
4 Thomas Langstaffe
5 Anthony Dixon
6 John Burnett
7 Thomas Pletts
8 George Robinson
9 William Wright
10 Philip Potter
11 John Stabler
12 Thomas Tomlin
13 Leonard Spenceley
14 Matthew Lee
15 William Dolphin
16 Francis Hesletine

17	Thomas Tomlinson		32	Henry Summers
18	George Lambert		33	Henry Jackson
19	William Guy		34	Charles Milner
20	Matthew Hogg		35	John Hilton
21	William Hillary		36	John Emmerson
22	Giles Burton		37	Robert Harrison
23	George Plant		38	James Robinson
24	George Harrison		39	Thomas Hallam
25	John Blaides		40	Thomas Whitell
26	James Russell		41	Wm. Hodgeon, Grinton
27	James Reynolds		42	Matthew Storrah
28	John Alderson		43	William Spence
29	Henry Porter		44	John Buckton
30	Joseph Clemminson		45	William Fletcher
31	Matthew Bell		46	Wm. Hodgeon, Newsham

Inlisted October 14th.

47	Francis Pickering		48	Thomas Allanson

Inlisted October 21st.

49	George Wood		50	Henry Carter

7TH COMPANY OF NORTH RIDING.

Christr. Crowe, junr., *Capt.* | Foster Coore, *Lieutenant.*
George Crowe, *Ensign.*

		Enlisted 1745.			£	s.	d.
Sep. 30.	Ralph Shaw, *Serjeant* ...	6 days to October 5th.			0	9	0
	Christ. Ramshaw, *Serjeant*	6	,,	,,	0	9	0
	Rd. Baynes, *Drummer* ...	6	,,	,,	0	7	6
	Stephen Pearl, *Corporal*	6	,,	,,	0	7	6
Oct. 1.	Andrew Stockdale ...	5	,,	,,	0	5	0
	Matt. Bridgewater	5	,,	,,	0	5	0
	Thos. Moore	5	,,	,,	0	5	0
	Jno. Horner	5	,,	,,	0	5	0
	Fras. Procter	5	,,	,,	0	5	0
	Wm. Langdale	5	,,	,,	0	5	0

					£	s.	d.
Oct. 1.	Stephen Bywell	...	5 days to October 5th.		0	5	0
	Rd. Windle	...	5	,, ,,	0	5	0
Oct. 2.	Wm. Kelly	...	4	,, ,,	0	4	0
	Thos. Appleby	...	4	,, ,,	0	4	0
	Geo. Graham	...	4	,, ,,	0	4	0
	Robt. Storrer	...	4	,, ,,	0	4	0
	Michael Alpha	...	4	,, ,,	0	4	0
	Jno. Law	...	4	,, ,,	0	4	0
	Wm. Blencairn	...	4	,, ,,	0	4	0
Oct. 3.	Thos. Cooke	...	3	,, ,,	0	3	0
	Geo. Menas	...	3	,, ,,	0	3	0
Oct. 4.	Thos. Buckle	...	2	,, ,,	0	2	0
	Thos. Greathead	...	2	,, ,,	0	2	0
	Michael Hunter	...	2	,, ,,	0	2	0
	Robt. Smalwood	...	2	,, ,,	0	2	0
	Thos. Wind	...	2	,, ,,	0	2	0
	Thos. Robinson	...	2	,, ,,	0	2	0
	Fras. Moore	...	2	,, ,,	0	2	0
	Jerem. Robinson	...	2	,, ,,	0	2	0
	Saml. Musgrave	...	2	,, ,,	0	2	0
	Wm. Taylor	...	2	,, ,,	0	2	0
Oct. 5.	Josh. Lightfoot	...	1	,, ,,	0	1	0
		First week's pay to October 5th.			£6	7	0
Oct. 7.	Thos. Robinson	...	7 days to October 14th.		0	7	0
	Wm. Wells	...	7	,, ,,	0	7	0
Oct. 9.	Charles Girfoot	...	5	,, ,,	0	5	0
	Thos. Brown	...	5	,, ,,	0	5	0
	Jona. Johnson	...	5	,, ,,	0	5	0
Oct. 10.	Jno. Hewson	...	4	,, ,,	0	4	0
	Sylvester Firby	...	4	,, ,,	0	4	0
	Jno. Raynard	...	4	,, ,,	0	4	0
	Jno. Ward	...	4	,, ,,	0	4	0
Oct. 11.	Christr. Morland	...	3	,, ,,	0	3	0
	Zach. Haw	...	3	,, ,,	0	3	0
	Wm. Wilkin	...	3	,, ,,	0	3	0
	Thos. Ward	...	3	,, ,,	0	3	0
	Thos. Thompson	...	3	,, ,,	0	3	0

					£	s.	d.
Oct. 12.	Christr. Boynton	...	2 days to October 14th.		0	2	0
	Robt. Horner ...	...	2	,, ,,	0	2	0
	Rd. Hall, *Corporal*	...	2	,, ,,	0	2	6
	Rd. Richmond ...	...	2	,, ,,	0	2	0
	Fras. Metcalfe ...	...	2	,, ,,	0	2	0
	Daniel Longpray	...	2	,, ,,	0	2	0
	John Graham ...	...	2	,, ,,	0	2	0
	Michael Rochester	...	2	,, ,,	0	2	0
	Ralph Scott ...	...	2	,, ,,	0	2	0
	Wm. Haykins ...	...	2	,, ,,	0	2	0
	Thos. Pratt ...	...	2	,, ,,	0	2	0
	John Collinson ...	...	2	,, ,,	0	2	0
					4	4	6
Pay for the men in the First Column, 8 days to Oct. 14th					13	8	0
					£17	12	6

1745.   *Dr.*   EXPENSES OF MY COMPANY.

Sept. 30. To Sir Conyers Darcy's Note on Gregory Elsley, esq., for £99   9   0

Cr.

					£	s.	d.
	Allow'd for Bounty and Trophy Money			...	20	0	0
Oct. 5.	First week's pay of 32 men as per Roll			...	6	7	0
14.	Second	,,	55	,, ...	17	12	6
21.	Third	,,	55	,, ...	19	17	3
28.	Fouth	,,	55	,, ...	19	17	3
					83	14	0
Oct. 29. Remains due in my hands			... ...	...	15	15	0
					£99	9	0

SIR,   KIPLIN, *October* 29*th*, 1745.

The above is the Account of the Expenses of my Company with the particulars of every person's pay and when enlisted, by which their remains due in my hands, fifteen pounds fifteen shillings.

I am Sir,
Your most obedient humble servant,

(Seal)   CHRISTOPHER CROWE, JUNR.
A Chevron between 3 (*crows ?*).

(The Accounts continue down to Feb. 13, following. Total disbursements £425 14s. 6d.)

CAPTAIN WM. DANBY'S COMPANY.

SWINTON, *October* 15*th*, 1745.

SIR,

In obedience to my instructions, you receive on account of the progress I have made in raising my company. My officers are Mr. Jno. Hardcastle and Mr. Lonsdale, both of Masham. They are both of them possess'd of a very considerable landed estate. I have got my number of Serjeants and Corporals, two of whom seem to know their duty very well. My complement of private men has been full several days. They have begun their exercises, but we are at a great loss for the want of arms, which I have been obliged to supply by getting a number of wooden pieces made, which serve for the present. But I have not yet been able to meet with a Drummer, who was not either very exorbitant in his demands, or unfit for the service.

I propose, as soon as I am more at liberty, to do my self the honour of waiting upon you, and am, Sir,

Your most obedient, and most humble servant,

W. DANBY.

Captain Danby's Company.

Wm. Lambert } *Serjeants.*
Jonathan Hall

Thomas Bellerby } *Corporals.*
Edward Croft

Wm. Allman, *Drummer.*

Christr. Hinley	Jonathan High
Wm. Metcalfe	Jno. Johnson
John Wardrope	Wm. Ascough
Jno. Spenceley	Geo. Press
Jno. Taylor	Christr. Taylor
Jno. Wilson	Jno. Hunton
Robt. Smorthit	Thos. Hird
Geo. Metcalfe	Rd. Graham
Robt. Ruecroft	John Robinson, Masham
John Vitty	Wm. Reynard
Wm. Ibbetson	Geo. Duffield
Robt. Theakston	John Robinson, Swinton
Jno. Robinson, junr.	Jno. Cannon
Thos. Skaife	Wm. Clapham

Thos. Clarkson
James Taylor
Simon Towler
Austin Metcalfe
Wm. Helmsley
George Kay
Thos. Ripley
Geo. Hagstone
Thos. Wilkinson
Duke Smith
Robt. Wintersgill

Wm. Wilson
Wm. Staveley
Wm. King
Cavendish Cannon
Thos. Plews
Peter Carter
Thos. King
Christr. Walker
Wm. Hudson
Fras. Winderhouse

All inlisted on or before the 6th of Oct., 1745 (from which day the pay of the whole commenced), except five of the private men exchanged for others, and the Drummer, who enter'd upon his pay the 20th of the same month.

Captain Danby's account ends with— £ s. d.
1745. Feb. 14. In the allowance of 2s. per man (being 55)
to carry 'em home and to drink the King's health 5 10 0
„ In Mr. Lonsdale my Ensign's pay for 82 days at
half-a-crown each 10 5 0

Total disbursed £446 14 9

SOME WILLS FROM THE RICHMOND REGISTRY.

The abstracts of Wills here printed are from the Registry of the Archdeaconry of Richmond, the index to which is now appearing in these pages. It was in the year 1853 that attention was first specially directed to these Wills by the late Canon Raine, who published a selection from them in Vol. 26 of the "Surtees Society"; the testamentary records of the Archdeacon were at that time deposited at Richmond, and were subsequently removed to London. All of them are what are officially known as "Unregistered" Wills, that is, the Wills have never been transcribed into registers as they should have been. When, therefore, reference to them is required, the searcher has produced to him the original or a probate copy, some of which have suffered severely through neglect, and are now in many cases almost illegible or falling to pieces. Many of the Wills which when referred to by Canon Raine, presented no difficulties, are now scarcely decipherable, and it is to be regretted that these valuable records have not ere this, been taken in hand by some of the County Societies. Those here given relate chiefly to parochial clergy of the North Riding; but there are also some from Lancashire, and a noteable one from Cumberland. They are also within the same period as those printed in "Richmondshire Wills," *i.e.*, the 15th and 16th Centuries.

It may be mentioned that a number of abstracts of testamentary records of the clergy of the Yorkshire Deaneries of Catterick, Boroughbridge, and Richmond, of the 16th Century, will be found in Vol. xiv. of the "Yorkshire Archæological Journal."

H. D. Eshelby.

Arch. Richmond.   Regd. ✠ 22.

WILLIAM PLUNGAR.

Ego Wm. Plungar, Rector Ecclie [de K] yrtlyngton. To be buried in the church of Kyrtlyngton St. Michael Archangel. To a priest to celebrate for my soul and for the souls of my ancestors, xxj^m. It.

do cuil'et puero Rogeri Lound, xx^{li}. Residue to said Roger Lund and his wife Joan, for payment of my debts, and disposal for the health of my soul. [Exors., the said Roger Lu]nd, and Joan his wife, and John Nobill. Witness, John Munby Chaplain, John Burgh, an Austin Friar, &c. Dat., Saturday after the Feast of the Decollation of St. John Baptist, 1438.

Arch. Richmond. Regd. ✠ 36.

RICHARD CHESTER.

Ricardus Chest'....... To be buried in the church of B. M. of...... Residue to Simon Tho......, my exor., to dispose for the health of my soul. Witness, ... clerico de Nerby, and others. Dat., apud Loncastr, duod .... Anno dni., 1462. (No probate clause.)

This Will is headed, "Testa^m Ricardi Chest', Theologie sacre p'fessoris vicarij ecclie de loncastr'."

Arch. Richmond. Will regd. ✠ 8.

JOHN BRAMSFELD.

Joh'es Bramsfeld, vicarius de Grynton, compos men .... aliquantulum in corpore sen .... in mortis Articu .... Willelm' conyers armiger' Condo testamentum meum in his .... a'i'am meam deo omnipotenti b'te Marie ...... omnib' S'c'is .... Cancello de Grynton. Katherine, Ellen, and John, my servants. Abbey of Grynton (?). Katherine Grinlyn, my servant, extrix. Supervisors I make William Conyers, esq., William Conell, of .... and John Melys. Witness, Sir John Whytby, Sir Matthew ......aderyng, Sir Thomas Cart'. Dat., 18 April, c. 1474. (No probate clause.)

Arch. Richmond. ✠ 24.

NICHOLAS NICHOLS.

[Ego N]ichus Nichols, Cap^{nus}. To be buried in the church or churchyard of Munkton, and I give my best gown for a mortuary. To the parish church of Calthorne, xx^s. To the Nuns of Munkton, xx^s. To Sir Richard Baynbrige, x^s. To William Thornill, x^s.

Residue to my exors. Sir Richard Baynbryge and William Thornyll, to dispose for the good of my soul. (No witness.) Dat., 3 July, 1478. (No probate clause.)

Arch. Richmond.   Regd. ✠ 82.

STEPHEN BIRKHEAD.

I Stevyn byrkhede, prest. I gyve and bequethe my soule vnto almyghty God my maker and my redemer, vnto his mother o^r blyssyd lady saynt mary, and vnto all the glorious company in hevyn, and my body to be buryed affore the gylde alter in o^r ladys quere.

I gyf to o^r lady my best belt. Itm I will ev^{r}y p^{r}st beyng at my exeques viij^d. Item I gyff to ev^{r}y one of my suster childer xi^s the hole some thereof x^{li}. Itm yf the remynant of my gudes will extende therto, I wold a prest dyd pray an hole yere for my father and mother, my brother and suster soules. Itm I will that Willm. Cayrhous my said suster sone have my best standyng cupe and cou^{r}yng y^r of. Itm I gyff to Robert Cayro' my said suster sone my best pece of sylv^r. Itm I gyff to Isabell Cayro' my syster doughter the next best pece of sylv^r. Item I gyff to Kateryng my suster doughter the nexte best pece of sylv^r. Itm I gyff to Kateryng my suster doughter the next best pece aft^r that. Itm I gyff to Agnes my syst^r doughter my best maser, payng therfor to one callyd lucas iij^s iiij^d. Itm I gyff to Rowland Wilson my lyttyll masour. I gyf to sir Walter browne my best gowne, my best bonet, and a sylv^r spone. Item to Richard browne vj^s viij^d. It^m to Agnes my syst^r, my mother sylv^r crokes. Itm to Roger Thikket vj^s viij^d. Item to Xpofer Sporte vj^s viij^d. Itm to sir henry banke my best shorte gowne. Itm to sir henry halled my black jaket and my best dublett. Itm to John browne, Thoms. and Willm. his brethren, my blewe furryd gowne. Itm to Isabell Cayro' aforesaid, a pare of bedes of amber w^h sware gaudys gylted. Itm to Kateryn Cayro' and Agnes aforesaid, ayther a pare of bedys, the one of awmber, the other of euery. Itm to Richard Johnson wyff a sylv^r spone, and the like to Bryan Johnson, John Trykbek, and the three children of my host. Itm to James syster childeren ii sylv^r spones. Itm to Thomas Tempes a sylv^r spone. Item to his wyff a pare of lytyll bedes in my purse, a fether bed, and such other gere as she haith of myne. Itm to the same Thomas my cupborde. Itm to my host my best bed cov^{r}yng.

I give the residue of my goods to be disposed to my pore frends by my exors., whom I make sir Walt^r browne, Rowland Wilson, "Xpofer Xpoll Sporte," and Roger Trikket. I make my godfad^r M. Richard dukket my supervisor. Witness, Syr Allan Shepard, Thomes Tempes. Dat., 16 April, 1533. (No probate clause.)

Arch. Richmond.   Regd. ✠ 130.
JOHN SMYTH.

Ego Johes Smyth capellanus magr cantarie de West Tanfield. I give my horse for my mortuary. I give for my burial xx^s which I will shall be taken of suche malte as is within the chauntre. I will that all such things as are contained in a pair of indentures whereof Sir Robt. Symson hath the one part be left holle to the chauntre. Itm I giff a scistrone of Grestone and a worte trough to remayne as harelomes to the chauntre. To Sir Robert Symson and Sir Edward Thompson one silver spone each. To Thomas Butler one chare which Edmonde burnett did give me. To Isabell my sister my great cowe and my blue gowne which was my brothers. Cuthbert Warryner, Antony Waryner, Elsabeth Pacoke, Petor Smyth my brother, Robert Waryner's wife, Willm. Smyth my brother son, Peter my brother iij doughters. I gyff my new fetherbed to sir Willm. hyne Canon. Itm I gyff to s^d Willm. Gill a boke of myne, the which he hath in his kepyng. To Jenet Wilson a white heded cowe which I had of Warwyke, &c. To William Smyth my brother son v^{li} for which Thomas Smyth did sell "benkes" of mine. To Henry Chapman my kelter gowne. To Xpofer my servant my kelter jaket. To Robyn Waryner wyff my shorte gowne. And as for the money that I hadd with leonard waryner, I didd ware it on hym and more to. To Sir John Richmond my best bonet.

I make Willm. Smyth and John Smyth my brother sones my exors. to whom and to my supervisors Sir John Tunstall, p'son of Tanfeld, and Sir Richard Threpland, m^r of well, I give the disposal of the residue of my goods. Witness, Sir John Richmond, Sir Willm. Gille, Thomas Robinson, Nicoles Sanderson. Dat., 19 Aug., 1535. Debts to Maisteres Jane, Rauf Coke, Peter Walles, p'son Moniforthe (or Momforthe), Thomas Robinson and her husband (*sic*), and [blank] Whitesyde. (No probate clause.)

PARISH REGISTER OF CLAY COTON,
NORTHANTS.

(Transcribed by the Rev. Gordon H. Poole.)

Roger Packe was bur. the first of November.
Thomas Murcote and Elizabeth Ballard weare mar. the xvi. of October.

Anno 1575.

Rafe Billinge was bap. the iii daye of June.
Nicholas Wells was bap. the xvi. of Julye.
Nicholas Moulton was bap. the xxx. of July.
Isabell Murcote, the dau. of Thomas Murcote, was bap. the first daye of August.
Margerie West, the dau. of Richard West, was bap. the first of Januarie.
Thomas Ballard, fhe sone of John Ballard, was bap. the ii. daye of Februarie.
Nicholas Cartmell and Elizabeth Coles were mar. the xxviii. of December.
Nicholas Moulton bur. the xiiii. of August.

By me Robert Cleye, &c.

Agnes Reeve, the dau. of Richard Reeve, was bur. the last daye of August.
Alexander Belch was bur. the first of November.

Anno 1576.

Agnes Reeve, the dau. of Richard Reeve, was bap. the xi. of Aprill.
Willia. hulley Francis and John Billing weare bap. the xv. daye of June.
Marie Moulton, the dau. of Willia. Moulton, was bap. the xvii. daye of June.
Joane West, the dau. of Thomas West, was bap. the iii. day Oct.
Dorothie Cartmell, the dau. of Nicholas Cartmell, was bap. the iiii. of October.

* Continued from page 194, of Vol. for 1896.

Robert Webster, the sone of Michael Webster, was bap. the xii. daye of November.
John Billington was bur. the iiii. of Julye.
Henry Bell and Elizabeth Oldam weare mar. the xxth daye of Oct.

Anno domini 1577.

Henrye Heward was bap. the xxvii. of nomber.
Francis and Alice Paulmer weare bap. the viiith daye of Februarie.
Willia. Wood was bap. the xxi. of February.
Francis Paulmer was bur. the xxv. day of Februarie.
Willia. Wood was bur. the vi. day of Marche.

Anno domini 1578.

Agnes March was bap. the xxvii. of August.
Willia. Moulton was bap. the xxix. of August.
Richard Pratt was bap. the ix. of Nove'ber.
Katherine Murcote was bap. the vi. daye of December.
Marie Brewese was bap. the ix. of Marche.
Alice West, the dau. of Richard West, was bap. the xxiii. daye of Aprill.
Lambert Murcote was buried the xvii. of Dece'ber.
Alice Smith was burieth (*sic.*) the xx. of Januarye.
Edward Mariat was buryed the xv. of February.
Edward Seale and Francis Ballard mar. the xii. of Julye.

By me Robert Cleye, &c.

Bartholomew Mount and Elizabeth Walker mar. xx. of October.

Anno domini 1579.

Sara Cartmell, the daughter of Nicholas Cartmell, was bap. the xix. day of Aprill.
Agnes Smith, the dau. of Henry Smith, was bap. the xiii. daye of Maye.
Willia. Reeve, the sonne of Richard Reeve, was bap. the xix. daye of Julye.
John Burgesse, the sonne of John Burgess, was bap. the last day of September.
John Webster, the sonne of Michaell Webster, was bap. the xxvth daye of October.

Alice Woode, the dau. of Thomas Wood, was bap. the xii. day of November.

John West, the sonne of Thomas West, was bap. the ii. daye of Januarye.

Anno domini 1580.

Judeth Cartmell, the dau. of Nicholas Cartmell, was bap. the iiii. daye of Februarye.

John Hulley, the sone of John Hulley, was bap. the vth daye of August.

John Heward was bap. the xx. of August.

Agnes Ballard the dau. of John Ballard, was bap. the viii. daye of Januarye.

Nicholas Brewesse, the sonne of Willm. Brewesse, was bap. the last day of November.

John Heward was bur. the xxx. of August.

Richard Pratt was bur. the xxvii. of October.

Agnes Murcote, the dau. of Thomas Murcote, was bap. the ix. daye of Januarye.

John Smith and Alice Wood weare mar. the ii. daye of Maye.

Robert Halford and Agnes Mariat weare mar. the xxiii. daye of Julye.

Anno domini 1581.

Katherine West, the dau. of Richard West, was bap. the xxvi. daye of Marche.

John Moulton, the sone of Willa. Moulton, was bap. the last day of Marche.

John Smith, the sone of Henry Smith, was bap. the xxviii. day of November.

Matthias Webster, the sone of Thomas Webster, was bap. the xxth daye of Februarye.

By me Robert Cleye, &c.

Joane Heward, the dau. of Thomas Heward, was bap. the xxvii. daye of Februarye.

Marie Pratt, the dau. of John Pratt, was bap. the ix. daye of Marche.

Elizabeth Murcote, the wife of John Murcote, was bur. the ix. daye of September.

Anno domini 1582.

Richard Reeve, the sonne of Richard Reeve, was bap. the xxii. daye of Aprill.

Alice West, the dau. of Thomas West, was bap. the xxi. daye of September.

Richard Ballard, the sonne of Willia. Ballard, was bap. the iii. daye of December.

Alice Murcote, the dau. of Thomas Murcote, was bap. the xx. daye of Februarie.

Joane Heward, the dau. of Thomas Heward, was bur. the xxii. daye of August.

Agnes Williams, widdow, was bur. the xiith daye of Januarye.

Robert Jackson and Margaret Goddard weare mar. the xxvii. day of October.

Richard Ward and Agnes Ballard weare mar. the vi. daye of Julye (*sic.*) Januarye.

Anno domini 1583.

Thomas Brewesse, the sone of Willia. Brewesse, was bap. the xvi. daye of Aprill.

Elizabeth Murcote, the dau. of Willia. Murcote, was bap. the ii. daye of August.

Prudence Ballard, the dau. of John Ballard, was bap. the iiii. day of August.

Agnes Heward, the dau. of Thomas Heward, was bap. the xxi. daye of September.

Willia. West, the sone of Richard West, was bap. the first of November.

Willia. Wood, the sonne of Thomas Wood, was bap. vi. daye of December.

Elizabeth Murcote, the dau. of John Murcote, was bap. the xxviii. of Februarie.

Alice Cartmell, the dau. of Nicholas Cartmell, was bap. the xxvth of Februarie.

Joane Halford, the dau. of Robert Halford, was bap. the iiii. daye of Marche.

Elizabeth Murcote, the dau. of Willia. Murcote, was bur. the xxii. of August.

Alice Wood was bur. the xxiii. of December.

MARRIAGE BONDS

OF THE

DEAN AND CHAPTER OF YORK.*

By T. B. Whytehead, Esq., Chapter Registrar.

1667. Feb. 29. Henry Wright, of Tockwith, co. York, husbandman, and Jane Buck.
March 23. Joseph Harrison, ... and Catherine Goodricke.
May 29. James Woodhouse, junr., of Misterton, co. Notts., husbandman, and Elizabeth Pickaver, of Misterton.
Sept. 21. Andrew Bulmer, ... and Hannah Jennings.
Sept. 27. William Wilkinson, of Stockton, co. York, yeoman, and Anne Wilkinson.
Oct. 7. William Dawson, of Nunmounton, co. York, bricklayer, and Sicily Bell.
Oct. 27. George Hewley, of Westowe, co. York, gent., and Elizabeth Gaythorne.
Nov. 16. Henry Nevile, of York, glover, and Margaret Hooper.
Dec. 10. Thomas Blyth, of Popleton, co. York, gent., and Ellen Blyth.

1668. April 14. John Beverley, of York, gent., and Douglas Saltmarsh.
April 22. Richard Ploweman, of Donington, co. York, linen weaver, and Elizabeth Rawe.
June 10. Francis Blount, of Melton, co. York, gent., and Elizabeth Boswell, widow.
July 30. William Moore, of the City of York, trunkmaker, and Elizabeth Richardson.
Aug. 3. Richard Taylor, of York, tayler, and Anne Gilling, widow.

* Continued from page 180, of Vol. for 1896.

c

LICENCES ISSUED "SEDE VACANTE."

1664. April 20. Aislabie Anderson, of Berkwick-on-Tease, yeoman, and Susanna Barker.

April 1. Thomas Pickaver, of Leeds, yeoman, and Mary Simpson.

April 5. Joseph Hall, of Holden, yeoman, and Anne Northene.

March 30. Joseph Stones, of Tinsley, parish of Rotherham, and Ruth Gill. [Rotherham.]

May 17. Thomas Froud, of Barnsley, and Anne Lee.

April 7. Thomas Waite, of Fishlake, yeoman, and Marie Barber.

April 7. Thomas Wilkinson and Mary Whitehead.

April 6. Thomas Leadebeater, of Hessle, freemason, and Jane Wager.

April 20. George Harrison and Dina Normabell.

April 14. Henry Johnson, of Barmby Moor, gent., and Judith Myers.

April 13. John Fearbie, of Upper Poppleton, yeoman, and Mary Flint.

May 20. William Ruston, of Whitworth, yeoman, and Elizabeth Hopworth.

May 19, John Wilson, of Ealand, surgeon, and Mary Cranfield.

April 12. John Pickhaver, of York, clothmaker, and Joane Core.

April 11. Edward Waddington, of Bramham, gent., and Mary Pudsey.

May 19. George Fairebanke, of Halifax, carrier, and Margt. Dobson.

May 5. William Baxter, of Askham, and Juliana Berry.

May 18. William Huscroft, of Trumpitt, husbandman, and Jane Spetch.

April 11. John Greene and Sarah Roades.

April 11. John Wood, of Fairfield, husbandman, and Dorothy Wolphe.

1664. April 11. Thomas Wise, of Northlawes, gent., and Dorathie Raper.

April 9. Christopher Brearey, of York, gent., and Elizabeth Spatchurst.

April 9. Samuel Simpson and Lucie Thompson.

April 14. James Nicholson, of Rothwell, fellmonger, and Jane Burton.

April 20. Francis Spetch, of Fishlake, waterman, and Mary Robinson.

April 20. Robert Bean, of Halifax, clothier, and Mary Clayton.

May 21. John Dutton, of Royston, and Grizell Wood.

May 20. Robert Windle, of Huddersfield, and Ann Blackburne.

May 20. Joshua Jefferson and Ann Milner.

May 20. Joshua Dixon and Jane Pickard.

April 18. Robert Franck and Moriall Graystick.

April 18. Edward Boys and Elizabeth Peele.

April 16. Robt. Watson, of York, gent., and Ellene Standinn.

April 15. Thomas Curtis, of Leeds, gent., and Ann Loftus.

May 3. Isiah Holdsworth and Mary Hollum.

May 3. William Dawson, of Leeds, clothdresser, and Isabel Pavorwick.

May 2. Henry Smith and Mary Ward.

May 2. John Carver, of Dringhouses, blacksmith, and Marie Gill.

April 30. Christopher Thisslethwaite, of York, grocer, and Margaret Lee.

April 29. James Oddy, of Leeds, clothworker, and Mary Battie.

April 21. William Oddy and Elizabeth Oddy.

April 2. James Addison, of ...., husbandman, and Dorothy Richards.

April 28. Henry Ellison, of Ribston, gent., and Elizabeth Usher.

April 28. Richard Gunyin, of Kirby Wharfe, yeoman, and Elizaboth Dennis.

1664. April 28. Thomas Burley and Katherine Schora.

May 6. John Pollard, of ...., yeoman, and Mary Middlebrooke.

May 15. Christopher Wade and Dorothy Ware.

May 4. Thomas Kilburne and Elizabeth Jefferson.

May 4. William Hagar, of ...., yeoman, and Ann Shillitoe.

May 4. John Hall, of Kirkby Mallandale, yeoman, and Margaret Thompson.

May 4. Michael Hardcastle, of Great Preston, gent., and Elizabeth Clough.

.... Thomas Fairfax, of York, gent., and Mary Anderson.

April 22. William Popplewell and Alice Rhoades.

April 21. Richard Cookeson, of Darrington, yeoman, and Marie Thompson.

April 20. William Maw, of Thornton, yeoman, and Margaret Lawson.

May 7. William Maffy, of Spofforth, labourer, and Ann Hewthicke.

May 6. Thomas Brooke and Sarah Blackburne.

May 3. Thomas Boothroyd, of Thornhill, tanner, and Mary Robson.

May 21. John Cooper and Anne Moore.

May 21. Thomas Greggs, of York, cordwainer, and Rachel Haller.

April 27. Peter Hardistie and Grace Rawson.

April 25. John Barker, of Gawber Hall, co. York, yeoman, and Suzann Key.

April 25. William Lambert, of Rotherham, gent., and Isabell Windle.

April 23. John Thorpe and Judith Hall.

April 22. Francis Fawcitt, of Hesle, co. York, and Alice Carter.

Sept. 10. Benjamin Norcliff, of Gray's Inn, Middlesex, esq., and Jane Weddell, widow.

ROKEBY FAMILY: BIBLE FLYLEAVES.

For a number of years there has been in the possession of my family a Reference Bible, octavo, red lined, printed by the Company of Stationers, 1650. On the flyleaves of this Bible are the following entries of the family of Rokeby, of co. York, in a lady's handwriting.

Will Rokeby, eldest sone of Tho. Rokeby, of burnby, Esq., was maried to Eme Bury, daghtr. to Will Bury, of Grantham, Esq., at Skllow, the 9 of november, being wedend, 1653.

Eme Rokeby, ye eldest daughter of Will. Rokeby, was borne at Skllow at 12 aclock one saterday at night, beng ye 8 of Septembr, 1654.

Will Rokeby, ye eldest sone of Will Rokeby, of Ackworth, was borne at Skllow one friday at 3 a clocke in ye after noune, bing the furst of augest, 1656.

Elizabeth Rokeby, sekond daughtr. to Will Rokeby, was borne at Skllow the 27 of augest, beng friyday at 4 in the after noune, 1658.

at Skellow thes 3.

Gorge Rokeby, sekond sone of Will Rokeby, of Ackworth, was borne one friday, the 9 of november at 9 aclock at night at Ackworth parke, 1660.

Thomas Rokeby, 3 sone of Will Rokeby, was borne at Ackworth the 13 Jeneway, thurday, and died in march after at Ackworth parke, 1662.

Alexander Rokeby, 4 sone of Will Rokeby, was borne one ye 26 of may, byeing thursday, at 1 aclock at noun at Ackworth parke, 1664.

Jane Rokeby, 3 daughter of Will Rokeby, of Ackworth, was borne ye 24 of June, being Lordsday, at 4 clock in mor[n]ing, 1666.

John Rokeby, 5 sone of Will Rokeby, of Ackworth, was borne ye 3 of noumber, 67, being lordsday, at 11 a'clock at noune, 1667.

at Ackworth parke these.

Thomas Rokeby, 6 sone of William Rokeby, of Ackworth parke, was borne yˢ 27 of Jenewary, being friday, at or betwixt 12 or 1 a clock at noune, 70. at Ackworth parke thes 6, 5 boys and 1 gerell was borne.

Mary Rokeby, 4 daughter of William Rokeby, was borne at Skellow, yᵉ 12 of feberewary, being wedensday, at 1 a clock at night, 72.

Dorothy Rokeby, 5 daughter of Will Rokeby, was borne at Ackworth, yᵉ 2 of march, being satarday, about 4 clock in yᵉ after noune, 1674.

Susanah Rokeby, 6 daughter of Will Rokeby, was borne at Pontfrick, yᵉ 5 of September, being teusday, 2 in yᵉ after noune, and a bad time I had, but god did mightly suport me, 1676.

Ebenneser Rokeby, 7 son of Will Rokeby, was borne at Pontfrik, yᵉ 14 of Aprill, being lordsday, about 5 a clock in morng, 1678. 1 page cut out.

At the end of the Bible :—

1660. My deare unkell Byard died yᵉ 9 of Jenewary, being tusday, at 11 at night, bured on wedensday at night, 1660.

My deare aunt Byard died yᵉ last of September, being monday, and was bured on tusday, yᵉ 1 of October, she died about 4 a clock in yᵉ after noune, and was bured about 8 yᵉ next night, yᵉ both died at Skellow, and was bured at Ouston Church, 1668.

Thomas Rokeby, 3 sone of William Rokeby, died yᵉ — march, and was bured at Ackworth, 62.

George Rokeby, 2 sone of William Rokeby, died yᵉ 20 of June, at a 11 aclocke at night, being friday, and was buried 21 at evening at Ackworth, 1673.

Mary Rokeby, 4 daughter of William Rokeby, died yᵉ 30 of June, at 9 a clock in yᵉ morning, and was bured at 9 a clock yᵗ night, being monday, at Ackworth, 73.

Emm Mason, eldest daughter of William Rokeby, died 2 of Augest, being friday, about 4 a clock in yᵉ morning, and was burid about 8 yᵗ night, She died at pontfrick and was bured ther, 1678.

R. GROSVENOR BARTLETT,
Corfe Castle.

DURHAM MARRIAGE BONDS.

1665. Oct. 31. John Wood, of Frosterley, and Mary Coltus, spinster.
Oct. 31. William Pickering, of Ludworth, and Margaret Richardson, spinster.
Oct. 27. Peter Ostell, of Newcastle, gent., and Mary Errington, spinster.
Oct. 28. John Wilde, of Houghton-le-Spring, and Margaret Chilton.
Oct. 28. William Hickson, of Middlestone, and Isabella Caverley, spinster.
Oct. 24. Thomas Swinhoe, Mowson, Northumberland, esq., and Elizabeth Carleton, spinster.
Oct. 21. Nicholas Crosyer, of Sunderland, and Barbara Anderson, spinster.
Oct. 19. John Lauton, of Woodhorn, and Barbara Heaton.
Oct. 16. John Neile, of Denwicke, and Jane Turner, widow.
Oct. 11. Cuthbert Hutchinson, of Framwellgate, and Jane Salley, spinster.
Oct. 7. Thomas Garthfoot, of Thornley, and Jane Patterson, spinster.
Oct. 14. George Jopling, of Durham, and Dorothy Peacock.
Oct. 14. Robert Harrison, of Oughton, and Elizabeth Williamson.
Oct. 4. John Marey, of Gateshead, and Margaret Green, spinster.
Oct. 3. John Smelt, of Chester, and Elizabeth Thompson.
Sept. 30. Richard Newton, Eltringham, and Jane Bancks, widow.
Sept. 28. Ralph Fell, of Newcastle, and Ann Matfin, spr.
Sept. 23. Robt. Richardson, Wolviston, and Barbara Finch, spinster.
Sept. 23. Richard Jackson, Lampton, and Mary Hall, spr.

1665. Sept. 23. Matthew Melledge, of Escomb, and Elizth. Smelt, spinster.

Aug. 17. Robert Atkinson, of Hilton, and Mary Parkin, spinster.

Sept. 5. Richard Chapman, of Billingham, and Dorothy Routledge, spinster.

Sept. 5. Nicholas Rowell, of Elvet, and Jane Laxe, spinster.

Sept. 2. James Burdon, of Stockton, and Mary Hixon.

CARLISLE MARRIAGE BONDS.

1729. May 12. William Anesley, of Newcastle, and Mrs. Elizth. Loury.

1730. March 13. Geo. Hartley, of Darlington, gent., and Deborah Baynes, of Appleby, spinster.

July 13. Rowland Shaw, of Bowes, co. of York, and Elizth. Tonstall.

July 15. Cuthbert Stobs, par. Hexham, and Ann Lee, of Renwick, spinster.

1731. Dec. 28. William Smith, of Coatham, gent., and Elizabeth Wilson, spinster.

March 4. Francis Salkeld, par. Allendale, gent., and Rebecca Harrison, spinster.

June 5. Lancelot Sanderson, of Staindrop, yeoman, and Agnes Orton, spinster.

Sept. 6. Robert Huck, of Whorlton, yeoman, and Janet Shutt, spinster.

Aug. 15. Henry Smith, par. Haltwhistle, and Mary Bell, widow.

July 28. Edmund Hind, of Newcastle, spurrier, and Mary Urwin.

1732. Oct. 4. John Hall, of Manchester, yeoman, and Esther Dockera, spinster.

Oct. 4. Thomas Wyer, of Newcastle, and Elizabeth Glenwright, spinster.

ALLERTONSHIRE MARRIAGE BONDS.

1755. March 8. James Wood, of Northallerton, and Frances Etherington.
March 31. John Romes, of Staple Inn, gent., and Mary Clark.
April 10. Hugh Farnell, of Northallerton, and Mary Busby, spinster.
June 13. William Hodshon, of Northallerton, gent., and Jane Willey, spinster.
Nov. 3. John Ewbank, of Northallerton, gent., and Ellen Rymer, widow.

1756. May 8. Thomas Fell, of Stockton, and Ann Cust.
May 5. Paul Morcan, of Northallerton, gent., and Mary Wilkinson.
June 30. Robert Mason, of Northallerton, and Ruth Wood, of Northallerton.
July 11. Christopher Attley, of Kirby Sigston, and Elizabeth Stonehouse.
Sept. 1. William Walker, of Northallerton, gent., and Sarah Clark.

1757. Feb. 2. John Neesham, of East Cowton, and Mary Trenholm, widow.
Aug. 23. John Milburn, par. Darlington, woolcomber, and Ann Johnson.

J. J. Howe,
Durham.

PECULIAR JURISDICTION OF St. LEONARD'S HOSPITAL, YORK.

Certain old registers of this Hospital have recently come to light, which reveal the existence of a peculiar jurisdiction hitherto unknown, apparently even to Dr. Marshall, exercised before the Reformation within the liberty of the Hospital.

The jurisdiction in probate and other matters seems to have included various parts of York, Newton-on-Ouse, Beningbrough, North and South Cave, Gisburn, Pikhill, Eskylby parish Burneston, Heslington, Carnaby, Great Broughton, Hotham, Bromfleet, Topcliffe, Rufford, Over Helmsley, Easthorpe parish Pocklington, and Saxton.

Most of the wills belong to Newton-on-Ouse, the present Peculiar indexes of which begin only in 1682, but there are wills from all the above places from 1421 down to the Reformation.

There are so many bequests for burial in the Hospital Church, that it almost looks as if this circumstance was by itself sufficient to give the Hospital jurisdiction.

Amongst many others, we notice the wills of several Kydalls of Newton, in 1432, 1436, and 1474; John Aslaby, janitor of St. Leonard's, 1440, and his wife, 1445 [? ancestors of the Aislabies of Studley] ; Lady Agnes Constable, widow of Sir Robert Constable, 1495; Wm. Frankyssh of North Cave, 1421 ; R. Thornton, rector of Almonbury and vicar of Silkston, who died at Rome, intestate, 1471.

There are also many inquests on sudden deaths by the King's Coroner within St. Leonard's Liberty; amongst others, one in 6 Hen. VIII., on the death of Henry Sutton, aged 4, and John Talliour, aged 5, who, climbing up a "maske fatte" in the Hospital Brewery, just as modern children might do, were there drowned.

Also proceedings in cases of defamation, incontinency, &c., within the Liberty.

A curious account is given of what was done in the case of clerical felons in 1512, for on the 5th March in that year a certain George Akeryg, late of St. Mary's Abbey, Merewall, co. Warwick, stole a silver girdle from the image of St. Mary in St. Mary's Abbey, York, and straightway fled to St. Leonard's Hospital, which is only a few yards distant, and there acknowledged the felony, and remained there till the 10th of the same month, after which, before the Coroners of the City and of the Hospital, he petitioned "to be abjured the realm," and accordingly this was done by the Coroners, and he was forbidden ever to return into the realm without the King's special mandate, and was shipped off from the Port of Hull.

There are also some interesting lists of obits within St. Leonard's Church, 13 Ed. III. to 10 Rich. II.

ACT BOOKS OF THE PREROGATIVE COURT OF YORK.*

1680. March 8. Norman, Anne, Burton Salmon. Adm. to son Wm. N.

March 9. Walker, Robert, Coopen, Durham diocese. Will to widow Margaret.

March 9. Heron, John, senr., Stockton, Durham diocese. Will to son Peter Heron.

March 9. Fawcett, Thomas, Hornby par. Smeaton Magna. Will to son Geo. Fawcett.

March 9. Flower, Geo., Sockburne. Will to widow Margt.

March 9. Swainston, John, Stockton-on-Tease. Will to widow Jenet.

March 9. Raisbeck, Jacobus, Stockton. Adm. to widow Frances.

March 11. Bosvile, Chas., Selby. Will to widow Deborah.

March 15. Truman, Mary, Gedling, widow. Will to dau. Mary, ux. Joseph Hieron.

March 15. Green, Mary, Losco, co. Derby, spinster. Will to Mary, ux. Joseph Hieron.

March 15. Dale, Anthony, Melmerby, co. Cumberland, gent. Will to widow Dorothy.

March 18. Clark, Thos., Middleham. Adm. with Will to widow Anne, to use of son Thos. Clark.

March 15. Scott, Leonard, Hull. Adm. to daughters Anne ux. John Lillie, and Mary, ux. John Leighton.

March 19. Ashton, Sir Ralph, St. Andrew's, Holborn, co. Middlesex, bart., but at Whalley, co. Lanc. Will to widow Elizth.

March 21. Thompson, Geo., Danby Parva. Will to widow Mary.

March 22. Clark, Robert, Cawood. Adm. to Marm. Maw of same, to use of Susanna his wife, sister of deceased (Helen Beane, now ux. Nich. Beane, of Nunnington, mother of deceased, renouncing.

* Continued from page 190 of Vol. for 1896.

1680. March 24. Tong, Thos., Bedderne, York, clerk. Adm. to widow, Ellenora. [Bond 11 Nov., 1681, by said Ellenora, Thos. Kirk, and Sarah Burnley.]

1681. March 25. Doue, Edward, York, silkweaver. Will to widow Jane.

March 26. Childers, Wm., Bole, co. Nott., but dying at St. Botolph's, outside Aldersgate, London. Adm. to sister Elizth. Childers, spinster.

March 29. Headon, Geo., Brompton, near Northallerton. Will and Codicil to John Prissick and Christr. Prissick.

April 4. Stafford, Sir Thos., London, knt. Adm. (as to goods left unadministered by widow Mary) with will annexed, to Thos. Howgrave, gent.

April 4. Stafford, Lady Mary, London, widow. Adm. (as to goods left unadministered by daughter Cath. Killigrew) with will annexed, to Thos. Howgrave, gent.

April 5. Acklam, Margaret, Howden, widow. Will to father Stephen Arlush.

April 6. Leavens, Wm., Rocliffe. Adm. to Fra. Duckworth of York, merchant, and Wm. Jepson of Brotherton, gent.

April 14. Chadwick, John, Butterworth Hall, par. Rochdale, co. Lanc. Will to brother Jordan Chadwick and widow Sarah.

April 15. Bretherick, Bethell, Brotherton. Adm. (by decree) to John Greene of same.

April 16. Burdon, Thos., South Shields, co. Durham. Will to widow, Isabella.

April 20. Adams, Michl., Manchester. Adm. to widow Mary.

April 26. Richardson, Henry, Heslington. Will to son Thos. Richardson.

May 5. Bradley, William, Keasden head par. Clapham. Adm. to nephew [nepos] Wm. Bradley, LL.D.

May 11. Stansfeild, John, Inchfield in Huddersfield, Chester diocese. Will to John Scolefield.

May 13. Crosby, Leonard, York. Adm. (by decree) to Abraham Faber, of York, gent.

May 18. Ashburne, Robert, York, bookseller. Will to Geo. Atkinson.

1681. May 25. Gerrard, Rd., Grayes Inn, gent., but dying at Drayton, co. Bucks. Adm. with will, to Anne ux. Bernard Greenvile, esq., principal creditor.

May 25. Shuttleworth, Rd. Forcett, esq. Will to widow Margaret.

May 25. Buckton, Thos., York, glazier. Adm. to widow Helen.

May 28. Foster, Helen, Clapham. Adm. to husband Wm. Foster.

June 2. Day, John, Hartwith, par. Kirkby Malzeard. Will to Charles Clapham and Fras. Day.

June 2. Midgley, Robt., Winewall, par. Colne, co., Lanc. Will to Barnard Hartley and son Robt. M.

June 3. Walker, Hannah, æt. 12, daughter of Robt. W., late of Barrow, co. Linc., decd. Curation to Peter Thompson, of Hull.

June 6. Tillitson, John, St. Gregory, London. Adm. with will to John Tillitson, of London, gent., principal creditor (John Hargreaves and Rd. Hindle, exors., renouncing.) (Another grant, Jan., 1683.)

June 6. Williamson, Margt., Bridekirk, co. Cumberland, widow. Will to Matthias Miller, "nepos" of decd.

June 7. Wood, Wm., Laughton-in-le-Morthing. Will to Nich. Pearson

June 20. Netherwood, Robt., Darlington, co. Durham. Will to widow Isabella.

June 20. Todd, Robert, Long Cowton. Will to Simon Taylor.

June 29. Pannell, Josua, Stockton, co. Durham. Adm. to widow Alice.

June 30. Oliver, Margaret, Intakes par. Hexham, widow. Will to Alice, ux. John Garbit, Anthy. Sharpe, junr., and John Sharpe.

June 30. Little, Thos., Hexham. Will to John Jobson.

June 30. Stobart, John, West Wood par. Hexham. Will to dau. Mary ux. Edward Browell.

June 30. Robson, Wm., Grundridge par. Hexham. Adm. to widow Elizth.

1681. June 30. Thirlwall, Geo., East Grundridge par. Hexham, Adm. to son Peter T.

June 30. Nixon, Jane, Lightsheele par. Allandale, widow. Adm. to son Thos. N.

June 30. Atkinson, John, Kirk Heaton. Will to widow Ellenor.

June 30. Atkinson, Jacob, Joseph, Thomas, Luke, Alan. Isabella, and Rebecca, infant children of John A., late of Kirk Heaton, co. Northumberland, deceased. Tuition to Ellenora, A. of same, widow.

June 30. Armstrong, Jacobus, son of William A., late of Allandale, decd. Tuition to Francis A., father of decd.

June 30. Stokoe, John, Robt., Margaret, and Anne, infant children of Wm. S., late of Hexham, decd. Tuition to Robert Riddell and John Rowland, gent.

July 2. Betson, John, Holtby. Adm. with will to brother Geo. B.

July 2. Betson, Geo., Holtby. Adm. to son Geo. B.

July 6. Lord, Hy., Firths par. Rochdale. Will to widow Elizth.

July 13. Dodsworth, Thos., Barton, gent. Will to sister Mary, ux. John Killinghall.

July 15. Drake, John, Dunington, clerk. Will to s n Humphrey D.

July 15. Holdsworth, Thos., clerk, Dean of Middleham. Will to nephew and niece, Anne and John H.

July 21. Pepper, Thos., Temple Cowton. Will to Leonard Smelt and John Smelt, esqrs.

July 23. Tebb, George, Aysenby juxta Topcliffe, Will to widow Anne.

July 27. Brearey, Mark, York, merchant. Adm. to brother Wm. Brearey, LL.D.

July 29. Smith, Elizabeth, Selby. Will to John Barehead, of York.

July 30. Buttery, Wm., Dalton. Adm. to John Buttery, of Sutton under Whitstoncliffe.

Aug. 1. Jackson, Geo., Pickering. Will to widow Barbara.

Aug. 1. Peckett, Geo., Nun Monckton. Adm. to wid. Mary.

LANGTON OF LANGTON,

co. Lincoln.

In a short paper in the Report of the Associated Architectural Societies, 1894, containing some ancient records relating to the manor of Langton and its Lords, I was obliged for want of evidence to leave it doubtful who it was of the Langton family that married Sarah, the daughter and eventual co-heir of Alan de Mumby, and was the father of Gilbert and Richard de Langton, the first members of the family of whom I then had any certain knowledge. I am now able to produce what I hope may be considered sufficient evidence that Osbert de Langton was the ancestor I sought for. I have been brought to this conclusion in this way. I found in the index to the charters in the Kirkstead Cartulary (B. M. Vespasian E. xviij.) a reference to charters of an Osbert de Langton. Then in the volume of Lincoln "Final Concords" I found mention of a Gilbert, son of Osbert, who A.D. 1202, quit-claimed all right in a bovate of land and 2 tofts in Langton to Ingeleis, who was the wife of Daniel, and Simon her son, and his heirs. On the next opportunity I searched the Kirkstead Cartulary, and found a charter (Ulsebi xxxv) of Ralph de Grendal to which Gilbert son of Osbert de Langton was a witness. A charter by which (xxv) Osbert de Langton granted to Kirkstead the whole land which Simon son of John held of him in the territory of Langton, the witnesses being Philip son of Robert de Tat'sal, Simon de Driebi, Hugh son of Robert de Hagwrdeham, Eudo de Alford, Henry de Wodehal. And what is still more convincing, the following charter :—

(xxiiij.) "Know, &c., that I Amfredus de Cheu have granted &c., to the Church of S. Mary and the Monks of Kyrkested in pure and perpetual alms v selions, and common pasture for xl. sheep in the fields of Langeton, &c.

Witnesses. Henry, Chaplain of Langeton, Osbert de Langeton, and Gilbert and Robert and Richard his sons, Simon son of Thomas de Langeton, Eudo de Sut'bi, &c."

There is mention of Henry, Chaplain of Langton, in A.D. 1219 (Bishop's Registers) which gives some clue to the date of the charter, and we may, I think, safely conclude that Osbert de Langton had by Sarah de Mumby his wife, three sons, Gilbert, the eldest, who presented to the Church of Langton in 1219, died without surviving male issue. As did also Robert. And Richard succeeded, as son and heir to his mother, whose son and heir, John de Langton, was the plaintiff in a suit 45 Henry III. with reference to the Mumby inheritance.

Mr. Langton, now of Langton, is, I believe, the only landowner in the County of Lincoln, who can prove descent in the direct male line from an ancestor who resided in the same parish and held some of the same lands at the beginning of the 13th century.

W. O. Massingberd.

STONEHOUSE: A CLEVELAND CATHOLIC FAMILY.

The great veneration my father bore to his grandmother Elizabeth Stonehouse, who claimed for her family continuous Catholic descent, and the tradition that the Christopher Stonehouse mentioned in Morris's "Troubles of our Catholic Forefathers," belonged to the family, led me to make some search. By the Hinderwell Registers, it is seen that she was daughter of Roger, son of Roger S. by Mary Hutchinson his wife; her mother being Elizabeth Pindar or Pinder (a witness to her Will spells it Pindar), daughter of Thomas Pinder and Elizabeth Stoope. Pinders and Pounders, &c., of Brotton, and Hutchinsons, of Grinton and Middleton Tyas, abound in the Recusant lists. But Stoope or Stowpe, of Marske, Brotton, &c., appear too frequently in the Jury lists, and it is suggestive that a Thomas Pinder took the Oath of Supremacy about 1700 (?), and that a William Ratcliffe also took the Oath, although before the date of a Marriage Licence in 1637 of William Ratcliffe, of Hinderwell, mercer, and Joan Stowpe, of Guisbro', spinster. Elizabeth Stonehouse used specially to mention her relatives going with the ladies of the Ratcliffe family to Stokesley (?) to be fined for Recusancy. The North Riding Record Society's publications fully confirm this at Quarter Sessions held at many places.

This search has led me to make some discoveries of interest to some families, besidss some religious orders. I append a chart, giving shortly certain particulars of those I can join to Christopher, and some particulars of a little nest of recusants.

In Foley's "Records of the English Province of the Society of Jesus," some particulars of Andrew Stone occur. The industrious compiler would seem to have made mistakes about this Jesuit Father. He describes him as born at Eastbrow or East Brow, and supposes this to be Easby, of which there are two in Yorkshire. If Foley had consulted a Gazetteer or Directory he would have found a more similar name in East Row, a hamlet in the joint township of Newholm-cum-Dunsley, in the parish of Whitby. Again when

Foley came across the name Stonas, following Andrœas, he naturally took it for Latin, instead of *broad Yorkshire* for Stonehouse. This enables us to identify him with the nameless priest, the brother of Anne and Mary Stonehouse, daughters of " Christr. Stonehouse, a good man and most constant Catholic dwelling in Dunsley," in Morris's "Troubles of our Catholic Forefathers," (Series I., page 222—5), and with Christopher Stonas, of Whitby, and his wife, " recusantes old," and with Xpofer Stonas (with others), suspected to be secretly married, not known where, in Peacock's " Yorkshire Catholics." We then see that Foley's conjecture that Andrew Stonehouse's mother might have been a Fairfax is wrong, and that the first wife (I learn it was his *first* wife from a different MS. from that quoted by F. Morris) belonged to the greater family of Smith. Mr. Waddington, of Grosmont, informs me of a Marriage Licence—William Stonehouse, of Whitby, and Margery Fairfax, of ———, in 1613, but that the marriage did not take place at Whitby. It may have been a secret marriage, of which the only registers are found in the Recusant lists.

The "North Riding Record Society" further furnishes us with the names of other members of the family in the list of recusants.

Margery Stonas, of Newholm, widow, was a recusant in 1636 and 1641. The relationship is not apparent; nor that of "John Stonas, husbandman, of Whitby, recusante old," in 1604, 1612, 1614, evidently an older man than Christopher, and his wife Alison or Ellis, a recusant in 1611, 1612 and 1614, but who conformed once, perhaps temporarily, in 1616; nor Jane wife of Alexander Stonas, of Eskdaleside, yeoman, recusant in 1629, Joseph Stonas, labourer, and Alice his wife, and Dorothy wife of Rowland Stonas, in 1641. These all relate to Whitby parish.

Peacock's " Yorkshire Catholics " gives some others of the name spelt Staynhouse, &c., at Skelton-in-Cleveland. These also appear in the " North Riding Record Series." Although John and Alice are described as "poore laborers" in 1604, in 1597 in the "Yorkshire Feet of Fines," John Stonehous and Alice his wife appear as defendants in a suit concerning ten acres of meadow in Skelton. John Stonehouse was a recusant in 1604, 1611, 1614, when he is called " John *Stonas*, of Stanghow," this being part of Skelton, and in 1616. Other entries there are, Richard S., of Lofthouse, 1623; Anne, wife of James S., of Danby, husbandman, 1624. Richard S., yeoman, of Brotton, 1625 and 1641. Robert S., tailor, 1627, called labourer in 1632; Anne his wife, 1629. Joseph S., labourer, 1633. George S., labourer, 1637, all of Egton. Elizabeth Stonas, supposed wife of Wm. Bartram, tincker, 1627. (In Peacock, 1604, Mr. W. Bartram, pewterer supposed to have two priests in his house). John S. and Annie his wife, 1690, all of Stokesley. Richard S., yeoman, and Anne S., spinster, and Ellice S., spinster, in 1614, of Kilton-in-Brotton. Nicholas Stonas, of Kirkleatham, in 1674. Thomas and Thomas (2), Annie his wife, and Mary S., of Hilton (? Kilton-in-Brotton), in 1674, and Maria Stonas, Anne, Henry and Anne his wife, of Brotton, in 1690.

From a conjunction of names, I have been inclined to think that Ursula Stonehouse's maiden name may have been Wright, not of Ploughland, but of York, (Apothecaries and recusants who gave two sons to the Church). An Ursula Joye, widow of Wm. Wright, lord mayor 1518 and 1535, died in 1543 (Surtees Society, vol. 57), and the name would be likely to survive in the family.

JOSEPH S. HANSOM.

27, *Alfred Place West,*
   South Kensington, S.W.

Christopher Stonehouse, "a most constant Catholic, dwelling in Dunsley," born at ——— about 1564, helped mother's means by making straw hats, taught to work jet and amber by master whom he converted, and he dying, C. S. taught his son. Hired house and lived pretty well. Harboured priest, desiring if one were captured in his house, he might be martyred with him, but never any was taken. Persecuted all his life long. Imprisoned when eldest dau. born. Escaped from York Castle, 23 Aug., 1593. Recusant old, and secretly marryed in 1604. Recusant 1611-12. On jury panel of Whitby Strand, 1 July, 1614. Chris. Stonas, of Whitby, yeoman. Recusant 8 July, 1614, and 9 July, 1616. Probably alive 1626, dead before 1632. Buried at ———. (A Christr. Stonehouse, apothecary, was buried at S. Dionis Backchurch, London, 1625. Harllian Society.)

═ Ursula ———, "secretly marr'd, not known where," before 1604. Recusant old Recusant in 1611-12-14-16-23 and 26, where she is described as "wife of Chris. Stonas, jeater," implying that he was then alive.

Frances Smith, a good Catholic, died when her eldest daughter was ten years old.

|

Anne Stonehouse, born 1592-3. Priests provided her places in Catholic houses. With Lady Ingleby (who was a recusant in 1616, at Lythe), and later with Lady Palmes, dau. of Lady Babthorpe. Professed laysister Order of S. Augustine, 21 Oct., 1618, d. Louvain, 14th Sept., 1656, aged 64; a good, obedient, Religious, very laborious, and charitable.

Thomas, jeater or jet worker, born 1594. recusant 1612-14-16. (A Thomas Stonehouse, recusant of Whitby 1674.)

Cuthbert, jeater, b. 1594, recusant 1611-12-14-16-18.

Andrew, b. at East Row, 1597. Student at S. Omer four years, and philosophy three months in Spain. Entered English College, Rome, 18 Oct., 1617, where he assumed the name of John Cuthbert, and "made good progress in learning piety and modesty." Ordained priest 19 April, 1623. Gee says, Andrew Stonehouse, near London, 1624, became a Jesuit in 1634. Made solemn vows 18 Feb., 1647. On Yorkshire Mission 8 Feb., 1647 and 55, as Andreas Stonas. Prisoner in York Castle, March 1657, to Sept., 1660, as John Fairfax. Died at ———, Yorkshire, 31 August, 1663, aged 66. Other *aliases*:—Andrew Stone, John Stone, Andrew Town.

Mary, born about 1602. Recusant, described as of Eskdaleside, dau. of Tho. (*sic.*) Stonas, jeater, in 1618, and of Dunsley, 1621, and 1623 when described as servant of Henry Fairfax, of Dunsley. After father's death, her brother (the priest) took care of her and persuaded her to become a religious. Served Mr. Clifford at Antwerp. Professed laysister Order of S. Augustine, 1 Feb., 1633, died at Louvain, 26 May, 1674, aged 71. "A downright good religious."

Christr. ═ Alice ———, junr, la- recusant borer, of 1623-26 Dunsley, and 1636 recusant 1623 and 1626.

STARTFORTH PARISH REGISTER,

CO. YORK.*

Transcribed by Mark W. Bullen, Esq., by kind permission of the Rev. Hartley Jennings, the Vicar.

Sepultor' nomina, 1690.

Rob. Raine, sepult' fuit 23° Novembris.
Maria Brench vid. sep. 28° Nov.
Jana Chapman, 29° die.
Willielm. fil. Joh. Jamson, 13° Decembris.
Will. fil. Rich. Waller, sepult 15° Febr.
Maria Laidman, vid. 17° Februarii.
Maria fil Guielmi Grainger, 25° Februarii.
Martha uxor Guielmi Soulbie, 12° Martii.

Sepultor' nomina, 1691.

Isabella fil. Car. Borckbeck, sepulta 22° Aprilis.
Elis Moore, vid. sepulta 6° Maii.
Matt. fil. Joh. Clarkson, sepult' 23° Maii.
Margaret uxor Jacobi Scot, sepult' 1° Junii.
Carol. Emmerson, sepult' 17° Augusti.
Doroth. Waterman, sep. 24° Octobris.
Christ. Garnet, vid. sepuit 6° Novembris.

3b.

Eliz. Todd, wid. sepulta fuit, 16 Novembris.
Christ. Laidman, sep. 20° Novembris.
Margareta fil. Tho. Applebie. sep. 22° Novembris.
Rob. Holy-day, sepult' 3° Decembris.
Anna Waterman, wid. sep. 7° Decembr.
Dor. Harker uxor Tho. Harker, sep. 8 Dec.
Rich. Nelson, sepultis 25° Decembris.
Gul. Thompson et Elinor Dent in matrimonium conjuncti fuere 23° Octobris, 1692.

* Continued from page 152 of Vol for 1896.

Connubia, 1691.

Thomas Appleby et Margaret Simpson in matrimonium coniuncti fuere 9° die Februarii.

Henrie Colling et Eliz. Fielding in matrimonium coniuncti fuere 29° Septembris, 1692°.

Baptizati, 1691°

Eliz. fil. Gulielmi Clarkson, baptizibatur, 10 die Mensis Martii.

Baptism', 1692.

Edward fil. Gulielmi Grainger, baptiz. 3° Aprilis.
Sarah fil. Christo. Finley, baptiz. 14th Aprilis.
Ruth filia Guelielmi Hayton, baptiz. 28° Aprilis.
Tho. fil. Tho. Clarkson, baptiz. 3° Julii.
Jana fil. Thoma. Richardson, baptiz. 6° Augusti.
Phillis fil. Rich. Waller, baptiz. 23° Augusti.
John fil. Rich. Marshal, defuncti, baptiz. 3° Octobris.
Feliz Musgrave, baptiz. 23° Octobris.
Tho. fil. Gul. Soulbie, baptiz. 27° Novembr.
Dorothea fll. Joh. Kipling, baptiz. 19th Martii.

Baptismata, 1693.

Margareta fil. Joh. Laidman, bapt. 6° Aprilis.
Jonathan fil. Gulielmi Thompson, baptiz. 23° Aprilis.
Jana fil. Tho. Foster, baptiz. 3° Augusti.
Eliz. fil. Tho. Chappethoe, baptiz. 14° Januarii.
Margareta fil. Xtoferi. Grainger, baptiz. 28° Februarii.

4.
Sepultor' nomina pro Ano. 1692.

Maria Copeland vid sepeliebatur, 9° mensis Aprili.
Sarah fil. Gulielmi Richardson, sep. 17° Aprilis.
Joana Brench, sepeliebatur 4° die Maii.
Rich. Marshall sepultus fuit 14° Maii.
Isab. fil. Tho. Coates sepulta fuit 13° Julii.
Wiil. Hayton sep. 13° Augustii.
Maria uxor Laurentii Addison sepulta 19° Septemb.
Laurentius Addison sepultis 3° Octobris.
Chr. Finley sepultis 3° Decembris.
Phillis Scot vid sepulta 26° Decembris.
Elinor Cheeseborough sepult' 26° Januarii.

Eliz. Newbie vid. sep. 3 Februarii.
Jona Clarkson vid. sepult 28° Februarii.
Anna Foster vid. sep. 27° Februarii.

Sepultor' nomina, 1693.
Edw. fil. Gul. Hayton sepultus fuit 7° Maii.
Maria uxor Gulielmi Tilburne sep. 10° Junii.
Ambrosius fil. Rob. Burnes sep. 23° Junii.
Sarah fil. Christo. Finley sep. 1 Julii.
Filia Gulielmi Jamson sep. 2 Julii.
Christ. uxor Tho. Kipling sep. 5° Julii.
Rich. Todd juvenis sepultais 15° Augusti.
Tho. Foster sepeliebatur 20° Septembris.
Cha. Grainger sepeliebatur 4° Decembris.
Anna Appleby sep. 6° Jan.
Jana Finley sep. 11° Januarii.
Tho. Bowes, sep. 13 Januarii.

Connubia, 1693.
Rich. Colling et Maria Garnet conuncti fuere in matrimonium secunda die Augusti·
Tho. Morgan and Eliz. Maudd conuncti fuere ....
Gulielm Tilburne et Elinor Emmerson ....

4b.
Baptism., 1693.
Ambrosius fil. Rob. Barnes, baptiz. 29° Martis.
Randulphus fil. Tho. Coates, baptiz. 17° Septembris.

1694.
Joab fil. Geo. Harker, batiz. 22° Aprilis.
Rich. fil. Car. Finley, baptiz. eod. die.
Maria filia Gulielmi Kelley, baptiz. 24 Maii.

Sepultor' nomina, 1693.
Elizab. fil. Radulphi Binyan sep. 28° Januarii.
Elizab. fil. Tho. Foster sep. 31° Januarii.
Christo. Garnet sepultus fuit 3° Februarii.

1694.
Randall Milburne sep. fuit 11° Junii.
Fleetwood uxor charissima Gulielmi Lambton Generosi sepulta 5° Julii.

Date.	Name.	Residence.	Document.	Reference.
1563	Chaloner, Janet.	Goldsborough.	W.I.	—
1565	,, Johanne.	,,	P. Act.	B. 10.
1557	,, Ranolde.	Flasbie.	W.I.	—
1591	,, Richard.	Flaxbie.	W.	—
1581	,, Roger.	Goldsboro'.	W.I.T.	—
1558	,, William.	,,	W.	—
	Chamber, *see* Flessher and Chambers.			
1577	Chambers, Agnes.	Thornton Steward.	W.I.	—
1559 ?	,, (Chawm')Xpofer.	,,	W.I.	—
1589	,, Jenet.	Harmeby.	W.I.	—
1557	,, (Chamer) Margt.	Patrick Brompton.	P. Act.	C. 43.
1560	,, ,, Richd.	Thornton Steward.	I.	—
1575	,, ,, Robt.	Asenbie.	Note.	D. 111.
1575	,, Simon.	Thornton Steward.	W.	D. 107.
1560	,, (Chamers),Thos.	Richmond.	I.	—
1560	,, ,, ,,	Allerton.	I.	—
1549	,, (Chamer), ,,	Bowthe.*	W.	C. 28.
1531	,, (Chamber),Walt.	Helsyngton.	W.	+ 130.
	Chamer, *see* Chambers.			
1575	Chapman, Alice.	Swayneby.‡	W.I.	—
1573	,, Edmond.	,, ‡	W.I.	—
1601	,, George.	Cotherston.	W.I.	—
1578	,, John.	,,	W.I.	D. 154.
1605	,, Robert.	Startforth.	W.I.	—
1578	,, Roger.	Carperby.	W.I.	—
1588	,, Thomas.	Thornton Rust.	W.I.	—
1542	Charder, Edmd., clk.	Grinton.	W.	—
1587	,, James.	Reeth.	W.	—
1547	,, Jeffra.	,,	W.	—
1563	Charnley, Alice.	Broughton.¶	W.	—
1561	,, Janet.	Wodplompton†	W.	—
1559	,, John.	,, †	W.	—
1562	,, ,,	,, †	W.	—
1561	Chatborne, Catherine.	Ellsweeke.	W.I.	—
1560	,, Thomas.	,,	W.I.	—
1550	Chater (Chatter), Geo.	West Bolton.	W.I.	—

* ? In Dalton-in-Furness.   ‡ Also of Pickhall.   † ? In co. Lancaster.
¶ Attested by Sir Roger Charnocke, Curate of Broughton,

D

Date.	Name.			Residence.	Document.	Reference.
1608	Chery, Robert.			Kearton.	W.I.	—
1462	Chester, Richd., clk.			?Lancaster.	W.	+ 36.
1557	Child, Agnes.			Whixley.	W.	—
1597	,,	Margery.		Marton.	W.	—
1582	,,	Peter.		Norton Luto.	A.	F. 128.
1597	,,	Richard.		Marton.	W.I.	—
1542	,,	William.		Copgrave.	W.	—
	Claghton, *see* Claughton.					
1606	Clapham, Xpofer.			East Witton.	W.I.T.	—
1566	,,	Isabell.		Crakall.	W.I.	—
1563	,,	James.		East Witton.	W.I.	C. 98.
1597	,,	,,		,,	W.I.	—
1589	,,	John, clk.		Jourvaux.	W.I.	—
1563	,,	Robert.		Bedale.	W.	—
1596	Clark (Clerk), Agnes.			Kirk Hamerton.	W.	—
1577	,,	,,	Anth.	Disforth.	A.	F. 56.
1577	,,	,,	Christ.	,,	W.I.	—
1598	,,	,,	,,	Kirkby.	W.I.	—
1608	,,	,,	,,	Nunmonkton.	W.I.	—
1582	,,	,,	Elizth.	Asenby.	A.	F. 125.
1532	,,	,,	George.	Topcliffe.	W.	+ 81.
1595	,,	,,	Giles.	Fingall.	W.I.	—
1590	,,	,,	Helen.	Grenehamerton.	W.I.	—
1564	,,	,,	Henry.	Lancaster.	W.I.	—
1576	,,	,,	James.	Askrig.	I.	—
1591	,,	,,	Janet.	Burton.	W.T.	—
1542	,,	,,	,,	Topcliffe.	W.	—
1543	,,	,,	John.	Marton.	W.	—
1549-	,,	,,	,,	Kirkby More.	W.I.	—
1552	,,	,,	,,	Watlehous.	W.I.	C. 7.
1566	,,	,,	,,	Scotton.	W.	B. 23.
1558	,,	,,	,,	Brampton.	W.	—
1598	,,	,,	,,	Kirkby.	W.I.	—
1580	,,	,,	Leonard.	Thirne.	W.	—
1554	,,	,,	Lionel.	Norton Luto.	W.I.	—
1580	,,	,,	Luce.	Little Crakall.	W.I.	—
1566	,,	,,	Margt.	Kirkby Hill.	W.I.	B. 25.
1598	,,	,,	,,	Minskip.	W.I.	—

Date.	Name.			Residence.	Document.	Reference.
1572	Clark (Clerk),		Michl.	Scorton.	W.I.	—
1565	,,	,,	Miles.	Kendal.	W.I.	—
1559	,,	,,	Richard.	Ellingthorp.	W.I.	—
1565	,,	,,	,,	Smeton.	W.I.	—
1578	,,	,,	Robert.	Humberton.	W.I.	—
1586	,,	,,	,,	Kirkby Mores.	W.I.	—
1553	,,	,,	Thomas.	Humberton.	W.I.	—
1558	,,	,,	,,	Elingthorp.	W.I.	—
1558	,,	,,	,,	Scorton.	W.I.	—
1566	,,	,,	,,	Langthorpe.	A.	B. 21.
1581	,,	,,	Thomas.	Greenhamerton.	W.I.	—
1581	,,	,,	,,	Marton Moors.	W.I.	—
1587	,,	,,	,,	Marton Burghshire.	W.I.	—
1602	,,	,,	,,	Bedale.	W.I.	—
1604	,,	,,	,,	Little Crackall.	W.I.	—
1549	,,	,,	William.	Ellingthrop.	W.I.	—
1559	,,	,,	,,	Scorton.	I.	—
1564	,,	,,	,,	Asynby.	W.I.	B. 8.
1564	,,	,,	,,	Kirkby Hill.	W.	—
1570	,,	,,	,,	,,	W.	—
1571	,,	,,	,,	Bedale.	W.I.	—
1576	,,	,,	,,	Hardrowe.	W.	D. 111.
1589	,,	,,	,,	Kirkhamerton.	W.	—
1610	Clarkson (Clerkson),		Barthol.	Richmond.	W.I.	—
1539	,,	,,	Brian.	Grinton.	W.	+ 193.
1559	,,	,,	Cuth.	Marsk.	W.I.	C. 89.
1587	,,	,,	,,	,,	A.	—
1574	,,	,,	Edward.	Grinton.	W.T.	D. 57.
1552	,,	,,	Elizth.	Richmond.	W.T.	C. 1.
1588	,,	,,	,,	Smerber.	W.T.	—
1591	,,	,,	George.	Hivelett.	W.	—
1589	,,	,,	Giles.	Kirk Ravensworth.	A.	—
1592	,,	,,	Henry.	Wensley.	W.I.	—
1574	,,	,,	Isabel.	Richmond.	W.	D. 56.
1558	,,	,,	Janet.	Askrigg.	W.I.	—
1560	,,	,,	John.	Richmond.	W.	—
1559	,,	,,	,,	Yffiett.	W.	—

Date.	Name.	Residence.	Document.	Reference.
1599	Clarkson (Clerkson), John.	Newstead.	W.	—
1564	,, ,, Mich., clk.	Easby.	W.I.	—
1571	,, ,, Richard.	Crackpot.	W.I.	—
1577	,, ,, ,,	Bretonby.	W.I.	D. 126.
1562	,, ,, Robert.	Cockerham.†	W.I.	—
1589	,, ,, Thomas.	Kirk Ravensworth.	A.	—
1583	,, ,, Wm.	Marsk.	W.I.	—
1584	,, ,, ,,	,,	W.	—
1589	,, ,, ,,	Newsham.	W.I.	—
1587	Clarvaux, Richard.	Croft.	W.I.	—
1590	,, ,,	,,	Commission	—
1532	,, William.	,,	W.	+ 173.
1540	Claughton, Peter.	Thornton.*	W.	+ 181.
1531	,, (Claghton), Wm.	,, *	W.	+ 75.
1606	Claxton, John.	Richmond.	W.I.	—
1583	,, Thomas.	Fletham.	W.I.	—
1564	Clayton, Charles.	Heigholme.	W.I.	C. 110.
1558	,, James.	Manfeld.	W.I.	—
1579	Cleasby, Dorothy.	Newton Morell.	W.	—
1554	Cleasby, John.	Ellerton.	W.I.	—
1550	,, Leonard.	Cleasby.	W.I.	—
1599	,, Matilda.	Richmond.	W.I.	—
1562	,, Ralph, gent.	Thintoft.	W.I.	—
1549	Clementson, Agnes.	Aldborough.	W.I.	C. 95.
	Clerk, see Clark.			
	Clerkson, see Clarkson.			
1605	Clifton (Clyfton), Peter.	Minskip.	W.I.	—
1563	,, ,, Wm.	Kirkham.†	W.	—
1587	Close, Agnes.	Spenceley.	W.	—
1576	,, Catherine.	Whayteyside.	A.	D. 120.
1587	,, Emote.	Spenceley.	A.I.	—
1562	,, John.	,,	W.I.	C. 95.
1575	,, John.	Healey.	W.I.	D. 102.
1580	,, Laurence.	Whyteyside.	W.I.	—
1590	,, Mark.	Harcayside.	W.I.	—
1558	,, William.	Richmond.	W.I.	—

† ? Co. Lancaster.   * ? In Lonsdale.

Date.	Name.	Residence.	Document.	Reference.
1572	Close, Sir Wm., clerk.	Topcliffe.	W.I.	—
1516	Clowman, Ralph.	St. Clement Danes.*	W.	+ 136.
1550	Cobsie, John.	Bolton Swayle.	W.	—
1558	,, Leonard.	,,	W.	—
1588	,, William.	,,	I.	—
1576	Cockrell, Thomas.	Manfeld.	W.I.	D. 116.
1585	Coghill, Thomas.	Knaresboro'.	W.	—
	Coke, see Cook.			
1427	Cook, Cecilia.	———	W.	+ 37.
1610	,, Ellinor.	Killinghall.	W.I.	—
1603	,, George.	Brearton.	W.	—
1577	,, Henry.	Topliff.	W.I.	F. 55.
1567	,, Miles.	Marton.	W.	B. 32.
1577	,, Nicholas.	Manfeld.	W.	D. 132.
1600	,, Peter.	Ripley.	W.	—
1561	,, Richard.	Bolton Swale.	W.	—
1563	,, ,,	Brearton.	W.I.	—
1570	,, ,,	Hutton Conyers.	W.I.	—
1559	,, Robert.	Staveley.	W.I.	—
1564	,, Thomas.	Scotforthe.†	W.I.	—
1568	,, ,,	Richmond.	W.	D. 24.
1570	,, ,,	Gayles.	W.I.	—
1596	,, ,,	Raynton.	W.I.	—
1557	,, William.	Kendal.	W.I.	—
1568	,, ,,	Brereton.	I.	—
1585	,, ,,	Picall.	W.I.	—
1550?	Cokye, Thomas.	[blank]	I.	—
1599	Cole, John.	Snape.	W.I.	—
1563	Coleson, William.	Middleton Tias.	W.	C. 102.
1581	Colley, Richard.	Wath.	W.T.	—
1580	Collier, Henry.	Copgrave.	W.T.	—
1577	Collinge, Elizabeth.	Whixley.	W.	F. 47.
1559	,, Thomas.	,,	W.T.	C. 86.
1560	,, Xpopher.	Ravensworth.	W.I.	—
	— See also Cowling.			
1584	Collingwood, Janet.	Kirkhamerton.	W.I.	—
1610	,, John.	,,	W.I.	—

*Co. Middlesex; mentions Doveridge and Somersal, co. Derby.   †? Co. Lanc.

Date.	Name.	Residence.	Document.	Reference.
1608	Collingwood, Robert.	Kirkhamerton.	I.T.	—
1553	Collinson, Agnes.	Richmond.	W.I.	—
1476	,, Robert.	Stanwix.	W.	+ 15.
1551	,, ,,	Richmond.	W.	—
1556	,, Thomas.	Staveley.	W.I.	—
1591	Collyer, William.	Grinton.	W.I.	—
1599	Collyn, Edward.	Kirkby Hill.	W.I.	—
1585	,, (Collen), Margt.	Ravensworth.	W.	—
1586	,, ,, Matt.	Richmond.	W.I.	—
1585	,, ,, Robt.	K. Ravensworth.	I.	—
	— See also Collinge and Cowling.			
1591	Colman, Agnes.	West Tanfield.	W.I.	—
1580	Comelache, George.	Grymsarghe.*	W.	—
1554	Constable, Ralph.	Thintoft.	W.	—
1566	,, Robert.	Bedale.	W.I.	—
1558	Conyers, Alice.	Richmond.	W.I.	C. 66.
[1574	,, Cuthbert, and Dakers, Ann, Marriage Licence.			D. 55.]
1541	,, Giles.	Apleton.	W.	+ 211.
1567	,, John.	Gatenby.	A.T.	—
1590	,, Ralph.	North Gaile.	W.I.	—
1554	Conyers, Wm., Esq.	Marske.	W.	—
1557	,, ,,	,,	W.I.	C. 44.
1587	,, [blank], gent.	Warlabie.	W.I.	—
1605	Coppin, Cuthbert.	Richmond.	I.	—
1573	Corkbie, John.	Cowborne.‡	W.	D. 32.
1579	,, (Corbie), Richd.	Redmire.	I.	—
1554	,, ,, Thos.	Caterick.	W.	—
1563	Corlus, Richard.	Garstang.†	W.I.	—
1541	,, Robert.	Cockerham.†	W.	D. 200.
1562	,, Thomas.	Garstang.†	W.	—
1574	Corneforth, John.	Richmond.	W.I.	D. 64.
1570	Corner, Edward.	,,	W.I.	D. 167.
1598	,, ? Edward.	,,	A.	—
1573	,, Ralph.	East Witton.	W.I.	D. 28.
1574	,, William.	,,	A.	D. 50.
1558	Cotes, Alan.	Ellerton.	W.I.	—
1572	,, Anthony.	Barningham.	W.I.	—

* ? In Preston, co. Lancaster.   ‡ ? In Caterick.   † ? In co. Lancaster.

Date.	Name.	Residence.	Document.	Reference.
1552	Cotes, Edmund.	Askrig.	W.I.	—
1585	,, Ellen.	Ellerton.	A.	—
1558	,, (Coot), Giles.	West Dalton.	W.I.	—
1602	,, Henry.	Whaston.	W.I.	—
1577	,, John.	Askrig.	W.	—
1552	,, ,, clerk.	Vicar of Picall.	W.I.	C. 12.
1572	,, ,,	Grinton.	W.I.	--
1585	,, ,,	Ellerton.	W.I.	—
1576*	,, Leonard.	[blank]	Note.	D. 111.
1576*	,, ,,	Grinton.	W.	—
1579	,, ,,	Forcett.	W.I.	—
1604	,, Nicholas.	Tanfeld.	W.I.	—
1597	,, Richard.	Ravenseat.	W.I.	—
1598	,, ,,	Richmond.	W.I.	—
1552	,, Thomas.	Delthwayte.	W.	C. 4
1575	,, ,,	Bowes.	W.	—
1583	,, ,,	East Dalton.	W.I.	—
1598	Cotesworth, Richard.	Romaldkirk.	W.I.	—
1508	Cotforth, William.	Watermott.	W.I.	—
1599	Cottingham, Henry.	Richmond.	W.I.	—
1599	Cottingham, John.	Richmond.	A.	—
1587	,, Thomas.	Fencott.	W.I.	—
1560	Cottom, Elizabeth.	Ribchester.	W.I.	—
1564	Colton, Hewan.	Askrig.	W.I.	—
1589	,, (Cowlton), Jas.	,,	W.I.	—
1573	,, Margery.	,,	W.	D. 42.
1598	,, Thomas.	,,	W.I.	—
1575	[Coverham, Libel Action, re the Firmar there.]			
1542	Coward, Richard.	Smeton.	W.I.	—
1570	,, ,,	Knaresboro'.	W.I.	—
1563	Cowbron, Laurence.	Kirkham.	W.I.	—
1607	Cowlinge, Catherine.	Marske.	W.I.	—
1560	,, Christopher.	K. Ravensworth.	W.I.	—
1564	,, ,,	Kendal.†	W.	—
1591	,, ,,	Feldom.	A.	—
1589	,, Edward.	East Dalton.	W.I.	—
1560	,, (Colling), Hy.	Richmond.	W.I.	—

* Probably identical. † Co. West.

Date.	Name.	Residence.	Document.	Reference.
1539	Cowlinge, John.	Richmond.	W.	+ 165.
1597	,, ,,	Dalton.†	W.I.	—
1570	,, Lucie.	Richmond.	W.I.	—
1546	,, Margaret.	,,	W.I.	—
1568	Cowling, Ralph.	Richmond.	W.	—
1565	,, ,,	,,	W.I.	—
1557	,, Richard.	,,	W.I.	—
1602	,, ,,	Marske.	W.I.	—
	See also Collinge and Collyn.			
1585	Cowper, Christopher.	Kirklington.	W.	—
1544	,, John.	Aldingham.‡	W.I.	—
1563	,, ,,	Urswick.‖	W.I.	—
1566	,, Matilda.	Greenhamerton.	W.I.	—.
1576	,, Richard.	Scotton.	W.I.	—
1577	,, ,,	Manfeld.	W.	D. 130.
1579	,, Robert.	Scotton.	A.	—
1609	,, Sydray.	Cundall.	W.I.	—
1598	,, Thomas.	Staveley.	W.I.	—
1565	Cowpertwhaite, Jas.	Lankerigge.§	W.I.	—
1566	,, Robert.	Markethestede.§	W.I.	—
1596	Cowpland, Peter.	Reeth.	W.I.	—
1603	Cowtonn, Henry.	Boroughbridge.	W.I.	—
1556	,, James.	Aldburgh.	W.I.	—
1593	,, William.	Aglethorp.	W.I.	—
1576	Coulton, John.	Over Dunsforth.	W.I.	—
1549	Cowton, Richard.	,,	W.I.	—
1593	,, (Cowlton), Rd.	Kirkhamerton.	W.I.	—
1559	,, Thomas.	Dunsforth.	W.I.	—
1556	,, William.	,,	W.I.	—
1577	Cradock, Henry.	Romaldkirk.	P. Act.	D. 134.
1572	,, Richard.	Downholm.	W.	—
1566	Craggs (Crag), James.	?Dent.*	I.	—
1577	,, ,, ,,	,, *	W.I.	—
1549	,, ,, Richard.	,, *	W.	—
1583	,, William.	Knaresbro'.	A.	—
1599	Craven, John.	Redmire.	W.I.	—
1574	,, Richard.	Scriven.	W.I.	—

† Bond of Ravensworth.   ‡ ? In Furness.   ‖ Co. Lanc.   § Co. West.   * In Lonsdale.

The Index Library (British Record Society, Limited). Annual Subscription—One Guinea. Published Quarterly. CONTAINS INDEXES, CALENDARS, AND ABSTRACTS OF BRITISH RECORDS. Calendars already completed—Prerogative Ct. of Canterbury, 2 vols.; Northampton and Rutland Wills; Chancery Proceedings, 3 vols; Royalist Composition Papers; Signet Bills; Berkshire Wills; Lichfield Wills; Gloucestershire Wills; Gloucestershire Inquisitiones post mortem. Calendars in progress—Prerogative Court of Canterbury Wills; Sussex Wills; Dorsetshire Wills; Chancery Proceedings; London Inquisitiones post mortem; Wiltshire Inquisitiones post mortem. *Hon. Sec.*:—E. A. FRY, Esq., 172, Edmund Street, Birmingham. *Agent*:—CHAS. J. CLARK, 4, Lincoln's Inn Fields, W.C.

The East Anglian; or, Notes and Queries on subjects connected with the Counties of Suffolk, Cambridge, Essex, and Norfolk. Edited by the REV. C. H. EVELYN WHITE, F.S.A., Rector of Rampton, Cambridge. Annual Subscription, 5s. post free. Ipswich: F. PAWSEY, The Ancient House. London: ELLIOT STOCK, 62, Paternoster Row.

Maine Historical and Genealogical Recorder. A Quarterly Magazine, the prime object of which is the publication of whatever may be secured of historical interest pertaining to our own State, and whatever of family history may be gathered from different sources that interest the sons and daughters of Maine, wherever located. Original Records, Documents, or other papers suitable for a publication of this kind solicited. Advertisements inserted at the usual rates. Published in Portland, Maine, at $3.00 per annum in advance. S. M. WATSON, *Editor and Publisher.*

Fenland Notes and Queries, Edited by Rev. W. D. SWEETING, M.A., Maxey Vicarage, Market Deeping. A Quarterly Journal devoted to the Antiquities, Geology, Natural Features, Parochial Records, Family History, Legends and Traditions, Folk-lore, Curious Customs, etc., of the Fenland, in the counties of Huntingdon, Cambridge, Lincoln, Northampton, Norfolk, and Suffolk. Price 1s. 6d. per quarter, by post 1s. 8d. A year's Subscription, if paid in advance, 6s. post free. Peterborough: GEORGE C. CASTER, Market Place.

Somerset and Dorset Notes and Queries, Edited by F. W. WEAVER, M.A., Milton Clevedon, Evercreech, Somerset, and C. H. MAYO, M.A., R.D., Non-Res. Canon of Sarum, Long Burton Vicarage, Sherborne, Dorset.
Vol. V. commenced March 1896. Parts issued Quarterly. Subscriptions, 5s. per annum, payable in advance to either of the Editors, to whom all communications should be addressed.

Bye-Gones: for Wales and the Borders. Established 1871. Quarterly, 5s. per annum. "Appears a wholly admirable publication, both in intention and execution."—*Saturday Review.* WOODALL, MINSHALL & Co., Oswestry.

Genealogical Queries and Memoranda. A Quarterly Magazine devoted to Genealogy, Family History, Heraldry, and Topography. Edited by GEORGE F. TUDOR SHERWOOD. Annual Subscription *(payable in advance)*, 3s. 6d. or $1; Single Numbers, 1s. or 25 cents. Genealogical Queries and Memoranda shows alphabetically, under Surnames and under Counties, whose genealogies are being investigated, and the points in them that require elucidation. It may be asserted that in nearly every case a query indicates the existence, in private possession, of a collection of evidence regarding the family referred to. It enables those interested to communicate with one another. It gives circulation to queries on heraldry and prints the answers to them. It catalogues pedigrees and collections of family history in print and MS., its aim being ever to open up fresh ground. It gives clues to other sources of genealogical information. All communications to be addressed GEO. F. TUDOR SHERWOOD, 99, Angell Road, Brixton, London, S.W.

Mr. Coleman's Catalogue, (No. ccxxiii.) of Charters, Deeds, Wills, Court-Rolls, Rent-Rolls, Pedigrees, Maps, Heraldry, Topography, &c., now ready. Also his two Alphabetical Lists of 1000 Old Wills each, price together 2s. 6d. JAMES COLEMAN, Genealogical Bookseller, 9, Tottenham Terrace, Tottenham, London, N.

The Scottish Antiquary; or, Northern Notes and Queries. Increased to 48 Pages, with Illustrations, price 1s. A Magazine of Archæology, Etymology, Folk-lore, Genealogy, Heraldry, &c. Edited by the Rev. A. W. CORNELIUS HALLEN, M.A., F.S.A. Scot. Mem. Coun. Hist. Soc. Issued Quarterly. Annual Subscription (payable in advance), 4s. *All Letters and Subscribers' Names to be sent to the Editor,* THE REV. A. W. CORNELIUS HALLEN, PARSONAGE, ALLOA.

APRIL 1897.

THE
Northern Genealogist.

CONTENTS:

	PAGE		PAGE
Notes and Queries	57	Papist Returns, 18th Century	84
Cumberland Wills	59	Clay Coton Parish Register	92
Lincoln Marriage Bonds	63	Marriage Bonds of the Dean and Chapter of York	96
St. Peter's, York—School Register	67		
Fangfoss Register Transcripts	72	Some Notes of Roman Catholics in Lincolnshire	102
Act Books of the Prerogative Court of York	75	Startforth Parish Register	105
		Some Richmond Wills	109
Durham, Carlisle, and Allertonshire Marriage Bonds	79	Supplement—	
Some Colonial Wills	82	Richmondshire Wills	33

Subscription 10s. 6d. per annum.

YORK:
PRINTED BY JOHN SAMPSON, 13, CONEY STREET.

WORKS BY THE SAME EDITOR.

EARLY LINCOLN WILLS; an Abstract of all the Wills and Administrations recorded in the Episcopal Registers at Lincoln, 1280—1547, 8vo. 21/-.

LIBER ANTIQUUS HUGONIS WELLS, Episcopi Lincolniensis; comprising the Endowments of Vicarages in Oxfordshire, Bucks., Beds., Hunts., Herts., Northants., Rutland, and Lincolnshire. 1209—1235, 8vo. 10/6.

LINCOLN MARRIAGE LICENCES; an Abstract of the Allegation Books preserved in the Registry of the Bishop of Lincoln, 1598—1628, 8vo. 15/-.

ELY EPISCOPAL RECORDS; a Calendar and Concise View of the Records preserved in the Muniment Room of the Palace at Ely. Compiled by direction of the Rt. Rev. Alwyne, Lord Bishop of Ely, 8vo. 42/-.

REPORTS on the Registry of the Bishop of Lincoln, and on the Records of the Corporation of Grimsby. Compiled for Her Majesty's Hist. MSS. Commission.

YORK WILLS INDEXES, 1544—1553, 1554—1568, and 1568—1585. Compiled for the Yorkshire Archæological Society. (*In Progress.*)

NOTES ON THE HERALDS' VISITATION OF LINCOLNSHIRE in 1634. With Supplements containing Indexes of the Wills in the Consistory Court and the Court of the Dean and Chapter at Lincoln, 8vo. (*In Progress.*)

The Northern Genealogist is issued quarterly, in January, April, July, and October, and is supplied to subscribers only, at 10s. 6d. per annum, payable in advance.

Notes, Articles, or Queries, on Antiquarian subjects, will be gladly received, as also Books or Articles for review.

Terms for Advertisements can be had on application.

The Editor personally undertakes Genealogical and Antiquarian Researches in any part of the Kingdom, and, in questions not involving such research, will be happy to give to Subscribers, free of charge, any advice or assistance in his power.

Transcripts or Abstracts of Wills, &c., in London, or in the York or other Provincial Registries, are supplied according to Scale of Charges to be had on application.

All communications to be addressed to

A. GIBBONS, F.S.A.,

Heworth, York.

NOTES AND QUERIES.

It would be of great use to many Genealogists if a list could be compiled of the dates and present place of deposit of old Manor Rolls, and perhaps if we print a few such notes as a specimen, some of our readers may be kind enough to add to them for a future issue:—

Wakefield, 1273, to present date. (Wakefield Manor Office.)
Swaledale Manors (Healaugh and Muker), 1686 to 1849. (Messrs. Rogers and Hudson, Richmond, Yorkshire.)
Thornton-cum-Bishopside, commence 1665. (Messrs. Wise and Son, Ripon.)
Kirkby Malzeard, Fountains, & Hutton Conyers. (Marquis of Ripon.)
Bradford, 1569 to 1696. (Nydd Hall.)
Allerton Mauleverer, Henry 4 to Philip & Mary. (Nydd Hall.)
Burley-in-Wharfedale, 1 Henry 4 to 2 & 3 Philip & Mary. (Burley Hall.)
Bishopthorpe, 1621 to 1814. (Archbishop of York.)
Cawood, 2 & 3 Philip & Mary to 1840. (Archbishop of York.)
Wistow, 13 Elizth. to 1840. (Archbishop of York.)
Menston, 49 Ed. 3 to 17 James 1. (Farnley Hall.)

* * * * *

Some proceedings in a matrimonial cause of about the time of Elizabeth, preserved amongst the muniments of the Dean and Chapter of York, give the following curious list of gifts during courtship. The suit was brought by one Edward Walker, against Dorothy Vavasour *alias* Walker, late of Copmanthorpe. Edward Walker says he is married to Dorothy, and prays for a declaration that the marriage is valid. Dorothy's answer is not to be found, but her further answer (from which it may be surmised that she pleaded precontract) is as follows:—

In prim:s the said Henry Vavasor in signe and token of matrimony, gave unto the said Dorothy a ring of gold with a stone called a Jacent, which she received thankfully.

2. Item, a hope of gold having writyn in it—*Amor vincit omnia*; and an other posie on the out syde, viz.—*No hope but in God.*

3. Item, a hope of gold having writen on the oute side—*Truthe trieth trowthe.*

4. Item, a tablett of gold with a grene stone; another of an emerode set in it.

5. Item, fyve angelles of gold.

6. Item, a .... of sylver and gilt.

7. Item, half a ryall of gold of Kyng Edwardes coyne.

8. Item, a pare of cremesyn sattan sleves. All which the said Henry gave and the said Dorothy received in token of matrimony contracted and to be solemnized between them.

* * * * *

Colthurst of Edisford. Required the earlier Yorkshire pedigree of this family. The Visitation of Somerset, 1573, p. 15, gives, " Henry Colethurst, yor Br. of Colethurst of Edisford, Yorks." as the father of Matthew Colthurst, of Wardour Castle, Wilts. (d. 1559), from whom the Somerset branch. Edmund Colthurst, of Hinton, co. Somerset, son and heir of the said Matthew, married Elinor, daur. to Thomas de la River, of Yorkshire. Can anyone tell me the abode of this family of De la River, in Yorkshire? A John de la River was buried at Hinton Charterhouse, co. Somerset, 2 Jan., 1573-4.

R. G. BARTLETT,
Corfe Castle, co. Dorset.

Otway—Fleming. Can any reader tell me in what way the poet, Thomas Otway, was connected with, or related to the family of Fleming (Le Fleming, of Furness)? I remember seeing the connexion made out some years ago, but I did not take a note of it at the time, and I quite forget where I saw it and what the connexion was.

FREDERICK W. RAGG,
Marsworth Vicarage, Tring.

Fairfax. £15 reward will be paid by the Editor for evidence (satisfactory to the College of Arms) of the identity of Joseph Fairfax, bapt. at Saxton, co. York, March 27, 1706, with Joseph Fairfax, buried at Windlesham, co. Surrey, June 22, 1783, aged 77. A reward will also be paid for any information as to the family, which may prove of service as a clue to the above.

CUMBERLAND WILLS.

Sir Timothy Fetherstonhaugh, of Kirk Ouswould, co. Cumberland, knight. 20 Oct., 1651. Being readie to sacrifice my life for my loyaltie to my dreade Sovereigne, Kinge Charles the Second, and in full and perfect memorye, praised be God, &c. To be decently buried as my friends shall think fit. Part of my estate to be sold "to paie children's porcons and maintaine you my dear wife." Residue of goods to wife Dame Bridgett F., extrix. to educate my children. Dated at Chester Castle, "signed and declared to be my last Will and Testament to my sonne-in-law Barnard Kirkbride, Oswould Bird." Proved at York, 1661-2. [xliv. 168.]

Patricius Senhouse, of Hameshill, par. Bridekirk, co. Cumberland, gent. (Short Abstract.) 9 Feb., 1681. To Anthony Wilkes, senr., of Papcastle elder, and Richard Tubman, of Talentire elder, my tenement in Hameshill, burgage houses in Cockermouth, and lands in Soulfeit and Saundayre, upon Trust for my wife Elizth. for life, and then for my sons Patricius, Thomas, John, and Humphrey Senhouse, successively in tail male, with remainder to my daughter Elizth. Senhouse in tail general, with remainder to Patricius Beeby, sonne of John Beeby, of Cookhirst, co. Cumberland, gent. Bequests to my two sisters Frances Senhouse and Isabell Senhouse, and some small bequests to servants and others. Wife extrix. Proved at York, 6 April, 1682. [lix. 272.]

William Ferryes, of Whitehaven, co Cumberland, merchant, 27 June, 1710. Wife Grace £50 per annum for life, and six rooms in my new house at Whitehaven during widowhood. Younger son Gale Feryes and daughter Elizth. F. £1000 each, and if the ships *Cumberland* and *William & Grace* do arrive at Whitehaven in safety, £200 each more, at 21. All my leaseholds in Ireland to eldest son Wm. F. in tail. Residue of goods to son Wm. To the Protestant Dissenting Minister at Whitehaven, for the time being, £5 a year till son Wm. attain 21. Friends Wm. Gilpin, esq., John Gilpin, merchant, Elisha Gale, merchant, John Gale, junr., merchant, and

Clement Nicholson, merchant, to be exors. My exors. to continue Abraham Chambers to collect my effects. Daur. Elizth. my silver tankard in Ireland, and half-a-dozen silver spoons, &c. Witnesses, Thos. Dixon, Abraham Chambers, and Jos. Spooner.

Codicil, 29 July, 1710. £200 more to wife. Witnesses, Thomas Lamplugh, Thomas Dixon, and Abraham Chambers. Proved at York, 10 Dec., 1711. [lxvii., 360.]

Thomas Benson, D.D., 27 Dec., 1726. [lxxix. 462.] To be buried in the South Ile of Carlisle Cathedral. Wife Mary my freehold and customary lands at Kendall for her life, and then to my friend and nearest kinsman Lieut-Col. Geo. Benson for life, and then to his only remaining son Thos. my godson, and in case of his death without issue then to Geo. Benson, grandson of the said Colonel Benson, by his eldest son John. To my wife the tithes of Botcherby; also my house in Abbey Street for life, and then to my friend and relation the Rev. Edward Burket. To the Vicar of Stanwix who shall succeed me, my lease of the tithe corn of Rennyholm. To the poor of Stanwix and Dalston, £50 each parish. Note from Mr. Alderman John How for £20 to be remitted for the use of the Charity School. Said Mr. Edward Birket £100. Godson, Rd. Bolton, son of Mr. Thomas Bolton, Rector of Graystock £100. Godson, Thomas, the son of my friend Mr. Edward Hutchinson £100. My relation and servant Ellinor Hudson £100. My friend and agent at Kendall, Mr. Wm. Bracken £50. Catherine daughter of said Wm. Bolton £50. All my servants half-a-year's wages. Residue to wife, extrix. Witnesses, Edwd. Carlile, Edwd. Birket, James Hilton. Proved at York, 29 Aug., 1727.

Geo. Brownrigg, of Wigton, co. Cumberland, gent., 20 Jan., 1726. House and garth at Wigton, and the furniture therein, to my now wife for life, and then to my granddaughter Mary Brownrigg. Lands in Crosthwaite, purchased of Wm. Dover and his wife, to my granddaughter Elizth. Brownrigg. Granddaughter Ann B. £100, and a close near Applethwaite. Grandson Wm. B. two closes of land. Son Geo. B. and his wife a guinea each. Grandson Henry B. a guinea. To said Mary B. £50. To said Elizth. B. £100. Son Geo. B. my lands in Gofforth, to be sold to raise portions for his younger children, particularly £200 to my grandson Henry. Ten of the poorest families in Under Skiddow xx^d each. Son Geo. exor. Supervisors, my cousins John Tubman of Cockermouth, and Richard Winder, of same. Witnesses, John Kaye, Jeremiah Grave, James Kaye. Proved at York, 26 June, 1727. [lxxix. 426.]

Sir George Fleming, bart., LL.D., Bishop of Carlisle, 13 April, 1743. [xci. 337.] To be buried in Carlisle Cathedral near where my wife is buried. Furniture mentioned in Inventory on page 82 of my Register Booke at Rose Castle to remain at Rose Castle for ever for the use of the See. Extrixes. to deliver to the next heir male of the ffamily the ancient gilded silver bowl with the family arms thereon, which my great great grandmother Agnes Fleming left and desired that it should be kept as a lucky piece of plate, as also the silver bason given by my great uncle John Fleming in 1662 to my father and his heirs male. Extrixes to deliver to the next heir male of my father Sir Daniel Fleming, knt., all such his MSS., printed books, and maps, now in my possession as could be obtained from the exors. of my brother Sir Wm. Fleming, bart., according to Sir Daniel's Will of 1697. My own books to my grandson Humphrey Senhouse, son of Humphrey S., esq. Residue of goods and my lands at Thursby, co. Cumberland, to my three daughters Mary, ux. Humphrey Senhouse, of Netherhall, esq.; Catherine, ux. Joseph Dacre Appelby, of Kirklinton, esq.; and Mildred, ux. Edward Stanley, of Ponsonby, esq., extrixes. Witnesses, Jos. Nicolson, Thos. Young. Proved at York, 25 Aug., 1747.

Barbara Relffe, of Cockermouth, co. Cumberland, widow, 20 April, 1724. I intend shortly to convey to my trusty friend John Harrison, of Mearley, co. Lanc., esq., my customary lands (described) at Cockermouth, upon trust. I declare the said trust to be for my nephew and grandson (sic.) Thos. Gibbon, younger son of my late brother-in-law the Rev. Dr. Thomas G., Dean of Carlisle, in tail, with remainder to his brother, my nephew, Williams G. and his heirs, but subject after the death of my brother Wm. Bird to the payment of £5 a year to his wife Elizth. Bird for life. To my said nephew anp grandson Thos. Gibbon in tail, my burgage and close called Sepulchre or St. Hellins, in Cockermouth. To my unkind sister Dame Dorothy

Hasell, widow, 1 guinea, and to her son, my nephew, Edward H., esq., 1 guinea. Brother-in-law Joshua Blackwill, gent., 1 guinea, and to my sister Lettice, his wife, £20, and to their son, John B., 1 guinea, and to May, his wife, £200. Nephew Williams Winder (who is now beyond the seas), son of my said sister Lettice by her former husband £300, if it please God he lives and returns into England. Sister Mary Gibbon, widow of my said late brother, Dr. Thomas G., £100. Said nephew Williams Gibbon £300. Said nephew Thos. Gibbon £200. Niece Barbara Gibbon, daughter of said Dr. G., £800, and to her sister, my niece, Dorothy G., £400. My half sister-in-law Lucy Bird, and her sisters Elizth. and Isabella Bird £50 each. Lucy, daughter of my half brother-in-law Wm. Bird, £20 at marriage or 21. Mrs. Mary Reinalds, wife of ...... Reinalds, of Spittle Fields, London, a near relation of my late dear husband, £20. Said John Harrison for his faithful services to me £100, and to Anne, his wife, 1 guinea. Wm. and James Bird, sons of my said brother Wm. B., £5 each. Grandson .... son of my said husband's kinsman Mr. Wm. Sawbridge, of London, mercer, £20. Cousin Dorothy Halson (*sic.*) daughter of my late uncle Miles Halson, £50. Timothy Hallen and Frances, his wife, 1 guinea each, and to their daughter, Dorothy Hallen, £20. Granddaughter Anne, daughter of Mr. John Tubman, of Cockermouth, £20. My godson, the son of Rd. Whinfield, of Cockermouth, 1 guinea. Anne widow of my said husband's late half brother James Bird, deceased, £20. Poor of Cockermouth the interest of £100, and poor of Graystock £50. Said nephew Williams Gibbon and said niece Barbara Gibbon, exors. Supervisor, the said John Harrison. Witnesses, Jo. Irvin, Thomas Potter, Jo. Tubmall. Proved at York, 20 Feb,, 1727. [lxxix. 597.]

Wm. Pearson, of Tallantire, par. Bridekirk, co. Cumberland, yeoman, 18 June, 1772. Wife Mary Pearson all my household furniture except the clock in the kitchen, which I give unto my son Wm. Pearson. Son Bell Pearson and daughter Sarah Pearson all my monies on Bonds and Notes equally between them; also my live stock. Son Bell Pearson £100, to be paid him by my son Wm. P. out of my lands. Wife Mary Pearson, extrix. (Signed by mark.) Witnesses, John Bell, Thomas Smith, Robert Dodgson. Proved at York, 30 May, 1777.

LINCOLN MARRIAGE LICENCES.*

1662. July 22. Caborne, Christopher, of Well, gent., and Sarah Wingfeild, of same, spinster. Surety, Robert Harell, of same, husbandman. [Hogstropp.]

1640. May 26. Caborne, John, of Salfletby St. Peter, gent., æt. 26, and Helen Caborne, of same, spinster, æt. 16. Surety, John Hareby, vicar of Mumby. [Salfletby.]

1667. Aug. 8. Caburne, John, of Saltfletby St. Peter, gent., and Ffrances Lawson, of North Sumercoates.
[N. Sumercotes or N. Thoresby.]

1668. March 11. Cade, George, of Boston, husbandman, æt. 36, and Helen Welton, of same, spinster, æt. 26. Their parents are dead. Application by Nicholas Hunt.
[Boston or Skirbeck.]

1662. Jan. 20. Caister, Stephen, of Bottesford, yeoman, and Sarah Ormerod, of same, spinster. Surety, William Caister, of same, yeoman. [Bottesford, Messingham or Ffroddingham.]

1664. Jan. 16. Caldron, William, of Stevenby, husbandman, and Elizth. Barker, of Sewstern, co Leicester, widow. Surety, Hugh Searston (signed Searson), of Colsterworth, mercer.
[Stevenby, Colsterworth, North Wytham or Gunby.]

1583. June 30. Act Book.—Callis, Wm., of Louth, and Elizth. Wyndell, of Great Grymesbie. [Lincoln Archdeaconry.]

1606. Feb. 14. C.—Calton, Nicholas, of Bletshoe, co. Bedford, gent., and Martha, daughter of William Ffishe, of Southill, co. Bedford, gent. Surety, Thomas Eakins, of Catworth, co. Hunt., gent.

1663. Oct. 9. Calverley, Samuell, of Boston, merchant, and Elizth. Cuffen, of same, widow. Surety, Robert Bustard, of same, gent. [Boston, Wrangle or Skirbeck.]

1669. April 5. Camocke, William, of Stamford, linnen draper, æt. 24, and Hester Ffowler, of Easton in the parish of Stoake, spinster, æt. 22. Surety, Richard Serjeant, of Corby.
[Corby or Stoake.]

* Continued from page 12.

1669. May 27. Canand, Richard, of Ffreeston, husbandman, æt. 24, and Elizth. Rackley, of same, widow. Application by Thos. Goodwin, of Boston. [Freeston, Fishtoft or Skirbeck.]

1569. Jan. 20. Ael.—Cantinge, Edward, of Rasonne, and Agnes Hewette, of Owersbie. [Owersbie.]

1667. July 22. Cappe, John, of Catherup, mason, æt. 27, and Sarah Barton, of Ffulbeck, spinster, æt. 20. His father and her mother consent; his mother and her father are dead.
[St. Mark.]

1634. Sept. 29. F.—Carden, Christopher, of Hundleby, æt. 53, and Sara Maulum, of same, widow, æt. 51.
[St. Peter in Eastgate.]

1611. June 20. Carr, Edward, of Sleeford, yeoman, and Suzan Be...on, of Donington, widow. Bond by Robt. Lambert, of Sleeford, yeoman. [Donington.]

1665. Feb. 16. Carr, Robert, of Grayingham, husbandman, and Katherine Becke, of Scotter, spinster. Surety, John Mawnall, of Scothern, yeoman.
[St. Peter at Arches, Harpswell or Hemswell.]

1663. Sept. 15. Carre, William, of Whapload, husbandman, æt. 20 (?), and Alice Ellis, of Ffleet, widow, æt. 30. Surety, John Nusam, of Whapload, carpenter.
[Pinchbecke or Whapload.]

1667. Feb. 21. Carington, John, of Swaiton, husbandman and widower, æt. 50, and Jane Garland, of same, spinster, æt. 26. His parents are dead; hers consent.
[Swaiton or Sempringham.]

1662. Oct. 27. Carrington, William, of Cayster, clerk, and Anne Holder, of Ffaldingworth, spinster. Surety, Arthur Carrington, of Mercate Raysin, gent.
[Ffaldingworth or Rothwell.]

1639. April 11. Carsly, Robert, of Donington-in-Holland, yeoman, and Sara Allott, of Lincoln, widow. [St. Peter at Goats.]

1603. July 26. C.—Carter, Ralph, of Graffam, co. Hunt., and Anne Underwood.

1662. June 20. Cartwright, Thomas, of Lea, husbandman, and Dorothy Silsthorne, of same, widow. Surety, Thomas Watson, of the Close of Lincoln, gent.
[Scampton or Burton by Lincoln.]

1670. May 14. Caskin, William, of the City of Lincoln, chandler, æt. 22, and Elizth. Gree, of St. Peter at Arches, Lincoln, spinster, æt. 22. Her parents and his mother consent; his father is dead. [Canwicke.]

1663. Oct. 29. Casterson, Robert, of Whapload, yeoman, and Ffrances Roote, of Market Deepinge. Surety, William Briggs (?), of Empringham, co. Rutland, husbandman.
[All Hallows, Stamford.]

1664. Jan. 6. Castledine, Nicholas, of Boston, yeoman, æt. 56, and Helen Wilson, of Lower Tointon, widow, æt. 60. Bond by Robert Wood, of .... gent., and Joshua Harwood, of Ffreeston. [St. Paul in Bail.]

1664. July 5. Cateline, Jonathan, of Horbling, clerk, and Katherine Dillingham, of Oundle, co. Northants, spinster. Surety, Benj. Dillingham, of Oundle, clk. [Thurning, co. Hunts.]

1669. May 17. Cater, William, of Market Rasin, cordwinder, æt. 24, and Elizth. Parr, of the Bail of Lincoln, spinster, æt. 20. His father and her mother consent. Surety, Wm. Cater, of Market Rasin, cordwainer.
[St. Mary Wigford or St. Martin.]

1569. Jan. 6. Ael.—Catskynne, Nicholas, curate of Kealbie; license to preach in Deaneries of Grimsby, Louth, &c.

1617. Oct. 27. F.—Cattell, Matthew, of Langtoft, mercer, æt. 30, and Margaret Hudson, of Markett Deepinge, widow, æt. 30. Application by Gregory Stawper, of Corbie, yeoman.
[Market Deepinge.]

1669. May 17. Cattell, Robert, of Market Deeping, and Mary Sharpe, of St. James Deeping, widow. Surety, Richard Roe, of Langtoft, yeoman.
[Langtoft or Stamford All Saints.]

1667. March 13. Cave, William, rector of Salfletby All Saints, æt. 28, and Hester York, of same, widow, æt. 33. His mother consents; her parents are dead. Surety, Richard Cracroft, of the Bail of Lincoln, draper.
[Salfletby St. Peter or St. Clement or Skidbrook.]

1663. April 22. Cawdron, Robert, of Helpringham, gent., and Elizth. Wood, of Sleeford, widow. Surety, John Spenley, of Helpringham, yeoman, and Hugh Walter, of the City of Lincoln, clerk. [Heckington or Helpringham.]

1662. Sept. 25. Cawthorpe, Francis, of Glamford Brigg, gent., and Anne Cutler, of Wintringham, widow. Surety, Michael Cawthorpe, of Lincoln, gent.
[Wintringham or Winterton.]

1628. June 13. Cawton, Thomas, of Eagle, yeoman, æt. 50, and Helene Wrighte, of same, spinster, æt. 26. Her parents consent. Bond by William Barker, of Harby, yeoman.
[Eagle.]

1665. May 30. Cely, Richard, of Sibsey, and Sara Shepheard, of Leverton, spinster. Surety, Thomas Burton, of Sibsey, clerk. [Sibsy, Stickney, St. Peter at Arches or
St. Paul in Bail.]

1602. June 9. C.—Chaderton, Robert, and Anne Yarrowe.

1648. Nov. 23. Challance, John, of Anwicke, husbandman, and Sarah Everitt, of same, spinster. Surety, Thomas Challance, of same, yeoman. [St. Paule or Anwicke.]

1663. May 26. Challenge, Richard, of Stubton, yeoman, and Elizth. Eman, of same, widow. Surety, John Wilkinson, of same, yeoman. [St. Margarett or St. Michael.]

1628. Feb. 5. Chamberlaine, George, of Bratoft, tailer, and Margt. Hodge, of same, spinster. Bond by Richard Ithell, of Steeping Magna, gent. [Bratofte.]

1666. March 15. Chamberlaine, William, of North Willingham, yeoman, æt. 25, and Anne Whelpdale, of Nettleton, spinster, æt. 20. His parents and her mother consent; her father is dead. Surety, Peter Dickson, of North Willingham, wheelewright.
[St. Peter in Eastgate or St. Paul in Bail.]

1662. Oct. 3. Chambers, Henry, of Kingston-upon-Hull, co. York, gent., and Elizth. Perman, of Thorpe Tilney in the parish of Timberland, widow. Surety, William Standish, of Thorpe Tilney, gent. [Metheringham.]

1668. Jan. 22. Chapman, John, of Panton, yeoman, æt. 38, and Susanna Melton, of same, widow, æt. 30.
[St. Peter in Eastgate or Panton.]

1665. June 13. Chapman, John, of Billingay, labourer, and Ruth Bellamy, of same, spinster. Surety, John Thompson, of same, labourer. [Billingay or Metheringham.]

ST. PETER'S, YORK.—SCHOOL REGISTER.*

1838. August 8. 251. Wm. Henry Fawcett, aged 12. Millwright, York. From Mr. Matthew's school, York. Left 14 March, 1844.

1838. Oct. 10. 252. Walter Pennington Creyke, aged 10. Son of Rev. S. Creyke, A.M., late Head Master of St. Peter's school, Rector of Wigginton. Left at Easter, 1839.

Oct. 10. 253. Samuel Johnson Butler, aged 15. Wine-merchant. From the New College school, Oxford. Left at Michaelmas, 1840.

1839. Jan. 17. 254. Francis Motley, aged 12. See 155. From Mr. Hough's school, Netherton, near Huddersfield. Left at Midsummer, 1842.

Jan. 17. 255. James Harris, aged 11. Son of Mr. Harris, New Street, York. From Mr. Gething's school, Darlington. Left at Xmas., 1841.

1839. April 6. 256. Richard Shaw, aged 13. Son of Rd. Shaw, esq., solicitor, Burnley, Lancashire. From Dr. Cowan's school, Sunderland. Left at Easter, 1841.

April 15. 257. Henry Smales, aged 11. Son of H. Smales, esq., York. From Mr. Storey's school, Haxby. Left at Midsummer, 1841.

1839. July 29. 258. Edward Powell, aged 15. Son of Rev. W. W. Powell, Ripley. From Mr. Heslop's school, Ripley. Left at Midsummer, 1840.

July 29. 259. Percy Hudson, aged 6. Son of Mr. Hudson, proctor. Never at school before.

July 29. 260. Charles Kirkby Robinson, aged 13. Son of Mr. Robinson, Acomb. From Mr. Haynes' school, Tadcaster.

July 29. 261. Jonathan Grant Robinson, aged 11. See 260. Left at Midsummer, 1843.

July 29. 262. Alexander Thiselton, aged 15. Son of C. Thiselton, esq., York. From Rev. J. Gray's school, Camberwell. Left at Midsummer, 1840.

* Continued from page 16.

1839. Oct. 10. 263. John Camidge, aged 13. Son of Dr. Camidge, York. From Fulnec school. Left at Midsummer, 1842.

1840. Feb. 1. 264. Thos. Camidge, aged 12. See 263. Left at Xmas., 1842.

Feb. 1. 265. Eskricke John Inman, aged 12. Son of ...... Inman, esq., Acomb. From the Proprietary school, York. Left at Easter, 1841.

Feb. 1. 266. Edwin Storry, aged 13. Son of Mrs. Storry, Tolston Lodge. From Mr. Guy's school, Howden. Left at Xmas., 1841.

Feb. 1. 267. George Langton Beckwith, aged 14. Son of Mrs. Beckwith. From the Proprietary school, York. Left October, 1841.

Feb. 1. 268. Augustus Comber, aged 12. Son of Rev. W. G. W. Comber. From Mrs. Bulmer's Preparatory school. Left at Xmas., 1841.

Feb. 1. 269. William Fryer, aged 14. Son of Mrs. Fryer. From Mr. Merry's school, Scarbro'. Left Midsummer, 1840.

1840. August 5. 270. Bowden Cattley, aged 11. Son of T. H. Cattley, esq., York. From the Proprietary school, York.

August 5. 271. Henry Thomas Cattley, aged 12. See 270. Left at Xmas., 1843.

August 5. 272. James Coultas, aged 14. Son of Mrs. Coultas, York. From school at Winteringham. Left at Midsummer, 1841.

August 5. 273. Francis Jennings Brown, aged 13. Nephew of Mr. G. Jennings. From Mr. Stubbs' school, Harrogate. Left at Midsummer, 1842.

August 5. 274. William Lee Johnstone, aged 13. Son of Mr. Spearman Johnstone. From Mr. Shackley's school, York. Left at Xmas., 1843.

August 5. 275. George Bainbridge, aged nearly 11. Son of Mr. G. P. Bainbridge, York. From Rothbury Grammar school, near Morpeth. Left at Midsummer, 1841.

August 5. 276. John Bainbridge, aged nearly 9. See 275. Left at Xmas., 1840.

August 5. 277. George Gurley, aged 15. Son of Mrs. Gurley. From Mr. Bush's school, Cockermouth. Left at Midsummer, 1842.

1840. August 5. 278. William Driffield, aged 13. Son of W. Driffield, esq., Knaresbrough. From the Grammar school, Knaresbrough. Left at Midsummer, 1841.

August 5. 279. William Holden, aged 9. Son of Mrs. Holden, Palace House, Burnley, Lancashire. Not at school before. Left at Midsummer, 1842.

1841. Feb. 3. 280. Thomas Amos Jennings, aged 10. Son of Mr. G. Jennings, Clifton. From Mrs. Bulmer's school. Left at Midsummer, 1842.

1841. July 29. 281. William Jennings, aged 8. See 280.

July 30. 282. Alexander Cattley, aged 10. See 270. Left at Xmas., 1842.

1841. August 2. 283. George Udny Hague, aged 12. Son of B. Hague, esq. From the Proprietary school.

August 2. 284. Edward Taylor, aged 16. Son of Mr. John Taylor, Staxton, Scarbro.' From Mr. Potter's school, Scarbro.' Left at Easter, 1843.

1841. Oct. 1. 285. Thomas Paul Coopland, aged 8. See No. ... From Miss Cave's school, Micklegate.

Oct. 1. 286. William Henry Potter, aged 13. Son of Mr. Potter. From his father's school, Scarbro.'

1842. Feb. 1. 287. Thos. Rupel Johnson, aged 14. ...... of Mrs. Rupel. From Mr. Shackley's school. Left Midsummer, 1842.

Feb. 1. 288. Eugene Thomas Curzon Whittell, aged 9. Son of J. F. Whittell, esq., Stamford Bridge. Not at school before.

Feb. 1. 289. John Thomlinson Walker, aged 12. Son of Mr. J. Walker, ironfounder, York. From Mr. Monkman's school. Left at Xmas., 1843.

Feb. 1. 290. Henry Wood, aged 11. See 235. From the Proprietary School.

Feb. 2. 291. Richard Bethel Earle, aged 14. Son of Mrs. Earle, Aughton, near Howden. From Beverley Grammar school. Left May 10th, 1842.

Feb 2. 292. Joseph Wilson, aged 10. See 177. From Rev. G. Toppin's, Rockliff Hall, near Carlisle. Left at Xmas., 1842.

1842. April 4. 293. Henry Richardson, aged 13. Son of Rev. Thomas Richardson. At St. Peter's school previously, but not registered.

April 4. 294. Robert Stephenson Bradwell, aged 14. Son of Mr. Bradwell, Micklegate. From Mr. Shackley's school. Left at Xmas., 1842.

April 4. 295. John Charles Bradwell, aged 13. See 294. Left at Easter, 1843.

April 4. 296. Henry Smyth, aged 10. Son of Mrs. Smyth. From Mrs. Bulmer's school.

1842. May. 297. Wm. Plows, aged 13. Son of Mr. Plows. From Mr. Ellerby's school.

1842. August 2. 298. Alick Lister Kaye, aged 9. Son of Sir John L. Kaye, bart. Not at school before. Left at Midsummer, 1843, on Sir John Kaye's leaving York.

August 2. 299. John Hopps, aged 10. Son of John Hopps, esq., surgeon. Not at school before. Left Sept., 1843.

August 2. 300. Kirkby Robinson, aged 10. Son of Mr. Robinson, Acomb. Not at school before.

August 2. 301. Frederick Evers, aged 8. Son of Mr. Evers, York. Not at school before.

August 2. 302. John Retallick Bellerby, aged 14. Son of Mr. Bellerby, York. From the York Proprietary school. Left at Midsummer, 1843.

1843. Jan. 18. 303. John Barry Simpson, aged 12. Son of H. Simpson, esq., Whitby. From Mr. Bretton's school, Whitby.

Jan. 18. 304. William Rhodes, aged 10. Son of Mr. Rhodes, York. From Mr. Shackley's school.

Jan. 23. 305. Edward Robinson, aged 11. Son of Rev. John Robinson. From Mr. Heslop's school. Left at Xmas., 1843.

Jan. 23. 306. John Carleton Robinson, aged $9\frac{1}{2}$. See 305. From Mrs. Gilby's school, Newark.

Jan. 23. 307. Harry Bell Johnstone, aged 12. See 274. Left Xmas., 1843.

Jan. 23. 308. Charles John Meuron, aged 9. Son of French Master at St. Peter's school. From Mrs. Bulmer's school.

Jan. 23. 309. Walter Cattley, aged 8. See 282.

1843. Jan. 23. 310. William Barber, aged 9. Son of J. Barber, esq., Brighouse, Halifax. Not at school before.

Jan. 23. 311. Fairless Barber, aged 8. See 310.

1843. Easter. 312. Charles Hessleton Rose, aged 8. Son of Rev. ... Rose. Not at school before.

Easter. 313. Michael Charles Cottam, aged 14. Son of Mr. G. Cottam, York. From Leeds Grammar School. Left at Michaelmas, 1843.

1843. Aug. 2. 314. William Garwood, aged 9. Son of Mr. Garwood, solicitor, Castlegate. From Mrs. Bulmer's school.

Aug. 2. 315. William Wood, aged 11. See 235. From the York Proprietary school.

Aug. 2. 316. Charles Masterman Smyth, aged 10. See 140. From Mrs. Bulmer's school.

1844. Jan. 317. Reginald Crawford, aged 12. Son of Mrs. Crawford, Scarbro' Parade. From a school at Carmarthen.

1844. April 15. 318. Thomas William Wilkinson, aged 8. Son of Mr. Wilkinson, York. Not at school before.

FANGFOSS REGISTER TRANSCRIPTS.

THE REGISTER COMMENCES IN 1755.

1701. L'day to 1702 L'day.
    Caid, Ann, dau. of Richard, bapt. March 28.
    Michaelfield, Cath., dau. of James, bapt. Oct. 12.
    Gilliott, Eliz., dau. of Robert, bapt. Nov. 30.
    Oliver, James, of Skertonbecke, and Eliz. Catton, of Fangfosse, married April 22.
    Oliver, Thos., of Skertonbecke, and Eliz. Overend, of Fangfosse, married May 13.
    Brambley, Christr., buried May 30.
            (Signed)   Jo. Silburne, *Curate*.
                        Edward × Catton, *Churchwarden*.

1702. Steell, Eliz., buried Sept. 28.
    Whitter, Eliz., buried Jan. 4.   (Signed)   Edward Catton.

1703. Micklefield, Mary, dau. of James, bapt. March 26.
    Malton, Xtiana., dau. of Robert, bapt. July 26.
    Gilliot, John, son of Robert, bapt. Oct. 10.
    Bell, William, son of Michael, bapt. Oct. 27.
    Caid, Eliz., dau. of Richard, bapt. Jan. 2.
    Etty, Mary and Jane, daus. of Edward, bapt. Jan 23.
    White, James, and Margaret Harper, of Youlthorp, married April 1.
    Ibbison, Robert, buried May 9.
            (Signed)   Richard Burton, *Curate*.
                        Edward Catton, *Churchwarden*.

1704. Catton, Anne, dau. of John, bapt. Dec. 10.
    Bell, George, son of Michael, bapt. Jan. 24.
    Micklefield, Sarah, dau. of James, bapt. March 13.
    Gilliot, Sarah, dau. of Robert, bapt. Nov. 11.
    Robinson, Jane, buried June 25.

1704. Micklefield, Sarah, dau. of James, buried April 18.
Terins, Susan, pauper, buried May 26, 1705.
(Signed) R. Burton, *Vicar.*

1705. Traine, Susanna, a poore woman, buried May 26. 4/-
Gilliatt, Sarah, dau. of Robert, bapt. Nov. 11. 2/-
(No marriages.)
Overend, William, and Tim. Overend, batchelors. 1/-

1706. Wood, Robert, buried Aug. 23.
Overend, Eliz., ux. Timothy, buried Nov. 6.
White, James, son of James, buried Feb. 17.
Micklefield, Jonn, son of James, bapt. Dec. 12.
Bell, Grace, dau. of Michael, bapt. Jan. 15.
Malton, Eliz., dau. of Robert, bapt. March 23.
(No marriages.) (Signed) Rd. Burton, *Vicar.*

1707. Fligg, Thomas, buried Feb. 8.
Fligg, Alice, buried Feb. 16.
Stothers, Eliz., buried March 1.
White, Robert, buried March 4.
White, Eliz., buried March 10.
White, James, buried March 18.
Fligg, Anne, bapt. Oct. 25.
Hart, Edward, of Newton, and Jane Dunne (?), of Fangfoss, married Oct. 15.
Harrison, Robert, and Eliz. Seamour, married Nov. 27.
(Signed) Rd. Burton.

1708. Smith, Mary, dau. of Roger, bapt. Aug. 20.
Catton, Edward, son of John, bapt. Oct. 17.
White, James, son of Margaret, bapt. Nov. 28.
Harrison, John, son of Robert, bapt. Feb. 27.
Malton, Robert, son of Robert, bapt. March 16.
Robinson, John, son of Jane, buried April 28.
Little, Jane, widow, buried Dec. 21.
(No marriages.) (Signed) Rd. Burton, *Vicar.*

1709. (No marriages.)
Bell, Michael, son of Michael, bapt. March 27.
Catton, Edward, son of John, buried March 9.
(Signed) Will. Overend, *Churchwarden.*

1710. Etty, Katherine and Eleanor, daus. of Edward, bapt. June 28.
Stothers, Benjamin, son of John, bapt. July 7.
Bell, Anne, dau. of Michael, bapt. Nov. 12.
(No marriages.)
Overend, Hammond, buried June 30.
Etty, Catherine, buried July 31.
Beaumont, Mr. James, buried Aug. 27.
Cade, Richard, buried Aug. 29.
Burton, Mary, buried Dec. 9.
Overend, Timothy, senr., buried Feb. 17.

       (Signed) R. Burton, *Vicar*.

ACT BOOKS OF THE PREROGATIVE COURT OF YORK.*

1681. Aug. 3. Bulcock, Wm., Twiston. Will to widow Elizth. (Brother Rd. B., renouncing.)

Aug. 5. Evans, Cath., Lincoln, spinster. Will to Thomas Hird, gent.

Aug. 9. Baskervile, Thos., Rochdale. Will to wid. Elizth. and son Josua B.

Aug. 9. Robinson, Hy., Dareley Banck. Adm. to widow Helen.

Aug. 24. Stokoe, Mary, Hexham, widow. Will to brother Anthony Woodman.

Sept. 2. Smith, Francis, æt. 17, son of Sir Jeremiah S., late of Osgodby, knt., decd. Curation to Robt. Ash, of York, gent.

Sept. 6. Fisher, Miles, Aspatrick, co. Cumberland. Adm. to sister Margt., ux. John Feaston.

Sept. 7. Lewen, Hy., Whickham, Durham diocese, gent. Will to widow Jane.

Sept. 15. Young, Michael, Castle Yard, co. Northumberland. Will to widow Elizth.

Sept. 19. Blakiston, John, Norton, co. Durham. Will to Jacobus Wood.

Sept. 24. Blakiston, Margt. and Wm., infant children of John B., late of Norton, decd. Tuition to Jacobus Wood and Thos. Chipchase.

Sept. 27. Nelson, Alison, Helperby. Adm. to son Thos. N.

Sept. 29. Heron, Elizth., dau. of Robt. H., late of Stockton-on-Tease, decd. Tuition to Elizth. H., of same.

Oct. 1. Pearson, Thos., Staynton Magna, clk. Will to sons Thomas and Henry P.

Oct. 8. Collingwood, Wm., Newsham, gent. Will to widow Merilia.

* Continued from page 47.

1681. Oct. 11. Wightman *alias* Johnson, Mary, ux. Edwd. Wightman, of Heslihgton. Adm. to her husband.
Oct. 12. Webster, Robt., Startforth. Will to dau. Elizth. W.
Oct. 17. Scadlock, Thos., Acom. Adm. to sister Margt. S., spinster.
Oct. 20. Holdsworth, Benj , son of Robt. H. Curation to Brian Dodsworth, of Woodhall Park.
Oct. 31. Allison, Elizth., Throssendale, but at Middleton, co. Durham, widow. Will to brother Wm. Wilkinson.
Oct. 31. Flower, Margt., Sockburne. Will to son Geo. F.
Oct. 31. Farndale, Geo., Stockton-on-Tease. Adm. to wid. Merilia.
Oct. 31. Grymes, Edward, Long Cowton. Adm. to widow Elizabeth.
Nov. 3. Scruton, Jacobus, York. Will to dau. Helenora, ux. Wm. Addinell.
Nov. 3. Moore, Thos., West Stockwith. Will to wid. Anne.
Nov. 4. Moore, Wm., Oswaldkirk, gent., but dying at York. Adm. to widow Helen.
Nov. 8. Wright, Richard, Dishforth. Will to wid. Dorothy.
Nov. 10. Kipling, Rd., Baldersdale. Adm. to widow Jane.
Nov. 14. Wheelwright, Gawen, Stanger, co. Cumberland. Adm. to widow Frances.
Nov. 15. Horner, John, Sikes Grainge in Netherdale, gent. Adm. to widow Anne.
Nov. 18. Bell, Rd., Copmanthorpe. Will to Rd. Fowell, Universal Legatee.
Nov. 18. Hood, John, Dringhouses, par. Acom. Adm. with Will to Wm. Hood, of same, to use of Wm. and John Hood, sons of deceased.
Nov. 9. Wade, Wm., Rigges. Adm. to son Wm. W.
Dec. 5. Braidwood, Alice, Hindley Hill, par. Allandale, co. Northumberland, widow. Will to son John B.
Dec. 5. Woodman, Anthony, Hexham. Will to John Armstrong and Thomas Howden.
Dec. 5. Pearson, Wm., Spittle, par. Hexham, gent. Will to sons Robt. and Wm. P.
Dec. 5. Bell, Joseph, Dotland, par. Hexham. Adm. to son Robert B.

1681. Dec. 5. Sharpe, Anthony, senr., Hexham. Adm. to widow Isabella.

Dec. 5. Winter, Wm., son of Robt. W., late of Spittle Sheel, par. Hexham, decd. Tuition to Wm. W., father of decd.

Dec. 5. Pearson, Wm., Whaley, co. Lancaster. Will to John Briggs.

Dec. 8. Barshard, Peter, Cawood. Adm. to widow Anne.

Dec. 13. Wharton, Jonathan, Barnardcastle. Will to sister Hannah W., spinster.

Dec. 14. Thompson, Thos., Clint. Adm. to wid. Martha T.

Dec. 15. Leek, Frances, Normanton, par. Southwell, co. Notts., widow. Will to Wm. Cartwright, esq. and Laurence Sturtevant, gent.

Dec. 10. Greton, Thos., Nottingham. Will to widow Anne.

Jan. 9. Lee, Matthew, Whitley, par. Allandale. Will to widow Frances.

Jan. 23. Harrison, Alexander, Brighton. Adm. to Robt. Ash, of York, gent., to use of Henry Allen, a creditor of deceased.

Jan. 20. Crombock, John, Wiswall. Adm. to dau. Dorothy, ux. Stephen Gay, clerk.

Feb. 4. Williamson, Wm., Dinsdale. Adm. to sons Wm. and Francis W.

Feb. 7. Squire, Beatrice, York, spinster. Adm. with Will to Mary Steel, widow of Thomas Steel, niece and extrix. of deceased.

Feb. 7. Steel, Thomas, York. Adm. to widow Mary.

Feb. 10. Binckes, Anne, York, wid. Will to son Edwd. B.

Feb. 16. Sawyer, Lady Anne, White Waltham, co. Berks., widow. Adm. to son Sir Robt. S., knt., attorney general to the king.

Feb. 17. Snowdon *alias* Danby, Thomasin, ux. Joseph Snowdon, of Borrowby. Adm. to her husband.

Feb. 18. Wilkinson, Edmund, Cloughouse in Extwisle. Adm. with Will to John Heape. (Mary W., widow of deceased renouncing and consenting.)

Feb. 18. Robert, Jacobus, senr., Mearclough. Adm. (by decree) to Edward Watson, of Cliviger.

Feb. 21. Otley, Wm., Kilwick. Will to dau. Anne O., spr.

1681. March 6. Arlush, Stephen, Knedlington, par. Howden, clk. Will to widow Anne.
March 18. Chapman, Wm., Newsham, co. Durham. Adm. with Will to sons Marmaduke and Peter C. (Isabel the widow renouncing and consenting.)
March 18. Skinner, *vide* Harthill Act Book.
March 18. Jenison, Matthew, Newark, co. Nott., esq. Will to son Matt. J., esq.
March 20. Fearby *alias* Hill, Mary, ux. Wm. F., of Upper Poppleton. Adm. to her husband.
Hill, *see* Fearby.
March 22. Almond, Anthony, How. Will to son Rd. A.
Jan. 12. Lodge, John, York. *See* City Act Book.

1682. March 30. Skinner, Wm., alderman of Hull. Will to son Wm. S., gent.
March 25. Garforth, Edmond, Lancaster. Adm. to brother Thomas G.
March 30. Stothard, Mary, Ulleskelfe. Will to Thomas S. and Isabella Harrison.
March 31. Herbert, Sir Thos., York. Will to widow Elizth.
April 4. Swittenham, Edmond, son of Elizth. S., of Tunstall, deceased. Tuition to Edward Wilson, esq.
April 5. Swittenham, Elizth., Tunstall. Adm. to Edward Wilson, to use of Edmond S., son of decd.
April 22. Browne, Mary, Wistow. Adm. to husband Rd. B.
April 6. Morland, Launcelot, Rownton. Adm. with Will to Philip Morland, to use of Robt. M., son of decd.
April 6. Senhouse, Patricius, Hameshill. Will to widow Elizabeth.
April 7. Trubshaw, Saml., Howden. Will to brother Wm. Trubshaw.
April 15. Jefferson, Robt., Carlisle. Adm. to widow Mary.
April 10. Cradock, Anthony, Bernard Castle. Adm. to daus. Mary, ux. Wm. Dobson, and Margt. ux. Wm. Dayle.
April 18. Blyth, Jane, Normanby, co. Lincoln. Adm. to husband Wm. B.
April 25. Grayson, Laurence, Kirklevington. Adm. to wid. Elizabeth.
April 26. Usher, Charles, Firkanders. Will to son Geo. U.

DURHAM MARRIAGE BONDS.

1665. Aug. 28. John Simpson, jun., of Durham, and Eliz. Heslop, widow.

Aug. 16. Edward Smith, of Lamesley, miller, and Isabella Sowbridge, widow.

Aug. 8. Arthur Blackbourne, of Elswick, and Anne Doune, spinster.

Aug. 8. Francis Taylor, of Rogerley, gent., and Ann Wilson, spinster.

Aug. 7. Robert Douthwaite, of Thornley, yeoman, and Jane Wearmouth, spinster.

Aug. 1. William Welsh, of Newcastle, merchant, and Margt. Bootfloore, spinster.

July 18. George Dennen, of Washington, yeoman, and Jane Arrowsmith, spinster.

July 14. Edward Dunwell, of Blaskiston, gent., and Ann Green, spinster.

July 14. William Waller, of Durham, and Ann Burton, spr.

July 8. Arthur Whitfield, yeoman, and Ann Steavenson.

July 12. John Simpson, of Newcastle, mariner, and Jane Fell, spinster.

July 9. Lionel Ayre, yeoman, and Eleanor Gaire, spinster.

July 1. George Lawes, of Urpeth, yeoman, and Katherine Hornsby, spinster.

July 4. Thomas Lampton, cooper, and Elizth. Bell, spinster.

June 4. John Garth, of Auckland, yeoman, and Jane Moore, spinster.

June 24. John Marley, whitesmith, and Ann Lawson, spr.

June 15. John Arundell, of Bishop Auckland, and Ann Hodgson, spinster.

June 10. Thomas Marley, of Kyo, and Phillis Craister, spr.

June 10. James Charlton, of West Rainton, and Isabella Ranson, widow.

June 3. John Crosby, of Durham, gent., and Elizth. Martyn, spinster.

1665. May 31. Charles Jackson, of Berwick, gent., and Margaret Backster, spinster.

June 3. Bryan Stobbert, of Auckland, and Elizabeth Todd, spinster.

June 3. Thomas Pott, of Northumberland, yeoman, and Isabella Hedley, spinster.

May 26. Robert Todd, of Newcastle, and Jane Todd, spinster.

May 22. Edward King, of Durham, and Mary Moorecroft, spinster.

CARLISLE MARRIAGE BONDS.

1732. Oct. 7. Anthony Reed, of Bishop Wearmouth, and Mary Hodgson, widow.

Aug. 10. John Pealt, of Carlisle, and Ann Troughton, spinster.

1733. Oct. 8. Thomas Nevison, of Whittingham, and Mrs. Jane Carlisle, aged 28.

Oct. 20. Nicholas Maughan, of Northumberland, and Mary Blacklock, spinster, aged 18.

1734. May 27. John Peat and Jane Donald, aged 21.

Dec. 21. Griffith Eaglesfield, of Edinburgh, and Mrs. Dorothy Gilpin, aged 23.

March 29. Mascall Brasse, of Easington, yeoman, and Sarah Ayre.

1736. Aug. 28. Joseph Robinson, of Barnard Castle, and Frances Hutchinson, spinster.

1737. June 22. William Troutbeck and Ann Rumney.

Nov. 28. Cuthbert Collingwood, of Newcastle, and Milcah Dobson.

May 28. Joseph Railton, of Hexham, and Ann Sturdy.

Oct. 25. Anthy. Kearton, of Swaledale, and Jennet Spooner, spinster.

June 4. George Middleton, of par. Sadberge, and Ruth Shaw, of Kirby Stephen.

ALLERTONSHIRE MARRIAGE BONDS.

1757. Feb. 15. James Armstrong, par. Cockfield, and Elizabeth Dennison, spinster.
Oct. 4. John Smithson, par. of Kirby Sigston, and Elizabeth Reeveley, widow.
Nov. 24. Edward Clark, of Deighton, and Alice Ridley.
Dec. 22. James Peacock, of Lazenby, and Mary Carter.
1759. March 12. Richard Weighill, of Osmotherly, and Ann Dunn.
June 15. John Graham, yeoman, and Jane Carter, spinster.
Aug. 21. William Ferguson, yeoman, and Elizth. Thompson, spinster.
1760. Feb. 25. Richard Stonehouse, of Yarm, and Mary Richardson, aged 22.
April 1. Roger Langdale, of Brompton, yeoman, and Elizth. Jackson.
April 1. George Davison, of Welbury, and Hannah Franklin, aged 21.
Dec. 29. Richard Hamilton, of Northallerton, and Catherine Pybus, both 21.
1761. Jan. 14. Thomas Dove, of Northallerton, and Mary Bowmer.

J. J. Howe,
Durham.

SOME COLONIAL WILLS.

Wm. Pullen, of London, merchant, 1 Oct., 1754. [98, fo. 292.] Joseph Richardson, of the Island of Jamaica, esq., and Jonas Butterfield, of London, gent., trustees of my estates, negroes, and effects, in Jamaica, upon trust to sell. Said Jonas Butterfield 10 guineas for mourning. To Camilla Parish in Jamaica, negro woman her freedom and £10 per ann. Jamaica currency for her life, and she to have any two of my negro women she shall choose for the term of her life. My servant boy James Urling £50 Jamaica currency, to be paid to him at the expiration of his time. Sister Elizabeth, ux. William Gibbeson, of Rippon, co. York, 10 guineas a year for life and 10 guineas for mourning, and to said Wm. Gibbeson 10 guineas for mourning. My two daus. Amy and Mary three negroes for life, and if either or both of them shall be minded to return to Jamaica, her or their passage to be paid out of my estate. Friend Peter Collgrave, of London, gent., a mourning ring. Cousin Wm. Pullin, one of my exors., 20 guineas for mourning. Friend David Patrick, the other of my exors., 10 guineas. Youngest son John (now in Jamaica) to be brought over to England. Residue to said Wm. Pullen and David Patrick, exors., for the maintenance of my three sons, Robt., Wm. and the said John, until 22, and then to be divided amongst them; if they all die, then to John Pullen, son of my said cousin Wm. Pullin. Witnesses, Jane Asquith, Peter Collgrave, Ralph Stresselicque.

Codicil, 3 Oct., 1754. Said friend David Patrick, 40 guineas more. My exors. to provide all necessaries for John Smith, of Knaresboro', until his affairs are settled in Jamaica. Witnesses, Jane Sugden, John Coles, James Farrer, junr. Proved at York, 14 Nov., 1754.

Richard Ware, heretofore of the province of New Jersey, in North America, and late of Hull, but now of Whitby, sail-maker, 7 April, 1792. [do. 313.] Am possessed of a tract of land formerly of Burlington in New Jersey, yeoman, decd., and afterwards of his surviving devisee Ann Dickinson, and afterwards of her daus. and co-heiresses, and their husbands, of whom I, and one John Clarkson, formerly of Burlington in New Jersey, but now or late of Whitby aforesaid, grocer, purchased the same as tenants in common, and it was by deed of 15 September, 1775 (duly registered in the proper Secretary's Office at Burlington, in Book A. T., fol. 201), released by said Clarkson to me, by the description of a tract of land in Roxbury, co. Morris, New Jersey province, beginning at Museconetung River, at an Ash Tree for a corner, &c., containing 479 acres, which lands are now or were formerly in occupation of Robt. Glass and Christr. Hoffman, and are of the value of £1,900 New Jersey currency. Am also possessed of another tract of land 422¾ acres, valne £1,200 New Jersey currency; and another tract 371 acres, value £1,200; and another tract 206 acres, and 740 acres of unlocated land value £112 (all minutely described). I give same tracts of land to my friend Joseph Turner, of Southwark, within the liberties of the City of Philadelphia, gent., and Martin Ryerson, of Amwell, co. Hunterdon, surveyor, as Trustees of my lands in North America, for my children Thos. Ware, Geo. Brown Ware, and Ann Guy, ux. John G., junr., of Hull, painter. My lands in Whitby and Scarbro' to my friends John Peacock, of Whitby, mariner, and Benjamin Gowland, of same, gent., upon trust to pay my father Christopher Ware £12 a year for life; to my said dau. Ann Guy £30 a year; my son Thos. Ware £20 a year; and my son George Brown Ware £25 a year, till said son George attains 22. Said Peacock and Gowland to be exors. Witnesses, Thomas Lawson, of Great Driffield, surgeon apothecary; Joseph Clement, of Great Driffield, and Thomas Cater, of Great Driffield, attorney-at-law. Proved at York, Nov., 1795.

PAPIST RETURNS.

City of York, and Part of Ainstie, 1735.

Articles enquired of:—

(1) What Papists? (2) What priest or person suspected to be such? (3) What house or place where mass is performed? (4) School? (5) Visitation or Confirmation by Popish Bishop? (6) Perversions to Popish religion? All answered in the negative unless otherwise noted here.

St. Michael.

James Lyth, keeper of publick house in Low Ousegate, and Sarah his wife. They have no children.

Margaret, wife of Rd. Farrar, upholder. She lives in Spurriergate. They have two children, infants.

James Robinson, keeps a little ale house in Coppergate.

Joseph Hous, mariner, and Cath. his wife. They live in ye Water Lane.

St. Maurice.

Robert Young, a gardener, and his wife, and her sister Eleanor Errington.

Bartholomew Scott, labourer, and his wife.

Elizabeth Shann, lately come from another parish to stay, during a year, in the family of Mr. John Preston (a brewer), to nurse a young child of his.

Trinity, Goodramgate.

Mr. Fras. Hasselgrave, a surgeon, (his wife being of the Church of England.)

John Saxton, a joiner, and his servant Elizth. Chambers.

Christian Rawden and Mary Wilson, both old widows.

John Wawd, a stay maker (his wife being of the Church of England) and his apprentice Chas. Kersher.

St. John Delpike.

Mrs. Vinter, widow and midwife, and her maiden daughter Ann Vinter, and her married daughter Mrs. Wilstrop, and ye widow Vinter's servant Ann .... [England.)

Thos. Robinson, a journeyman carpenter (his wife of the Church of ...... Wilstrop, ye husband of the said Mrs. Wilstrop, was perverted from ye Church of England to ye Popish religion about two years ago, in ye City of Paris. He has not shown himself at York for about a year last past.

Trinity, Micklegate.

Thos. Selby, esq. and lady, two daughters, footman, Jane Pallister, Mary Clark, Jane Little, servants.

Roger Mennel, senr., esq. and Lady. Susanna Wilkinson, Jane Rose, Cath. Judar, Anne Fowler, servants.

Roger Mennell, junr., esq. and Lady. John Blacket, Eliz. Parker, servants.

George Kingsley, gent. Jane Clark, servant.

Mr. Audrian, innholder, and wife.

Mrs. Conyers. Mrs. Clifton.

Lodgers :— Mrs. Palmes, Mrs. Metcalf, Mrs. Stanfeild, Mrs. Hodgson, Mrs. Walker, Mrs. Tidswel.

Servants :—Elizth. Tasker, Eliz. Benson, Frances Audars.

John Hird, labourer, and wife.

Wife of Arthur Morkil, cordwainer.
,, Thomas Foster, taylor.
,, Timothy Knowles, malster.
,, John Smelt, barber.
,, James Thompson, barber.

Supposed priests:—Mr. Pyot, Mr. Mennock.

Mass performed in a house. [Bishop visits.

School for girls kept by Mrs. Conyers and Mrs. Clifton. A supposed

Trinity, King's Court. None.

St. Helen, Stonegate.

Ellinor Ellis, widow, æt. 77, receives alms.

Ellinor Wilson, married, æt. 29, poor.

Elizabeth Croft, æt. 80, receives alms.

Mary Ingle, æt. 27; Eliz. Ingle, æt. 22; Margt. Ingle, æt. 19; Frances Ingle, æt. 16; four sisters, unmarried, washerwomen.

All Saints', North Street.

Margt. Cornforth and Ellenn Cornforth, spinsters.
Mary, wife of Joseph Hayton, carpenter.
Mary, wife of Christopher Darbyshire, porter.

All Saints', Pavement.

Mary, wife of John Greenwood, barber.
May, daughter of John Greenwood, barber.
Joseph Lodge, haberdasher of hatts; Jane, his wife.
Ellenor Moulden, senr. and Ellenor Moulden, junr., strangers at Mr. Lodge's.
Rebecca, servant to Joseph Lodge.
Thomas Waud, shoemaker, and his wife.

St. Saviour.

Wife of Miles Denton, labourer.   Widow Barnet.

St. Olave.

John Bell, and John and Thomas Bell, his sons, brickmakers.
Ignatius Hyde, translator, and Margaret, ux.
Thomas Hardcastle, bucklemaker.
Mary, ux. Montague Giles, brickmaker.
Ann Wilkinson, widow.

St. Martin's, Micklegate.

Stephen Tempest, esq.   John Cooper, his servant.
Wm. Hutchinson and Eliz. his wife.
Mary Hutchinson their daughter, a milliner.
Thomas Wilson, breechesmaker.
Benjamin Calvert, barber.
Jane Dunstan, widow.
Mary Turner, buttonmaker.
Dorothy Calvert, Ann Scarr, Mrs. Rooksby, widows.
Mr. Fothergale, gent.
Eliz. Wright, servant to Mr. Lumm.
Mathew Scarr, taylor.

St. Margaret.

Mary, ux. Matthew Turner, labourer.
Catherine Coates, a poor widow.

S. Mary, Castlegate.

George Thwing, Castlegate, sells coals; and Dorothy his sister, who lives with him. Both unmarried.

St. Helen.

Mr. Brigham. Thomas Patrick his servant.
Mr. George Reynoldson, upholder, and his wife. Henry Smith his apprentice.
Leonard Grimboldson, barber, and his mother.
Mr. Keregan, stage-player, his wife and two daughters. Sarah Hanley his servant.
Mr. Thos. Medcalfe, haberdasher, his wife and two daughters.
Widow Downing, ale holder.
Richard Bond, hackney coachman, his wife and two daughters. Cath. Rheims his servant.
Rd. Fleming, apprentice to a smith.

St. George-cum-Naburn.

Mrs. Mary Palmes, a maiden gentlewoman.
Mary, ux. Thomas Dickenson, yeoman.
Michael Stockdale, husbandman, and Mary his wife, and Frances Haddock his servant. No children.
There is said to be a design to have mass performed in Bryan Palmes' house when it is finished.

St. Dennis.

John Flemming, a labourer, and Margaret his wife.
Chas. Flemming, apprentice to .... Gregg, tayler, in St. Crux parish.
John Flemming, apprentice to George Woodhouse, barber, in St. Crux parish.
Richard Flemming, apprentice to John Hood, a whitesmith, in St. Helen's parish.

St. Cuthbert.

John Stapylton, esq.; Mrs. Stapylton, his sister; Eliz. Perry, housekeeper; Bridget Waterhouse and another maid-servant, and one man-servant.
Rd. Walker, horse-rider; Judith Walker his wife, who are upon ye removal into the parish of Belfrey's in York.

Mr. ...... Dale, housekeeper; his wife, and a maid-servant (very lately come into the parish.)
Mrs. Hudson, sister to Mrs. Dale.
Rd. Curtis, gardener, and Grace his wife, and Edmund Munday his apprentice, who live in parish of St. Mary, Lay-thorpe.

St. Crux.

Mr. Charles Atkinson, grocer.
David Hewison, innholder, his wife, and daughter.
Christopher Hewison, cutler.
Francis Bredall, apprentice to an apothecary.

Nether Poppleton. None.

Moor Monkton. None.

Hutton Wansley.

John Neal, an hired servant to Elizabeth Vary.

Fulford.

Joan Foster, a gardener's widow in Gate Fulford.

Bishopthorpe. None.

Bilbrough. None.

Acaster Malbis.

Robert Marfield, tailor.   Simon Tasker, wheelwright.

PAPISTS, 1767.

Parishes that have places of worship served by Popish Priests or Reputed Priests.

City of York.

Parish.	Name.	Age.	Res. Yrs.
St. Cuthbert's	Mr. Thomas Nandike	44	$4\frac{1}{2}$
Fulforth	Mr. Watson	63	$\frac{2}{3}$
St. Michael Belfry	Mr. More, brother to Mrs. Dalton	40	2
	Mr. Thomas Daniel	50	25
	Mr. Thomas Ferby	28	3

Parish.	Name.	Age.	Res. Yrs.
Holy Trinity	Mr. Giffard	60	17
in King's Court	Mr. Nickson	34	3½
Holy Trinity	Mr. Joseph Robinson	49	1
in Micklegate	Mr. Robert Constable	61	2
		In City of York—	9

DEANERY OF AINSTIE.

Abberford	Mr. J. Steer	65	25
Barwick-in-Elmet	Mr. Winter	25	2
(D. of Norfolk's estate)			
Spofforth	Mr. Walmsley	...	...
	Mr. John Stone	45	...

DEANERY OF CRAVEN.

Broughton	Mr. Thomas Heatley	50	2
Mitton	Mr. Doyne (Jesuit)	35	2½
Ilkley	Mr. Jno. Watkinson	40	8

DEANERY OF BULMER.

Bransby	Mr. Meynell	29	3
(At Mr. Cholmley's)			
Coxwold	Mr.	...	...
(At Angram)			
North Kilvington	Mr.		...
(At Mr. Meynell's house)			

DEANERY OF CLEVELAND.

Crathorne & Appleton	Mr. Colburn	65	20
(In Mr. Crathorne's house)			
Egton	Mr. John Shepherd	52	16
(At Egton Bridge)			
Lythe	Mr. Parkinson	...	...
(At Ugthorp)			
Yarm	Mr. Syddall	67	35
(In Mr. Farmer's house.)		(*not so old*)	

G

Parish.	Name.	Age.	Res. Yrs.
Northallerton and Osmotherly	Mr. John Houseman (*quiet & inoffensive*)	65	12
Osmotherley	Mr. Thomas Watson	...	...
Leake (At Nether Silton)	Mr. John Eccles	38	3

Deanery of Rydale.

Gilling (In Lord Fairfax's house, and at Helmsley)	Mr. John Bolton	40	3
Hovingham	Mr. James Barrow (*very forward*)	42	...
		In North Riding—12	

Deanery of Nottingham.

Radford	Mr. Thomas Pickering	60	20

Deanery of Retford.

Blythe	Mr. George Shuttleworth	48	15
Worksop (At Duke of Norfolk's)	Mr. Taylor	33	8
		In Notts.— 3	

Deanery of Doncaster.

Clayton and Sandal Magna	Mr. Sanderson	50	16
Sheffield	Mr. John Lodge	43	11
	Mr. William Winter	30	2

Deanery of Pontefract.

Carlton	Mr. Rd. Nesfield	36	8
Pontefract	Mr. Rd. Barrow	50	2
Rothwell (In a house of D. of Norfolk's; a new fitted-up place)	Mr. Thos. Haddam (*yt was at Leeds*)	60	4
	In rest of West Riding—13		

Deanery of Harthill.

Parish.	Name.	Age.	Res. Yrs
Everingham (At Mr. Constable's)	Mr. William Fleetwood Reputed. (He is a Jesuit)	...	...
Holme in Spalding Moor	Mr. John Fisher	58	27

Deanery of Holderness.

| Skeckling | Mr. George Mayor | 39 | ⅔ |
| Swine | Mr. James Taylor | 38 | 4 |

In East Riding— 4

Hexhamshire.

Hexham (At Cogshaw Chapel)	Mr. George Gibson	30	12
(At Battle Hill Chapel)	Mr. Fairleman	30	12
	One Jesuit & one Secular		
St. John Lees	Mr. Newton	48	1

In Hexhamshire— 3

Jurisdiction of Ripon.

| Bishop Thornton | Mr. Richard Talbot | 27 | 3 |

In Riponshire— 1

Nov. 26, 1767. In the Diocese of York, including Peculiars. —

Total of Priests 45

PARISH REGISTER OF CLAY COTON,

Northants.

(Transcribed by the Rev. Gordon H. Poole.)

Anno domini 1584.
By me Robert Cleye, &c.

Richard Moulton, the sone of Willia. Moulton, was bapt. the xxvii. daye of Julye.

Margerie Burgesse, the dau. of John Burgesse, was bapt. the xxx. day of Julye.

Sara Pratt, the dau. of John Pratt, was bapt. the xxi. daye of Sept.

John Murcote, the sone of Willia. Murcote, was bapt. the iiiith daye of October.

Judeth Heward, the dau. of Thomas Heward, was bapt. the iiiith day of November.

Edward Brewesse, the sone of Willia. Brewesse, was bapt. the viith day of November.

Prudens Murcote, the dau. of Thomas Murcote, was bapt. the vith daye of Januarye.

Nicholas Webster was bur. the xx. daye of Julye.

John Webster was bur. the xxvi. of Julye.

Anno domini 1585.

Agnes Webster, the dau. of Michaell Webster, was bapt. the xxvi. daye of Maye.

Joane Ballard, the dau. of John Ballard, was bapt. the ii. daye of September.

Thomas Webster, the sone of Thomas Webster, was bapt. the xii. daye of September.

Nicholas Heward, the sone of Thomas Heward, was bapt. the xiiith daye of October.

John Jonson, the sone of John Jonson, was bapt. the xth daye of December.

Joane Ballard, the dau. of John Ballard, was bur. the iiii. daye of September.

* Continued from page 32.

John Randle was buried the viii. of December.

William Williams and Susan Perkins weare married the vith daye of December.

Avice Carter was buried the vi. of Januarie.

Margerie Webster was buried the xiiii. of March.

Anno domini 1586.

Agnes West, the dau. of Richard West, was bapt. the xvth daye of Maye.

Elizabeth Ballard, the dau. of John Ballard, was bapt. the ixth of September.

Edward Reeve, the sone of Richard Reeve, was bapt. the xith day of September.

Susan Wood, the dau. of Thomas Wood, was bapt. the xxx. of November.

By me Robert Cleye, &c.

Nicholas Cartmell, the sone of Nicholas Cartmell, was bapt. the xxiith of Januarie.

Thomas Williams, the sone of Willia. Willias., was bapt. the first day of Februarie.

Joane Murcote, the dau. of Thomas Murcote, was bapt. the iiiith daye of Februarie.

Margret Pratt, the dau. of John Pratt, was bapt. the first daye of Marche.

Agnes Heward, the dau. of Thomas Heward.

Agnes Heward, the wife of Nicholas Heward, was buried the xxi. of Aprill.

Anno domini 1587.

Richard Murcote, the sone of Willia. Murcote, was bapt. the 11 day of Aprill.

John Brewesse, the sonne of Willia. Brewesse, was bapt. the xxxth daye of Aprill.

Thomas Heward, the sonne of Thomas Heward, was bapt. the xxviiith day of Januarie.

Anno domini 1588.

Thomas Ballard was bur. the vii. of June.

William Murcote was bur. the vii. of Julye.

Willia. Ballard was bur. the vii. of Julye.

Margret Webster, the dau. of Michell Webster, was bapt. the first daye of Februarie.

Brigett Williams, the dau. of Willia. Williams, was bapt. the first daye of Februarie.

Henric Ballard, the sone of John Ballard, was bapt. the ixth daye of Marche.

Anno domini 1589.

William Webster, the sone of Thomas Webster, was bapt. the xiiith day of Aprill.

Edward Heward, the sonne of Thomas Heward, was bapt. the iiii. daye of Januarye.

Elizabeth Brewesse, the dau. of William Brewesse, was bapt. the vth of Januarye.

Thomas Burgesse, the sonne of John Burgesse, was bapt. the xxiiii. of Januarie.

Alice Wood, the dau. of Thomas Wood, was bapt. the xxviii. day of Februarie.

Edward Murcote, the sonne of John Murcote, was bapt. the xxviiith of Februarie.

By me Robert Cleye, &c.

William Williams, the sone of Willia. Willias., was bapt. the xxviiith daye of Marche.

Anno domini 1591.

Thomas West, the sonne of Henrye West, was bapt. the xxviiith day of August.

Thomas Mariat, the sonne of Richard Mariat, was bapt. the xxvith daye of October.

Margerie Heward, the dau. of Thos. Heward, was bapt. the 11 daye of Januarie.

John Ballard, the sonne of John Ballard, was bapt. the xiiiith daye of Januarie.

George Marche, the sonne of Edward Marche, was bapt. the xxxth daye of Januarye.

Richard Mariat and Alice Heward weare mar. the ixth daye of Aug.

Edward (*sic.*) and Marie Webster weare mar. the xxviith daye of September.

Edward Suffolke was bur. the xiith daye of Februarie.

Thomas Banburie was bur. the xiiith daye of Maye.

Anno 1592.

Margerie Heward, the dau. of Thomas Heward, was bapt. the xxviith of Maye.

Thomas Wood was bur. the xvii. of January.

Anno domini 1593.

Marie Williams, the dau. of Willia. Williams, was bapt. the xxx. daye of Marche.

Robert Heward, the sonne of Thomas Heward, was bapt. the vith daye of Julye.

Willia. Killingley, the sonne of Bartholl Killingley, was bapt. the xiiiith daye of Marche.

Anno domini 1594.

Alice Heward, the dau. of Thomas Heward, was bapt. the xvi. daye of August.

Elizabeth Mariat, the dau. of Richard Mariat, was bapt. the vi. of October.

Marie Richardson, the dau. of Richard Richardson, was bapt. the xxiiii. of November.

Thomas Scare, the sonne of Thomas Scare, was bapt. the xxx. day of December.

Robert Ballard, the sone of John Ballard, was bapt. the xvth day of Marche.

Thomas Hulley and Elizabeth Gethgale nupt. 29 Oct.

Thomas Barford was bur. the xxvii. of Julye.

By me Robert Cleye, &c.

Ano. dni. 1595.

John Sutton and Margerie Paulmer weare mar. the ii. daye of Nov.

Robert Heward was bur. the xxxth daye of Julye.

Thomas Mariat was bur. the xxx. of December.

John Paulmer was bur. the xxxth daye of Januarie.

Agnes March, the wife of Nicholas Marche, was bur. the iiiith day of Marche.

Anno Domini 1596.

Robert Britten and Margerie Storie weare mar. the xiiiith daye of October.

John Heward and Eme Reeve weare mar. the xxith of Februarie.

MARRIAGE BONDS

OF THE

DEAN AND CHAPTER OF YORK.*

By T. B. Whytehead, Esq., Chapter Registrar.

"SEDE VACANTE."

1683. June 26. Thomas Burgh, of Pocklington, labourer, aged 20, and Ellen Marre, of Hull, aged 24.
June 30. Geo. Bayley, of Adwicke-on-Dearne, yeoman, and Elizabeth Shepperd, of Bolton-on-Dearne, spinster.
[Doncaster.]
June 30. Joseph Scott, of Gildersom, and Elizabeth Lake.
June 30. Quintin Fearby, of York, merchant tailor, and Rose Raynold.
June 28. Jas. Wilson, of Leeds, aged 27, and Anne Buck, aged 28. [Leeds or Calverley.]
June 29. Geo. Bothamley, of North Owram, stapler, and Dorothy Nalson.
June 29. Robert Gleidhill, of Hanbury, yeoman, and Sarah Marsden.
July 19. Thomas Hobson, of Rotherham, wheelwright, and Sarah Hancock.
July 6. John Laughton, of Mexborough, yeoman, and Anne Oley.
July 15. Wilfred Peell, of Heckmondwike, yeoman, and Elizabeth Senior.
Aug. 20. Wm. Strickland, of Hunslet, baker, and Catherine Pickering.
Aug. 1. Jeremiah Hirst, of Tambersley, nailsmith, and Rebecca Marsh.
July 11. Joseph Brearley, of Bradford, gent., and Mary Wood.
July 30. John Cooke, of Barwick, cordwainer, and Isabell Settle.

* Continued from page 36.

1683. July 30. Thomas Wrigglesworth, of Asenby, yeoman, and Elizabeth Greaby.
July 23. John Beeston, of East Hardwick, gent., and Mary Horner, spinster.
July 13. Robert Roseman, of Guisbrough, chemist, and Mary Fox.
July 21. John Green, of Doncaster, husbandman, and Alice Law, of Carrhome, widow. [Doncaster.]
July 4. John Clapham, of Batley, baker, and Hanna Turner.
July 23. John Thomson, of Halifax, gent., and Mary Kershaw.
July 14. Thos. Holm, of Flixby, husbandman, and Jane Siker.
July 28. Rowland Belson, of York, tanner, and Elizth. Jansan.
July 10. Jas. Croft, of Wragby, husbandman, aged 43, and Margaret Ellis, of Ackworth, widow, aged 38.
[Pontefract.]
July 28. Richard Ward, of Methley, ropemaker, and Mary Emett.
July 11. Thomas Kitson, of North Owram, baker, and Mary Hollings.
July 14. Christr. Caburn, of Louth, aged 21, and Mary Bird, of Hull, spinster, aged 19.
July 7. Richard Baley, of Hesle, gent., aged 46, and Sarah Lealand, of Hesle, widow, aged 40.
July 8. Wm. Stapleton, of Paul, aged 26, tailor, and Jane Johnson, of Tunstall, aged 25, spinster.
July 5. Nathaniel Heyton, of Kingston-on-Hull, aged 30, butcher, and Margaret Cromp, of Hull, widow, aged 35.
July 3. Edward Wilkinson, of Sunderland, aged 27, sailor, and Mary Rosindill, of York, aged 20, spinster.
July 25. Richard Craike, of Marton, gent., and Frances Horner, spinster.
July 10. Robert Thornton, of Methley, yeoman, and Elizth. Lake.
July 9. Henry Pulleyn, of Harwood, yeoman, and Jane Dawson.
July 21. Peter Wools, of Ripon, aged 27, yeoman, and Phillis Bell, of Borrowbridge, aged 27.
[Ripon or Aldborough.]

1683. July 22. Thomas Stockton, of Swine, labourer, aged 21, and Elizabeth Wilson, of Burstwick, aged 20, spinster.
July 21. Robt. Riley, of Watton, yeoman, aged 38, and Lose Bainton, widow, of Swinkle, aged 36.
July 19. Ebenezer Robson, of Kingston-on-Hull, aged 26, tailor, and Anne Marshall, of Hull, aged 19, spinster.
July 5. Thos. Winter, of Penreth, aged 34, and Mary Rowell, of Heslarton, aged 21. [St. Olave's or Cathedral.]
July 6. John Willop, of Kighley, carrier, and Ann Roy.
July 11. John Robinson, of Bellingley, yeoman, and Elizth. Wilson.
Aug. 16. Peregine Lascelles, of Whitby, gent., and Mary Wigmore.
Aug. 6. William Guisburne, of Guisbrough, miller, and Marjery Wilkinson.
Aug. 6. Matthew Craven, of Hull, and Sarah Swanne, spr.
Aug. 30. George Parnell and Mary Parnell.
Aug. 10. Martin Ponston, of South Dalton, aged 40, and Dorcas Bigg, of York.
Aug. 18. John Scholfield, of Armethorpe, husbandman, and Mary Hopton, of Barmby-on-Dunn, spinster. [Doncaster.]
Aug. 13. Francis Fox, of Wakefield, gent., and Elizabeth Howston.
Aug. 11. Michael Watson, of Fylingdales, yeoman, and Elizabeth Knagges.
Aug. 10. John Copeland, of Newthorpe, Sherburn, husbandman, aged 23, and Barbarah Teale, of Ackworth, spinster, aged 25. [Pontefract.]
Aug. 15. Jeremy Taylor, of Burstall, yeoman, and Mary Brooke.
Aug. 5. Thomas Scofield, of Gomersall, baker, and Jane Hollings.
Aug. 7. Wm. Cooke, of Linton, and Mary Leyland.
Aug. 4. Richard Howard, of Wakefield, salter, and Susanna Norfolke.
Aug. 18. Jacob Rhodes, of Wakefield, malster, and Mercy Milner.
Aug. 9. Joshua Crosley, of Norland, Halifax, baker, and Elizabeth Towne.

1686. Nov. 11. Wm. Marshall, of York, cordwainer, and Frances Carter.
Nov. 10. Daniel Hogg, of York, sadler, aged 23, and Elizth. Morland, of York, spinster, aged 20. [St. Helen's.]
Dec. 6. John Pool, of Lawkland, gent., aged 32, and Anne Armestead, of Stainforth, spinster, aged 22. [Giggleswick.]
Nov. 30. Thomas Fox, of York, and Mary Procter, spinster.
Jan. 12. Edward Dixon, of Hull, sailor, aged 23, and Jane Radley, of St. Mary, Castlegate, York, spinster, aged 21.
[St. Mary, Castlegate.]
Dec. 22. Moses Calvert, of York, merchant, aged 35, and Anne Colton, of York, widow, aged 30. [St. Crux.]
March 9. George Taylor, of Raskelf, gent., and Mary Gatemanby.
Oct. 15. William Collinson, of Kirkby Misterton, esq., and Katherine Gascoigne.
Oct 15. Edward Hodgson, of Cockram, Lanc., husbandman, and Sisily Butterfield.
Oct. 18. Robt. Stabler, of York, and Elizth. Grant, spinster.
Oct. 25. John Needham, of Cawood, gent., and Bridgett Byles, spinster.
Nov. 1. Wm. Skelton, of Aislaby, butcher, aged 30, and Elizabeth Pearson, of Marton, spinster, aged 28.
[St. Mary, Castlegate or St. Michael, Spurriergate.]
Nov. 1. John Harrison, of Sheriff Hutton, yeoman, aged 30, and Mary Cobb, of Sheriff Hutton, spinster, aged 26.
[St. Trinity, Goodramgate.]
Nov. 22. Matthew Levett, of Holm-on-Wolds, yeoman, aged 40, and Mary Bayley, spinster, aged 21.
[St. Maurice, St. Denis or St. George.]
Aug. 31. Thos. Milnes, of Linton, husbandman, aged 27, and Ellen Wright, of Linton, spinster, aged 29.
[St. Trinity, Goodramgate.]
Aug. 28. Edward Walker and Meriana Knipe, spinster.
Sept. .... William Hunter, of York, clothworker, and Jane Langton, spinster.
Sept. 17. Thomas Milner, of Beverley, gent., aged 48, and Mary Oliver, widow, aged 40, of St. John's, Beverley.

1686. Sept. 13. Oswald Buckle, of York, upholsterer, aged 23, and Rebecca Thomlinson, of Brayton, spinster, aged 20.

Sept. 24. Thos. Lutton, of York, gent., and Anne Buck, spinster.

Sept. 25. Wm. Linthall, of Rocliffe, husbandman, aged 30, and Ursula Vicars, of York, spinster, aged 24.
[St. Mary, Castlegate or St. Crux.]

Oct. 6. John Mitchell, of York, baker, St. Mary, Castlegate, and Anne Harrison, of All Saints', Pavement, spinster.
[St. Olave's or Trinity, Goodramgate.]

July 27. Wm. Hood, of York, vinter, and Elizth. Redshaw.

Aug. 25. Thos. Yeates, of Ripon, felmonger, aged 23, and Mary Brandsby, of Ripon, aged 28, spinster.

Aug. 25. Thomas Brooke, of Wakefield, gent., and Merry Naylor.

Aug. 25. John Leng, of Wheldrake, cordwainer, aged 22, and Mary Clifford, of New Malton, aged 25, spinster.
[Old Malton or New Malton.]

Aug. 26. John Rodhouse, of Ripon, husbandman, aged 40, and Elizth. Feather, aged 38, spinster. [Kippax.]

Aug. 26. William Harrison, of York, chandler, aged 25, and Mary Thorpe, widow, of Crambe, aged 28.
[Cathedral or Crambe.]

July 27. Leonard Atkinson, of Leeds, clothier, and Mary Spence.

July 26. Wm. Fairfax, of Newton Kyme, esq., and Susannah Coates.

July 27. Joseph Dixon, of Thornhill, aged 24, mason, and Alice Rhoades, spinster, aged 30. [Bishopthorpe.]

Aug. 5. Josiah Hilary, of York, merchant, and Mary Dawson, spinster.

Aug. 9. John Egan, of Barnard Castle, aged 26, gent., and Elizth. Kitchen, of York, spinster, aged 19. [St Cuthbert.]

Aug. 10. Geo. Shield, of Sutton-on-Forest, brickmaker, aged 30, and Dorothy Taylor, spinster, of Huntington, aged 28.
[Sutton or Huntington.]

Aug. 16. John Gill, of Horseforth, tanner, aged 26, and Mary Marshall, spinster, of Thorner, aged 22.
[Guisley or Thorner.]

1686. June 27. Marmaduke Benson, of Coxwold, yeoman, and Sara Day, spinster.

July 7. Henry Whitby, of Whitby, gent., aged 26, and Judith Panton, of Grimston, spinster, aged 28.
[Cathedral or St. Helen's.]

July 6. Richard Russell, of Hull, barber and surgeon, and Ann Robinson, spinster.

July 9. John Adcock, of Tadcaster, yeoman, and Joanna Plumber, widow.

July 14. Samuel Cooper, of Guisley, aged 26, clothier, and Mary Spencer, of Kildwick, aged 25, spinster. [Kildwick.]

July 17. Richard Barker, of Newton-on-Ouse, husbandman, aged 30, and Martha Browne, spinster, aged 27.
[Holy Trinity, Goodramgate.]

July 23. Abraham Topham, of Kettlewell, yeoman, and Agnes Fawcett.

May 31. George Trewman, of Leeds, gent., and Dorothy Wright.

June 14. Eustas Casse, of Sawdon, yeoman, aged 22, and Ann Wilberforce, spinster, aged 17.
[Goodmanham or Brompton.]

June 17. Thomas Gibson, of Linton-on-Ouse, aged 21, gent., and Hannah Stephenson, aged 21, spinster, of Sowerby.
[Bransby.]

July 19. Thomas Tyndall, of Everingham, husbandman, aged 40, and Mary Chambers, aged 28, spinster.
[St. Margaret's, York.]

July 11. Robert Settrington, of Conysthorpe, yeoman, aged 38, and Dorothy West, spinster, aged 33. [Whenby.]

June 29. Ralph Clarke, of Thorpe, Kilburn, gent., and Isabell Coates, spinster.

April 24. Thomas Thackeray, of Hampsthwaite, butcher, and Jane Pott, spinster.

April 24. Charles Buchanan, of Hull, clerk, and Sarah Mirfield.

May 27. Ambrose Sayer, of Hutton Rudby, gent., aged 28, and Elizabeth Redman, of York, spinster, aged 22.
[Sheriff Hutton.]

SOME NOTES OF ROMAN CATHOLICS IN LINCOLNSHIRE.*

An account of Papists and reputed Papists within the diocese of Lincoln, according to the returns made thereof in 1780.

Ednam	2
Faldingworth	1
Fotherby	7
Frodingham	1
Fulstow	2
Grimoldby	9
Hainton (a Popish school)	112
Harlaxton	6
Holton-le-Clay	1
Horbling	1
Horncastle	2
Irnham	180
Kelsey, North	3
Kettlethorpe	3
Kingerby	4
Kirkby with Osgarby ...	14
Kirkby Underwood ...	1
Legsby	14
Lissington	2
Lincoln (a school by a woman but all Prot. children) ...	24
Louth	16
Ludford Parva	6
Manton	2
Marsh	10
Messingham and Botsford	11
Morton and Hacconby ...	2
Nettleton	21
Nocton	1
Norton Bishop's	2
Nun Ormsby	4
Ponton Magna	6
Raisen Market (a school)...	33
„ West	47
Rearsby	3
Ropsley	1
Saxilby	5
Scamblesby...	6
Scotter	9
Sibsey	1
Sixhill (25 of them children)	50
Snarford	2
Somerby with Humby ...	14
Somercotes, N.	2
Stainton by Langworth ...	11
Stamford	*3
Stewton	1
Torrington, E. with Wragby	16
„ W.	1
Thoresby, N.	6
Thorganby	5
Thornton-le-Moor	8
Ulceby	1
Utterby	2
Walcot	3
Waltham	4
Welton by Louth	2
Willingham, South ...	5

* Continued from page 208, of Vol. for 1896.

Willingham by Stow	...	1	N.B.—Falstrop not returned.		
Winterton ...	...	1			
Worletby ...	...	36			
Wrawby and Brigg	...	24	Lincolnshire	...	1061
Wyam and Cadeby	...	7	Leicestershire	...	211
Cockerington, near Leond.		1	Hunts. ...	...	30
Ludburgh ...	...	5			
Thurlby, near Bourn	...	2	Herts. ...	...	19
Wellingore ...	...	1	Bedfordshire	...	25
		1034	Bucks. ...	...	282
Mareham-le-fen	...	3			
Sleaford ...	...	1			1628
Tetney ...	...	23			
Total ...		1061			

ARCHDEACON'S VISITATION, 1604.

BIGBIE-CUM-MEMBRIS.

Gervasius Anne, gen.; Robertus Shierson, Michael, Margareta, and Rosa Matteus, famuli ejus; Carolus Nevell *als*. Walker, et Elizabetha ejus uxor; Jenetta Brown, vid.; Effam ux. Martini Graven; Maria filia dicti Martini; presented for manifest recusants, 5° Sept., 1604, citati non comparuerunt. Ideo sequest'.

WRAGGOE DEANERY.

Barbara ux. Thome Hennage militis, presented for recusant, 5° Sept., 1604, citata non comparuit. vii^s sequest'.

WRAWBIE.

Maria Townsende et Maria Pierson, famula dicte Townsend, presented for recusants, 6° Octobris, 1604, citate non comparuerunt. Sequest'.

Johannes Bell et Ricardus Gueste, gardiani, presented for omitting to presente Anthony Saltmarshe's wiffe and syster for recusants.

IMMINGHAM.

Edwardus Porkenton, gen. et uxor ejus, presented for recusants. Sequest'.

NOTES FROM PARISH REGISTERS.

Ashby-cum-Fenby, 1698, April 19. William Welford, of Hainton, and Elizabeth Simson, of Lowth, papists, w^r married at Th. Ashton's hous January 13, 1697. Certified this day.

Market Stainton, 1697. Theophilus Gregg, of Goldsby, and Jane Kirkham, of Market Stainton, both seperates, joyned themselves together as they pretended, November ye 7th,

West Rasen, 1742. Mary, the late wife of William Utterby, papist, buried Nov. 23rd.

Wyham-cum-Cadeby, 1767. Mr. Henry Kirby, a Romish priest. His circumstances I know not, aged 55 years, buried May 16.

Conisholme, 1773. Ann Bywater, a papist, buried Sept. 12th.

Grimoldby, 1787. William Caley, a papist gentleman, aged 67, buried April 24th. 1792, Mary Caley, a papist, aged 102, buried June 3rd.

The following entry, which occurs both at Belleau and Swaby in 1680, is suggestive, as to the omission of Non-conformists from the registers:—"All these with some other that were excommunicated, and sectaries not here mentioned, were all interr'd in wollen according to law, as appear'd by Mr. Boswell's certificates, all dated and brought in due time."

STARTFORTH PARISH REGISTER,
CO. YORK.*

Transcribed by Mark W. Bullen, Esq., by kind permission of the Rev. Hartley Jennings, the Vicar.

Maria uxor Mat. Scot sepulta fuit, 23° Junii.
Josephus Sanderson, medic., sepult' 24° Octobris.
Ambr. Simpson sepultus fuit 6° Decembr.
Maria Waterman vid. sep., 8° Januarii.

Connubia, 1693.

Rob. Kipling et Alicia Fielding in matrimonium conuncti fuere 1° die Februarii.

Connubia, 1694.

Rich. Coates et Margareta Grainger in matrimonium coniuncti fuere secundo die m. Septembris.

Tho. Kipling et Isabella Harker in matrimonium coniuncti fuere Octobr. 6°.

Joshua Clarkson et Catharina Cheesebrough in matrimonium, &c., 11 Octobris.

Tho. Waterman et Isabella Bolron in matrimonium coniuncti fuere 24° Januarii.

1695.

Franc. Allison, Bernard Castle et Margareta Colling in matrimonium 30 Junii.

5.
Baptism., 1694.

.... fil. Richard Colling, baptiz. 19° Julii.
.... fil. Tho. Hall, baptizatus 22° Julii.
Jana fil. Jeremia Bainbridge, baptiz. 29° Julii.
Gulielm fil. Rob. Laidman, baptiz. 25° Augustii.
Tho. fil. Rob. Barnes, baptiz. 10° Septembris.
Jacobus, fil. Thomae Richardson, baptizat 11° mensis Octobris.
Maria filia Caroli Birckbeck, baptiz. 23° Novembris.
Francisca fil. Gulielm. Mills, baptiz. 9° Decembris.

* Continued from page 56.

Joannes, fil. Jo. Milburne, baptiz. 12° Januarii.
Anna fil. Jo. Jamson, baptiz. 24 Februarii.
Rob. fil. Tho. Garstell, baptiz. 14° Martii.

Baptism., 1695.

Josephus fil. Roberti Naitby, baptiz. fuit 11° Julii.
Jan. fiil. Gul. Hanbie, baptiz. 18° Julii.
Sarah fil. Tho. Kipling, baptiz. 21° Julii.
Joannis fil. Radulphi Binyan, baptiz. 28° Julii.
Matt. fil. Matthei Dent, baptiz. 18° Augusti.
Michael fil. Gulielmi Clarkson, baptiz. 22° Aug.
Alicia fil. Rob. Kipling, baptiz. 29th Sept.
Gul. fil. Gulielmi Thompson, baptiz. 2 Octobris.
Rich. fil. Thomae Clarkson, baptiz. 27° Octobr.

5b.

Marcus fil. Jacobi Auds, bap. ....
Joannes, fil. Rich. Waller, baptiz. 2(o ?) ....

Baptism., 1696.

Christoph. fil. suppositit. Chr. Cradock de Bern. Castle, baptiz. 22° Aprilis.
Catharina fil. Josh. Clarkson, baptiz. 24° Junii.
Henry the son of Henry Jollin, of Starfor.. , baptized the ...... of July.
Isabell the daughtor of Charles Birkbeck, of Startforth, was bapt. the 7 of July.
Anne the daughter of Tho. Morgan, was baptized the 9 of July.
John the son of John Kipling, of Startforth, was baptized the 11 of Octobr.
Jane the daughter of Chris. Finley, was baptized the 18 Octobr.
Tho. the son of Tho. Waterman, was baptiz. the 8 of Novemb.
William the son of Geo. Harker, was baptized the 29 of Novemb.
Richard the son of Richard Coats, was bapt. the 26 of December.
Mary the daughter of Thomas Chapellowe, was baptized the 21 of January.
Edward the son of William Kelley, was baptized the 28th of Jan.
Tho. the son of Tho. Richardson, was baptized the 9 of March.
Anne the daughter of Matthew Dent, baptiz. 14 of March.
Mary, daughter of Geo. Dawson, bapt. 21 March.
James supposed bastard child of Jam. Clarkson, was baptized the 22nd of March.

6.
Sepultor' nomina, 1695 (*sic.*)

.... fil. Chr. Finley, sep. 30 Aprilis.
......uth Lightfoot, sepultus 9° Junii.
Maria fil. Radulphi Laidman, sepulta 11° Julii.
Abortiv. fil. Geo. Dawson, sepult' 13° Julii.
Gul. Thompson, sep. 26° Julii.
Guliel. fil. Rob. Laidman, sep. 15° Septembr.
Margaret fil. Tho. Morgan, sep. eod. die.
Alicia fil. Rob. Kipling, sepult' 30 Septembris.
Timoth. fil. Tho. Coates, sep. 14 Octobris.
Elinor Foster, spinster, sepulta fuit 12° Novembris.
Joannes Renison, sep. 25° Novembr.
Alicia Addington, sep. 2° Decembris.
Abortiv. Tho. Waterman, sep. 6° Decembris.
Gulielm. fil. Willelmi Thompson, sep. 22° die m. Decembris.
Anth. fil. Lionelli Michel, sepultus ultimo die Decembris.
Gulielmus Simpson de Egleston Abbey, sep. fuit 17° Januarii.
Ruth Hayton, sepulta 30 Januarii.
Gulielm. fil. Gulielmi Fielding Generosi, sepultus fuit 17° Februarii.

Sepultor' nomina, 1696.

Margareta uxor Joannis Wennington, sepulta fuit 30 Martii.
Alicia uxor Anth. Hambie, sep. 14° Aprilis.

6b. 1696.

Cuth. Hambie, sepultus fuit 2° mens............
Henry, the son of the supposed Henry Joblin, of Cle......... was bur. the 20 of July.
Barba. the daughter of Brian Birkebek, was buried the 12 of Octo.
Margarett Clerkson was buried the 20 of October.
Grase Loadman, wife of Robert Loadman, was buried the 24 of November.
Thomas Harker was buried the 29 of November.
Eliz. Finley, wife of Chris. Finley, was buried the 5 of Decem.
John Milburn, son of John Milburn, was buried the 6 Decemb.
Jane Hutchinson was buried the 21 of December.
Francis, the daughter of Will. Mills, was buried the 10 of January.
Bridgett Clerkson was buried the 13 of February.
Anne Banks buried the 22 of March.

1697.

Margaret Kipling was buried the eleventh day of May.
Sarah, the daughter of Geo. Race, of Deepdaill, buried the 20th of May.
Mark, the son of James Audd, buried June the 9th.
Chr. Dent buried July 11th.
Jane Naitbie buried August 20th.
Hugh Clifton was buried September the 5th.
Jane, the wife of William Kelley, was buried October the tenth.
Robt. Brench was buried the 9th of November.
A child of Geo. Harker buried Nov. 18th.
Lionel Michels maid-servant, buried Nov. 19th.
William, the son of Geo. Harker, buried Nov. 22.
Isabel, the wife of Tho. Atkins, buried December 19th.
Richard Grainger was buried December 31.

7.

Connubia, 1696.

William Thompson and Margarett Hodgson were married the 9th of Julii.
George Pearson, of Bowes, and Jane Foster, were married the 2 of May.
Will. Grainger and Anne Thompson were married the 6 of May.
John Thwaites and Margaret Harker were married the seventh day of June.
Geo. Procter and Margaret Kipling married 15th July.

Baptism., 1697.

Hannah, daughter to Tho. Kipling, was baptized April 1.
Mary, daughter to Rich. Colling, baptized April 10th.
Sarah, daughter to Jo. Boundy, baptized June 5°.
Will. the son of Will. Hambie, baptized Septemb. 2°.
Thomas, the son of Jo. Thwaites, was baptized the twelft of Sept.
Eleanor, the daughter of Will. Thompson, baptized Octob. 17th.
Jane, the daughter of Will. Hutchinson, was baptized December 16.
Timothy, son of James Scott, of Bd. Castle, bapt. Jan. the 1st.
Mary, the daughter of Jo. Vicars, was baptized Jan. 4th.
Mary, the daughter of Thomas Hall, baptized January 16th.
Phillis, the daughter of Will. Grainger, baptized Februaray 6th.

SOME WILLS FROM THE RICHMOND REGISTRY.*

Arch. Richmond.
SIR WILLIAM MANFELD.

Sir Wyll. Manfeld, pryst, of mekyll langton upon swall. "I gyff my sawll unto almyghty god, our lady sanct mary, and to all the holy company off heven, and my body to be erthed w^t in the qwere of sanct wylfryd."

I give to William Manfeld "a cow and an qwy," and to Leonard Manfeld xx^s. I will that Henry Manfeld "my brother son" pay to William Manfledd at ten years' end, iij^l vj^s viij^d. Sir Anton. Metcalf, Sir John Johnson. I give to "the kyrkwark," iij^s iiij^d. To Master Robt. Conyers "my leyes that I have off the benefeyes, and the order of Wyll Manffeld w^t all; also the resudew off my gudes not wyll, I gyff unto John Manfeld, Wyll. Manffeld, and Henry Manfeld," and make them my exors. Master Robt. Conyercs, supervisor. Witnesses, Sir John Johnson, John Wastell, John Wylson. Dat., 8 August, 1538. Proved, 14 May, 1539.

Inventory made 28 Oct., 1538, by Johen Sigeswyke, Johen Dayll, Johen Wylson, and Thos. Smyth. Sum vij^l ix^s xj^d, Debts lix^s iiij^d.

Arch. Richmond.   Regd. ✠ 191.
THOMAS POWER.

I Thomas Power, of Kyrlyngton. "I gyve my soull to almyghty god, and to his blyssed mother mary, and to all ye celestiall copany of heven; and my body to be buryed in the church erth of Kyrklyngton, and I make Maisteres Wandisford syrvaer of my wyll, and I gyve to hir v^s of gold; also I make Sir Robert Wilkynson and my broder John Power, myne executores."

* Continued from page 28.

To Cristofer Power, of Kyrklyngton, "v angells nobylls." Richard Power (the younger), my brother John Power and his wife, John Power (the younger), my mother, my sister Elizabeth, Elizth. Power. To Xpofer. Power "a cayt" that was his father's. To Richard Power (the elder) " my best cott." To Xpofer. Power, of Aynderby "oyn of my tawny coytts with yalow welts." Residue to Maistres Wandysford and to my exors. for the health of my soul. Witnesses, Maists. Christofer Wandisford, esqwyere, and John Walkare. Dat. 16 Jan., 1540. Proved (no date.)

Arch. Richmond.

LANCELOT FOSTER.

Sir lansloyth foster. "I gyffe my soule to god allmyghty, and to oure lady saynt mary, and to all the celestiall company off hevyn, and my body to be bered in ye churche of saynt columbe in thopclyffe, also I wyll that I shalbe honestly broght furth w^t dyryge off the qweyr the day of my beryall, also I wyll hayve iiij torchys."

I give to Margret Wyllson my sister "my syde gowne," and to Annesse Foster my sister "two shorte gowns and apayr of new hoyse cloyth." To John Wyllson my brother-in-law "my ledder doblet and my fustchan doblett." To o^r lady gylde xij^d, also I gyffe to the newe bell xij^d. Sir Thomas Hoghson, Sir John Plumpton, Thomas Grene, Xpofer. Grene, Catryne Grene, and Elzabeyth Grene. Res. to my sisters Margaret Wyllson and Annesse Foster, my extrices. Witnesses, Syr Thomas Hoghson, Wyllm. Pulland, and Sir John Plumpton. Dat., 12 June, 1541. (No probate clause.)

Inventory off the goods of Sir lansloot foster, prest, departyd to the mercy of god, psed. by thes iiijth men. yt is to say, Wyllm. Burnet, Robert Burton, Robt. Whype, and Robert Thomson. Includes "on pours on belt and on payr of knywes vi^d"; in half-yere wayges xiij^s iiij^d. Sma. vij^l v^s iiij^d.

Arch. Richmond,

WILLIAM ASKOY.

I Wylm. Askoy, prest, hool of mynd, and in full memory ferying the jeop'de of deth. "I geve my saull to God almighty, to o^r lady sanct Mary, and to all the gloriosse dompany of hevyn, and my body to be buryed in the pysch church yerd of God and sanct Romald, boshopp and m'tyr, w^t all the dewtyes of holy church thereto accustomed (now by the law), also I geffe to ev^{r}y p^{r}st for masse and dirige at the discretion of my executors at the day of my buriall. The reysydewe of all my goods, my detts payed, and fun'all expenses deduct, I give to Janet Askow my servant whom I orden my executrix to dyspose for the helth of my saull as may seym hir good booth for the pleasure of God and comforth for my saull." Witnesses, Thos. Sanderson, Nicholas Cloose, John Nicolson, priests. Dat., 20 Jan., 1544. (No probate clause.)

Inventory of goods priced by Thomas Wharts, Wylm. Morthm, Wyllm. Appleby, and Wylm. Bails. Imprimis, twoo kyen, the price xxiiij^s; Item iij old gowns, price vj^s viij^d; Item ij cou'letts, ij shets, price iij^s; Item ij old blankketts, price xij^d; Item on fedd^r bedd, price v^s; Item on brassce pott, price v^s; Item on charger, price xx^d; Item on Almyre, price iij^s; Item on chest, price xij^d; Item on rooke of hay, price vj^s; Sma. to^{lis}, lvj^s iiij^d. Debitorium dicti Wilmi. Imprimis, to Sir Thomas Sanderson xxx^s; Item to Wylm. Rownthwait ix^s; Item to Elsabeth Paty vj^s viij^d; Item to Cecil Cornends iij^s; Item the house farm iij^s iiij^d; Item to Sir Nicholas Cloose vj^s viij^d; Item the small expenses xix^s viij^d; Item to Janet Askow x^s, the which me lady Conyers sent hir x^s. Sma. to^{lis}, iiij^l viij^d.

Arch. Richmond.

JOHN WARDROPER.

Sir John Wardroper, preste, (of Bedall.) "Ye firste, I ...eqwethe my soule unto allmyghtie god, and to o^r laydie sancte marie, and to all ye holy copanye of heuen, and my bodie to be buried where it shall please god."

To every priest at Bedall and to Sir John Key vj^d. To John Wardroper and to Elizabethe Wardroper xl^s. To Geo. Wardroper, Robert's sonne, a fely fole and a yow and a lambe. Elizabethe Langthorne and her children. James Wardroper's children. George Langthorne. Residue to John Wardroper and Elizabethe. Dat., 22 April, 1556. Admon. issued to (   ) 13 Nov., 1556.

Arch. Richmond.

RICHARD MORE.

Richard More, of Borobrig, of the pishe of Aldburghe. "I bequethe my soule to god almightie, to our blessed ladie saynt marie, and to all the celestiall copany of heaven, and my bodye to be laud within the kirke garthe at Aldburghe."

I give my house and a little close, bought of Maister Tankerd, to Robert More my son, and his heirs, rem^r to my youngest son Wm. More, my wife having the rent during her widowhood. I give my lease or gifte of my father leyke, and the deeds therof to my son William. I give to my said sons xij^l, and if they die before full age, I will that the same remain to my brethren Robert and John More, with my house and close in Fishergate. I give my land in Langthroppe to my father Buckell, and John buccle his sonne, also yf barnard bekwith desyer yt, he to have it. I give to John Buccle my brother, a fillye that is at Vpsalle parke. To Emot Buccle, iiij wethers, and to her brother xiij^s iiij^d. Xpofer. Waring. Willm. Scruton's two children. To Robert my brother, a pare of hose clothe; and to my father Buccle, my beste cappe. To Wm. Leike, halfe a cowe hyde that lyeth in the great tubb undermost. William Petye. Robert Burnand. I make Xpofer. Waring, Wm. Scruton, my supervisors, to be good to my wife and two children. Residue to Elyzabeth my wife, and my two children, my exors. Witnesses, John Maison, Richard Marshall, Xpofer. Waring, Willm. Scruton, Robert More. Dat., 28 March, 1560. (No probate clause.) Inventory, dat., 3 ……, 15…

Date.	Name.	Residence.	Document.	Reference.
1587	Craven, William.	Scriven.	W.I.	—
1587	Crawe, John.	Boroughbridge.	W.	—
1586	,, ,,	Kirk Stanley.	W.I.	—
1567	Crawforth, Peter.	Hutton Conyers.	W.I.	B. 33.
1602	Croft, Agnes.	Conystropp.	W.	—
1551	,, Anthony.	Aldbrough.	W.I.	—
1557	,, Christopher.	Gayle.	A.	C. 43.
1577	,, ,,	West Laton.	A.	D. 125.
1579	,, ,,	,,	B.	—
1575	,, Edmund.	West Witton.	W.I.	D. 88.
1598	,, John.	Kirkhamerton.	W.I.	—
1579	,, Ralph, gent.	Coverham.	A.	D. 163.
1607	,, Robert.	Staveley.	A.	—
1575	,, Thomas.	Bolton Swayle.	W.	D. 84.
1579	,, Thomas.	East Witton.	W.	D. 157.
1579	,, ,,	,,	W.I.	—
1563	,, William.	,,	W.I.	—
1476	,, ,,	?Hulton.†	W.	+ 16.
1590	,, ,,	East Witton.	W.I.	—
1609	,, ,,	Grenehamerton.	A.I.	—
1607	Crosier, Lionel.	Caldwell.	W.I.	—
1573	Croke, Xpofer.	Barningham.	W.I.	D. 3.
1551	,, George.	Preston.†	W.	—
1573	,, Henry.	Richmond.	A.	D 43.
1580	,, James.	Barningham.	W.I.	—
1583	Crokey, Jane.	Burton Bishopdale.	A.	—
1565	Cropper, Richard, clk.	Pulton.†	W.	—
1587	Crosbie, Dorothy.	Richmond.	A.	—
1575	,, John.	Middleton Tyas.	W.I.	D. 73.
1559	,, Richard.	Richmond.	W.I.	—
1541	Croskill, Robert.	Lancaster.	W.	+ 204.
1564	,, ,,	,,	W.I.	—
1541	Cross, George.	Gosenaigh.†	W.	+ 203.
1570	Cudbart, Robert.	Burniston.	W.	—
1580	Cundall, Agnes.	Fingall.	A.I.	—
1566	,, John.	,,	W.	—
1585	,, ,,	Knaresborough.	W.	—

† ? Co. Lancaster.

E

Date.	Name.	Residence.	Document.	Reference.
1588	Cundall, William.	Fingall.	W.	—
1583	Currell, Xpofer.	Bolton Swayle.	W.I.	—
1597	Currer (Corrier), Elyn.	Wath.	W.I.	—
1608	Curtess (Courteous), Robt.	Grafton.	W.	—
1530	Curwen, John, clk.	Workington.*	W.	+ 64.
1531	,, Robert.	,,	W.	+ 80.
1544	,, Sir Thomas.	,,	W.	C. 24-25.
1557	Dacres, Edward.	Kirkhamerton.	W.	—
1579	,, Marmaduke.	Farnham.	A.	—
1579	,, Robert.	,,	W.I.	—
1598	,, Richard.	Kirkhamerton.	W.I.	—
1597	,, ,,	Staveley.	W.I.	—
1574	,, Ann, see Conyers, Cuthbert.			
1602	Daggett, Elizabeth.	Disforth.	W.I.	—
1580	,, Janet.	Topcliffe.	I.	—
1541	,, Jenet.	? ,,	W.I.	—
1547	,, Lancelot.	,,	W.I.	—
1577	,, William.	Picoll.	W.	D. 136.
1470	‡Dale, als. Flesshewer.	Great Fencots.	W.	—
1562	,, John.	Rainton.	W.I.	—
1581	,, ,,	Brakenberghe.	W.I.	—
1574	,, Thomas.	Knaresbro'.	W.I.	—
1590	Dalton, George.	Joleby.	Letter.	—
1592	Danby, Agnes.	South Cowton.	W.I.	—
1589	,, Edward.	Aysgarth.	W.I.	—
1587	,, Henry.	South Cowton.	W.I.	—
1585	,, Lancelot.	Great Langton.	A.	—
1558	,, Ralph.	,,	W.I.	—
1474?	,, Sir Robert.¶	———	W.	+ 11.
1586	,, William, gent.	Great Langton.	W.I.	—
1592	,, Thomas.	Newby Wisk.	W.I.	—
1539	Daniell, Ellis.	Ribchester.	W.	+ 150.
1599	Dan, John.	Richmond.	W.I.	—
1604	Dannson, Jennet.	Awdfield.	I.	—
1577	Darbie, John.	Norton Luto.	A.	—

* In co. Cumberland. ‡ Printed, Surtees Society, 1853; also in Clarkson's Richmond App. xxxii. p. ci. ¶ Chief Justice in Common Pleas.

Date.	Name.	Residence.	Document.	Reference.
1606-9	Davell, Richard.	Kirby Fletham.	I.	—
1592	Davison, John.	Farnham.	W.I.	—
1593	Davison, John.	Farnham.	W.I.	—
1573	,, Michael.	Romaldkirk.	—	D. 30.
1562	Davye, Letice.	Bysham.*	W.I.	—
1578	Davy, Thomas.	Rybbye-in-Kirkham.†	W.I.	D. 157.
1572	Dawson (Dowson), Alison.	Kirkby Hill.	W.I.	—
1584	,, Adam.	Gamerskell.	W.I.	—
1550	,, Alison.	Whixley.	W.	—
1570	,, Caterine.	Coverham.	W.I.	—
1589	,, Christopher.	Melmerby.	W.I.	—
1599	,, ,,	Richmond.	W.I.	—
1594	,, Godfrey.	Carleton-in-Coverdale	W.I.	—
1576	,, John.	East Cowton.	W.I.	D. 113.
1596	,, (Dowson), John.	Marske.	W.	—
1597	,, John.	Melmerby.	W.I.	—
1540	,, Peter.	Coverham.	W.	+ 176.
1570	,, ,,	,,	W.	—
1564	,, Ralph.	Preston.†	W.I.	—
1599	,, ,, ?(Rowland)	Easby.	W.I.	—
1553	,, Robert.	Carlton.	W.I.	—
1579	,, Roger.	Whixley.	W.I.	—
1576	,, Simon.	Melmerby.	Note.	D. 113.
1562	,, Thomas.	,,	W.I.	—
1566	,, William.	East Grinton.	W.I.	—
1570	Dekine, John.	Burniston.	W.	—
1557	Denny, John.	Hunton.	W.I.	C. 43.
1606	,, William.	,,	W.I.	—
1570?	Dent, Agnes.	East Laton.	W.I.	—
1552	,, Brian.	Romaldkirk.	W.	C. 2.
1576	,, Catherine.	Aldborough.	W.I.	—
1582	,, Christopher.	Baldersdale.	W.	—
1577	,, George.	Thorp.	Note.	D. 137.
1475	,, John.	Wycliffe.	—	+ 36.
1563	,, ,,	Romaldkirk.	W.I.	C. 103.
1573	,, ,,	,,	W.I.	D. 12.

*? In Amounderness Deanery. † ? In co. Lancashire.

Date.	Name.	Residence.	Document.	Reference.
1587	Dent, John.	East Witton.	W.	—
1590	,, ,,	Romaldkirk.	W.	—
1599	,, ,,	Bowbank.	W.I.	—
1581	,, Leonard.	Barningham.	W.	—
1597	,, Margaret.	Romaldkirk.	W.I.	—
1594	,, Michael.	,,	W.	—
1557	,, Nicholas.	,,	W.I.	C. 42.
1557	,, Robert.	Farnham.	W.	—
1588	,, ,,	Romaldkirk.	W.I.	—
1596	,, ,,	,,	W.I.	—
1609	,, ,,	Turnerholm.	W.I.	—
1573	,, Rowland.	Romaldkirk.	W.I.	D. 19.
1570	,, Thomas.	Aldburghe.	W.I.	—
1573	,, ,,	Romaldkirk.	W.I.	D. 45.
1578	,, ,,	Laborne.	W.	D. 149.
1583	,, ,,	East Witton.	W.I.	—
1590	,, ,,	Forcet.	W.	—
1593	,, ,,	Mynskipp.	W.I.	—
1562	,, William.	Romaldkirk.	W.	—
1575	,, ,,	,,	W.	D. 103.
1578	,, ,,	Bardon Dikes.	W.I.	D. 147.
1590	,, ,,	Mynskip.	W.I.	—
1570	Denton, Margaret.	Burneston.	W.I.	—
1565	,, William.	,,	W.I.	—
1577	,, ,,	Chaythroppe.	W.I.	—
1609	Dearlove, Alice.	Ripley.	W.I.	—
1571	,, John.	Scotton.	W.I.	—
1585	,, Richard.	Ripley.	I.	F. 138.
1534	,, Robert, clerk.	Knaresborough.	W.	+ 143.
1581	,, ,,	,,	W.I.	—
1569	,, William.	Scotton.	W.I.	—
1565	Dewes, Catherine.	Goldsburgh.	W.I.	B. 10.
1557	,, Miles.	Allerton Maleverer.	W.I.	—
1608	,, Robert.	Grafton.	A.I.	—
1542	,, William.	Kirkhamerton.	W.I.	—
1563	Dewhurst, Thomas.	Ribchester.	W.I.	—
	Dickinson, see Diconson.			
1599	Dickson, Agnes.	Kirklington.	W.I.	—

Date.	Name.	Residence.	Document.	Reference.
1592	Dickson, Christopher.	Kirklington.	W.I.	—
1599	,, Henry.	Balderby.	W.	—
1558	,, John.	Whixley.	W.I.	—
1548	,, ,,	Cleesby.	W.	—
1579	Dickson, John.	Rokeby.	W.I.	—
1593	,, ,,	Newbigging.	W.I.	—
1550	,, Miles.	Birthwade.	W.	—
1564	,, Roger.	Knaresborough.	A.	B. 3.
1538	,, William.	?Witton.	W.	+ 163.
1549	Diconson, Elizabeth.	Askrig.	W.I.	—
1600	,, Henry.	Kirkhamerton.	W.I.	—
1577	,, ,,	Disforth.	W.	F. 46.
1562	,, James.	Dalton.*	W.I.	—
1587	,, John.	Romaldkirk.	A.	—
1571	,, Margaret.	Lowne.	W.	—
1578	,, Michael.	Patrick Brompton.	W.	—
1583	,, Peter.	Burton Leonard.	W.	F. 132.
1563	,, William.	Lancaster.	W.I.	—
1569	,, ,,	Harrogate.	A.	B. 45.
1600	Dighton, Isabel.	Sutton Howgrave.	W.	—
1582	,, John.	Wath.	W.I.	—
1586	Dilworth, Helen.	Broughton.	W.I.	—
1600	Dinsdale, Geoffrey.	Sleddeldale.	W.	—
1586	,, Henry.	Snape.	W.I.	—
1559	,, Thomas.	Ainderby Steeple.	W.I.	—
1591	,, ,,	Gale.	W.	—
1576	Dobson, Francis.	Hornby.	W.	D. 112.
1588	,, Mable.	,,	W.I.	—
1557	,, Robert.	Ribchester.*	W.I.	—
1562	,, Thomas.	Plumpton.	W.I.	—
1577	,, William.	[No place]	—	D. 125.
1559	,, ,,	Snape.	W.I.	—
1587	Doclay, Thomas.	Rokby.	W.	—
1562	Dodding, Robert.	Kendal.	W.I.	—
1564	Dodgson, William.	Raynton.	W.I.	B. 8.
1587	Dodsworth, Agnes.	Jolby.	W.I.	—
1558	,, Christopher.	,,	W.I.	—

* Co. Lancaster.

Date.	Name.	Residence.	Document.	Reference.
1579	Dodsworth, Dorothy.	Halnaby.	W.	D. 155.
1571	,, Edward.	Aysgarth.	W.I.	—
1573	,, Gawin.	Eastbronton.	A.	D. 30.
1587	,, Leonard.	Halnaby.	W.I.	—
1564	,, Mabel.	Jolby.	A.	C. 114.
1609	,, Peter.	Aysgarth.	W.	—
1587	,, Robert.	Romaldkirk.	W.I.	—
1578	,, Vincent.	Langrig.	W.I.	D. 147.
1558	,, William.	Halnaby.	W.I.	—
1562	Dolfyn, James.	Garstang.*	W.I.	—
1558	Donkin, William.	Easby.	W.I.	C. 79.
1576	Donne, Anthony.	Ainderby.	W.I.	D. 111.
1591	,, John.	Eastlaton.	W.I.	—
1562	,, William.	Ainderby.	I.	—
1602	Dowe, Thomas.	Aldborough.	W.I.	—
	Dowson, *see* Dawson.			
1563	Dudell, Alice.	Ribchester.	W.I.	—
1608	Duffeld, Christopher.	Ellerton.	*Account*	—
1589	,, George.	,,	W.I.	—
1548	,, James.	Norton.	W.I.	—
1558	,, Miles.	Gilling.	W.I.	—
1558	Dunning, George.	Barton.	W.I.	—
1592	Durham, Anthony.	Fingall.	W.I.	—
1579	,, Christopher.	Studaye.	W.I.	—
1572	,, Henry.	,,	W.I.	—
1573	,, ,,	,,	W.	—
1584	Dutton, William.	Well.	W.	—
1606	Eamondson, George.	Knaresboro'.	W.I.	—
1580	,, Hugh.	Richmond.	W.I.	—
1603	,, Peter.	Knaresborough.	W.I.	—
1539	,, Richard.	Goldisborough.	W.	+ 170.
1559	,, Roger.	Well.	W.I.	—
1547	Earston (Eyrston), George.	South Cowton.	W.	—
1562	Eastby, Leonard.	Thintoft.	A.	C. 94.
1576	,, Nicholas.	Richmond.	A.	D. 111.
1589	Edrington, Richard.	Scruton.	W.I.	—

* Co. Lancaster.

Date.	Name.	Residence.	Document.	Reference.
1610	Edrington, John.	Scruton.	W.I.	—
1574	,, William.	Gilling.	W.	D. 65.
1586	Edward, James.	Romaldkirk.	W.I.	—
1608	Egland, John.	Bainbridge.	W.I.	—
1557	Eglesfield, William.	Borobridge.	A.	C. 47.
1574	Ellerton, Isabel.	Burneston.	W.I.	—
1570	?Ellerton, John.	Burneston.	W.I.	—
1587	,, Leonard.	Lartington.	Ad.	—
1582	Ellice, Anthony.	Knaresbrough.	A.	F. 126.
1593	,, Thomas.	Boroughbridge.	W.	—
1604	Elwood, Thomas.	Allerton.	W.I.	—
1587	Elsworth, Helen.	Goldisborough.	W.I.	—
1567	,, Robert.	Ripley.	P. Act.	B. 32.
1557	Elwan, John.	K. Ravensworth.	W.	C. 56.
1571	Emerson, John, clerk.	Earyholme.	W.I.	—
1564	English, Alice.	Aldborough.	W.	B. 5.
1558	,, Richard.	East Cowton.	W.I.	C. 75.
1476	,, William.	,,	W.	+ 15.
1563	,, ,,	Langton.	W.	C. 103.
1542	Eseak, Richard.	[No place]	Note.	+ 208.
1558	Eshe, Lancelot.	Patrick Brompton.	W.	—
	Eshton, see Ashton.			
1490	Eston, Simon.	Masham.	W.	+ 29.
1484	Eskrig, Chrisr. *capellanus*	Lancaster.	W.	+ 27.
	Etherington, see Edrington.			
1578	Evans, Richard.	Norton Conyers.	Note.	D. 147.
1575	Ewbank, Thomas.	Richmond.	—	D. 106.
1606	,, Thomas.	Melsanby.	W.I.	—
1585	Exelby, John.	Norton-in-Luto.	W.I.	—
1558	,, Thomas.	Topcliffe.	W.	—
1583	,, ,, gent.	Knaresboro'.	W.I.	—
1609	,, ,,	Norton Luto.	W.	—.
1530	Faddersawle, Richard.	Eu'sham.*	W.	+ 62.
1605	Fallowfield, Margaret.	Fingall.	W.I.	—
1559	Fargouse, Alice.	Bedale.	W.I.	—
1606	Farleton, Bartholomew.	Richmond.	I.	—
1588	,, Christopher.	,,	I.	—

* ? Heversham, co. Westmoreland.

Date.	Name.	Residence.	Document.	Reference.
1579	Farleton, George.	Richmond.	A.	D. 167.
1579	,, ,,	,,	I.	—
1559	,, Nicholas.	Marske.	W.	C. 89.
1598	,, Ralph.	Richmond.	W.	—
1572	,, Richard.	,,	A.	—
1584	Farmerye, Christopher.	Wath.	W.I.	—
1605	,, ,,	Asenby.	W.I.	—
1583	Farmerye, Robert.	Norton Luto.	W.	F. 138.
1551	,, William.	,,	W.I.	—
1592	,, ,,	,,	I.	—
1603	Farnham, John.	Watlas.	W.I.	—
1550	Farington, Hugh.	Ribleton.†	W.I.	—
1562	Farclowght, Richard.	Ribchester.	W.I.	—
1541	Farwell, John.	Catterick.	W.	+ 185.
1605	Faull, Richard.	Langthroppe.	W.	—
1575	Faule, *als.* Fawell, Tho.	Burneston.	W.	D. 85.
[1599	Faux, Anne,‡ with Kilborne, Henry.	Marriage Bond.]
1536	Favell, William.	Clyffe.	W.	+ 148.
1578	,, (Fawle), Wm.	Marton.	W.I.	—
1585	,, (Fall) ,,	Aldbrough.	W.I.	F. 156.
1583	Fawcett, Brian.	Newhouses.	W.I.	—
1551	,, Christopher.	Sedbergh.	W.	—
1595	,, ,, surgeon.	Richmond.	W.I.	—
1557	,, Edmund.	Bainbridge.	W.I.	—
1554	,, Giles.	Kidstones.	W.I.	—
1609	,, ,,	,,	W.I.	—
1582	,, George.	Nidd.	A.	F. 115.
1599	,, ,,	Aysgarth.	W.I.	--
1558	,, Helen.	Copgrave.	W.	—
1591	,, James.	Sedbergh.	W.I.	—
1597	,, Janet.	Laborne.	W.I.	—
1608	,, Jenkin.	Smerber.	I.	—
1537	,, John.	Overkellet.	W.I.	—
1556	,, ,,	Haulbank.*	W.	—
1555	,, ,,	Zedbar.*	W.	—
1571	,, ,,	Kidstones.	W.I.	—
1604	,, ,,	Brompton.	W.I.	—

† In Preston, co. Lancashire.   * ? If the same.   ‡ Sister of Guy Faux, the Conspirator.

The Index Library (British Record Society, Limited). Annual Subscription—One Guinea. Published Quarterly. CONTAINS INDEXES, CALENDARS, AND ABSTRACTS OF BRITISH RECORDS. Calendars already completed—Prerogative Ct. of Canterbury, 2 vols.; Northampton and Rutland Wills; Chancery Proceedings, 3 vols; Royalist Composition Papers; Signet Bills; Berkshire Wills; Lichfield Wills; Gloucestershire Wills; Gloucestershire Inquisitiones post mortem. Calendars in progress—Prerogative Court of Canterbury Wills; Sussex Wills; Dorsetshire Wills; Chancery Proceedings; London Inquisitiones post mortem; Wiltshire Inquisitiones post mortem. *Hon. Sec.*:—E. A. FRY, Esq., 172, Edmund Street, Birmingham. *Agent*:—CHAS. J. CLARK, 4, Lincoln's Inn Fields, W.C.

The East Anglian; or, Notes and Queries on subjects connected with the Counties of Suffolk, Cambridge, Essex, and Norfolk. Edited by the REV. C. H. EVELYN WHITE, F.S.A., Rector of Rampton, Cambridge. Annual Subscription, 5s. post free. Ipswich: F. PAWSEY, The Ancient House. London: ELLIOT STOCK, 62, Paternoster Row.

Maine Historical and Genealogical Recorder. A Quarterly Magazine, the prime object of which is the publication of whatever may be secured of historical interest pertaining to our own State, and whatever of family history may be gathered from different sources that interest the sons and daughters of Maine, wherever located. Original Records, Documents, or other papers suitable for a publication of this kind solicited. Advertisements inserted at the usual rates. Published in Portland, Maine, at $3.00 per annum in advance. S. M. WATSON, *Editor and Publisher.*

Fenland Notes and Queries, Edited by Rev. W. D. SWEETING, M.A., Maxey Vicarage, Market Deeping. A Quarterly Journal devoted to the Antiquities, Geology, Natural Features, Parochial Records, Family History, Legends and Traditions, Folk-lore, Curious Customs, etc., of the Fenland, in the counties of Huntingdon, Cambridge, Lincoln, Northampton, Norfolk, and Suffolk. Price 1s. 6d. per quarter, by post 1s. 8d. A year's Subscription, if paid in advance, 6s. post free. Peterborough: GEORGE C. CASTER, Market Place.

Somerset and Dorset Notes and Queries, Edited by F. W. WEAVER, M.A., Milton Clevedon, Evercreech, Somerset, and C. H. MAYO, M.A., R.D., Non-Res. Canon of Sarum, Long Burton Vicarage, Sherborne, Dorset.
Vol. V. commenced March 1896. Parts issued Quarterly. Subscriptions, 5s. per annum, payable in advance to either of the Editors, to whom all communications should be addressed.

Bye-Gones: for Wales and the Borders. Established 1871. Quarterly, 5s. per annum. "Appears a wholly admirable publication, both in intention and execution."—*Saturday Review.* WOODALL, MINSHALL & Co., Oswestry.

Genealogical Queries and Memoranda. A Quarterly Magazine devoted to Genealogy, Family History, Heraldry, and Topography. Edited by GEORGE F. TUDOR SHERWOOD. Annual Subscription *(payable in advance)*, 3s. 6d. or $1; Single Numbers, 1s. or 25 cents. Genealogical Queries and Memoranda shows alphabetically, under Surnames and under Counties, whose genealogies are being investigated, and the points in them that require elucidation. It may be asserted that in nearly every case a query indicates the existence, in private possession, of a collection of evidence regarding the family referred to. It enables those interested to communicate with one another. It gives circulation to queries on heraldry and prints the answers to them. It catalogues pedigrees and collections of family history in print and MS., its aim being ever to open up fresh ground. It gives clues to other sources of genealogical information. All communications to be addressed GEO. F. TUDOR SHERWOOD, 99, Angell Road, Brixton, London, S.W.

Mr. Coleman's Catalogue, (No. ccxxiii.) of Charters, Deeds, Wills, Court-Rolls, Rent-Rolls, Pedigrees, Maps, Heraldry, Topography, &c., now ready. Also his two Alphabetical Lists of 1000 Old Wills each, price together 2s. 6d. JAMES COLEMAN, Genealogical Bookseller, 9, Tottenham Terrace, Tottenham, London, N.

The Scottish Antiquary: or, Northern Notes and Queries. Increased to 48 Pages, with Illustrations, price 1s. A Magazine of Archæology, Etymology, Folk-lore, Genealogy, Heraldry, &c. Edited by the Rev. A. W. CORNELIUS HALLEN, M.A., F.S.A. Scot. Mem. Coun. Hist. Soc. Issued Quarterly. Annual Subscription (payable in advance), 4s. *All Letters and Subscribers' Names to be sent to the Editor,* THE REV. A. W. CORNELIUS HALLEN, PARSONAGE, ALLOA.

July 1897.

THE
Northern Genealogist.

CONTENTS:

	PAGE		PAGE
Notes and Queries	113	Cumberland Wills	144
Act Books of the Prerogative Court of York	116	Sir Roger Salvin	146
		Startforth Parish Register	150
Some Richmond Wills	124	Marriage Bonds of the Dean and Chapter of York	154
Givendale Register Transcripts	130		
Analytical Calendar of Lincolnshire Wills in the P.C.C.	132	Sandal Magna Register Transcripts	160
Waifs and Strays	138	Supplement—	
Clay Coton Parish Register	140	Richmondshire Wills	41

Subscription 10s. 6d. per annum.

YORK:
PRINTED BY JOHN SAMPSON, 13, CONEY STREET.

WORKS BY THE SAME EDITOR.

EARLY LINCOLN WILLS; an Abstract of all the Wills and Administrations recorded in the Episcopal Registers at Lincoln, 1280—1547, 8vo. 21/-.

LIBER ANTIQUUS HUGONIS WELLS, Episcopi Lincolniensis; comprising the Endowments of Vicarages in Oxfordshire, Bucks., Beds., Hunts., Herts., Northants., Rutland, and Lincolnshire. 1209—1235, 8vo. 10/6.

LINCOLN MARRIAGE LICENCES; an Abstract of the Allegation Books preserved in the Registry of the Bishop of Lincoln, 1598—1628, 8vo. 15/-.

ELY EPISCOPAL RECORDS; a Calendar and Concise View of the Records preserved in the Muniment Room of the Palace at Ely. Compiled by direction of the Rt. Rev. Alwyne, Lord Bishop of Ely, 8vo. 42/-.

REPORTS on the Registry of the Bishop of Lincoln, and on the Records of the Corporation of Grimsby. Compiled for Her Majesty's Hist. MSS. Commission.

YORK WILLS INDEXES, 1544—1553, 1554—1568, and 1568—1585. Compiled for the Yorkshire Archæological Society. (*In Progress.*)

NOTES ON THE HERALDS' VISITATION OF LINCOLNSHIRE in 1634. With Supplements containing Indexes of the Wills in the Consistory Court and the Court of the Dean and Chapter at Lincoln, 8vo. (*In Progress.*)

The Northern Genealogist is issued quarterly, in January, April, July, and October, and is supplied to subscribers only, at 10s. 6d. per annum, payable in advance.

Notes, Articles, or Queries, on Antiquarian subjects, will be gladly received, as also Books or Articles for review.

Terms for Advertisements can be had on application.

The Editor personally undertakes Genealogical and Antiquarian Researches in any part of the Kingdom, and, in questions not involving such research, will be happy to give to Subscribers, free of charge, any advice or assistance in his power.

Transcripts or Abstracts of Wills, &c., in London, or in the York or other Provincial Registries, are supplied according to Scale of Charges to be had on application.

All communications to be addressed to

A. GIBBONS, F.S.A.,

Heworth, York.

NOTES AND QUERIES.

The Rev. C. W. Foster, of Epworth, is compiling a Calendar of Lincoln Wills, 1280—1700, which will contain:—(1) An Alphabetical Calendar of the Wills and Administrations, from 1280 to 1547, recorded in the Episcopal Registers of the old Diocese of Lincoln, comprising the counties of Lincoln, Leicester, Northampton, Rutland, Huntingdon, Bedford, Hertford, Buckingham, and Oxford. (2) An Alphabetical Calendar of the Wills of the Consistory Court proved between 1507 and 1700, which are now deposited in the Probate Registry at Lincoln. (3) It is also proposed to add Alphabetical Calendars of the Wills proved in the various Peculiar Courts, and now deposited in the Lincoln Registry. The Testators' places of residence, and, as far as possible, their status, will be given; and an index of places will be added.

The Calendar, which will probably be completed in two royal octavo volumes, will be printed by the British Record Society, and will be issued to its members by instalments in ordinary course. Persons who are not members of the Society may obtain copies of one or both volumes, in parts as issued, at the subscription price of half-a-guinea a volume, by sending their names to the Rev. C. W. Foster, Epworth, Doncaster.

* * * *

Beho—Napier—Gibson. Notes in Vol. II. p. 31, *re* Beho, and Vol. III. p. 84, *re* Farrar, enabled me to amplify some family notes of Gibsons, descended from George Gibson, the keeper of a popular Inn in York, of which Drake says, " I must not omit a public Inn here (Finkle Street, perhaps merged in the Assembly Rooms, as George Gibson sold land in Lendal Street for the building) of great resort, though without a sign; good wine, with good usage, needs no inviting bush. The house is kept by Mr. George Gibson, and his stables, sufficient for two hundred horses or more, are in the Mint Yard."

Some notes of Paver's shewing that the Napiers seem to have been interested in land at Killingbeck, Leeds, suggested that the Gibsons might be connected with the John Gibson, Mayor of Leeds in 1700, who seems from Thoresby to have been a wine merchant.

Napier / Beho Family Pedigree

JOHN NAPIER, of York, merchant-tailor. Non-juror 1715. Declares freehold in Jubbergate. [alive 1737, d. 1741.]
= .... **BEHO**.
[A Paver Note says—a Mrs. Elizabeth N., alive in 1737, but?]
A Barbara Napier, mercer of York, freeman 1724.

THOMAS BEHO, of York, gent. Will, 23 Oct., 1751, proved at York, 1756. His name appears in N. Riding Record Society's publication, dealing with property.

Children of John Napier and ...... Beho:

Barbara N. [Barbara Ormanby, alive 1737, Killingbeck.] = ... **Ormandy**.
- Luke N. [alive 1737, Killingbeck.]
- Elizabeth N.

Clare N. = **Jas. Wheeler**, of Hemsworth, Hants.

Mary N. = ... **Ricard**.
- Mary Ricard, of Aberford, d. Burton Constable, 18 Feb., 1789, unmarried.

Catherine N. = **? Katherine Hartley**.
- John N.

Margaret N., papist 1735, having then two infant children, of Spurriergate, d. 1764, æt. 52. = **Rd. Farrar**, of York, upholder. Lord Mayor 1756 and 1769, d. 1780, æt. 75.

Anne N. = **Geo. Gibson**, of York, innholder, of Finkle Street, (Drake's *Eboracum*), freeman 1719.

Children of Mary N. and ...... Ricard:
(via Elizabeth F. = ... Gerard)
- 1. John.
- 2. Richard.
- 3. James.
- 4. Elizabeth F. = ... Gerard.
  - Evan Gerard.
  - Margaret Gerard.

Children of Margaret N. and Rd. Farrar:
- 5. Edward F.
- 6. Richard F.
- 7. Luke Farrar, who erected monument in St. Michael-le-Belfrey, York.

Children of Anne N. and Geo. Gibson:

George G., of York, silk-mercer in Coney Street, b. 1746, d. 1815. = **Mary**, dau. of Michael Walton (by Eliz. Beswick), son of Mich. Walton, father of Wm. Walton bishop of Trachonitis.

Anne G. = **Joseph Kaye**, of Liverpool. s.p.

Children of George G. and Mary Walton:

George G. = **Alicia**, dau. of John Wilks, son of Jn. W. of Coughton, Warwick.

Michl. G., of Liverpool & Leamington, Cotton-broker. = **Elizabeth**, daur. of John Reeve, of Coughton, Warwick, 5th in descent from Thomas Reeve, of Rowington, Warwick, d. 1612.

Entries in Square Brackets [ ] are from Paver's Notes.

There is a note of another Inn-holder, Christopher Gibson, of York, in 1651-2. I should be interested if any of your readers could give information of these first Gibson's, Napier's, and Beho's. Is Beho an English name? Thomas Beho's Will suggests that he had connections with Cambridge, Surrey, and Hants.

JOSEPH S. HANSOM.

27, Alfred Place West,
      South Kensington, S.W.

              *   *   *   *   *

Virginia and Maryland Parish Registers. Can any reader kindly give any information as to these registers, which are said to have been brought to England at the commencement of the Revolutionary War?

ACT BOOKS OF THE PREROGATIVE COURT OF YORK.*

1682. April 28. Blanchard, Rd., Acombe, esq. Adm. (by Decree) to son Rd. B.
 May 18. Robinson, Hy., Brigham. Will to Christ. Scingham.
 May 6. Johnson, John, Craike. Adm. to brother Thos. J.
 May 2. Smith, Matthew, York. Adm. with Will to Geo. Wright to use of Anne his wife, daughter of deceased.
 May 10. Wright, Anthony, S.T.B., York. Will to Geo. and Philippa Consett.
 May 10. Chipchase, William, Wolveston. Will to widow Anne, (also tuition of Anne and Thos. C., children of deceased.)
 May 20. Edman, Alice, Bramham. Will to John Smith.
 May 31. Shackleton, John, Worsthorne. Adm. to widow Jane.
 June 14. Bridgman, Hy., Bishop of Sodor and Dean of Chester. Will to widow Margaret.
 June 16. Ureing, John, Bow Lane, London. Will to widow Elizabeth.
 June 3. Tripp, John, Barton, co. Lincoln, gent. Will to Wm. Long and Geo. Froggitt.
 June 16. Bell, Philip, Burrowbridge. Will to brother Wm. B.
 June 16. Lockwood, Dorothy, York. Will to son John L.
 June 9. Conyers, Edward, Belman Lawne. Adm. to widow Dorothy.
 June 21. Jefferson, Ruth and Catherine, daughters of Robert J. late of Carlisle, deceased. Tuition to Mary J. their mother.
 June 21. Leaper, John, Bridlington. Adm. to widow Elizabeth.
 July 2. Fowler, Robert, York. Will to widow Margery.
 July 19. Lorde, Simeon, Royde. Will to widow Mary.

* Continued from page 78.

1682. July 19. Martin, John, Backbrough. Adm. to John Hird, to use of Ellen his wife, niece of deceased.

July 31. Brereton, Sir Thos., bart., Handford, Chester dioc. Adm. to John Levett of the Inner Temple, gent.

July 10. Craige, Thos., Hexham. Will to John Coulson and Thos. Craige.

July 10. Jefferson, Philip, Hexham. Will to son Thos. J.

July 10. Cooke, Wm., Hexham. Will to widow Margaret.

July 10. White, John, Allerton Towne. Will to Thomas White.

July 10. Urwen, Mabel, Hexham. Will to son Wm. U.

July 10. Yarrow, Gerrard, Hexham. Will to Benoni Carr.

July 10. Hobkirk, Archibald, Acomb, par. St. John Lee. Will to widow Anne.

July 10. Sharpe, Anthony, junr., Hexham. Adm. with Will to John S.

July 9. Rippon, John, York diocese. Adm. to widow Alice.

July 9. Leadbitter, Richard, Hexham. Adm. to Edward Robson.

July 9. Robson, Wm., Wall, co. Northumberland. Adm. to widow Isabella.

July 9. Johnson, John, Harlah bancke, par. Allandale, co. Northumberland. Adm. to widow Anne. Also Tuition of children John, William, Elizabeth, and Anne Johnson.

July 9. Fenwick, John, Hexham. Adm. to widow Bridget.

July 9. Fletcher, John, Acombe, par. St. John Lee, co. Northumberland. Adm. to Elizabeth Hutchinson, widow of deceased.

July 9. Woodmas, Thomas, Wooley, par. Allandale, co. Northumberland. Adm. to widow Anne.

July 9. Bee, Fras., Broadwoodhall, par. Allandale, co. Northumberland. Adm. to sister Barbara, ux. John Howden.

Aug. 9. Stoope, Isabella, Melwood Parke, co. Lincoln. Will to daughter Isabella Stanhope, widow.

Aug. 7. Portington, Elizabeth, Portington. Adm. to sister Anne Arthington, to use of Michael P., infant son of Henry P., esq., late of Portington, deceased. Also Tuition of said Michael.

1682. Aug. 29. Brockell, John, Barnard Castle. Adm. to widow Susanna. Also Tuition of Thos. and Ralph B. sons of deceased.

Sept. 9. Kendall, John, Parkeyate. Will to widow Agnes.

Sept. 25. Holme, Geo., Thornethwaite. Will to brother William H.

Sept. 11. Walker, Wm., Burne. Adm. to brother Thomas Walker.

Oct. 10. Feilden, Abraham, Swineshead. Will to Chas. Lord.

Oct. 10. Shackleton, Robert, Worsthorne. Will to sons Wm. and Laurence S.

Oct. 23. Hungate, Sir Fras., bart., Saxton, but dying at St. Paul's, Covent Garden. Adm. (by requisition from the Bishop of Worcester) to son Sir Philip H. bart.

Oct. 16. Killinghall, John, Hurworth. Adm. to widow Mary.

Nov. 16. Plaxton, Elizabeth, Pocklington. Adm. with Will to William Scorbrough.

Nov. 16. Plaxton, Wm., son of Elizabeth P., late of Pocklington, decd. Tuition to Wm. Southeron, gent.

Nov. 25. Sarton, Wm., London, but dying at Normanby, co. York. Adm. (as to goods unadministered by widow Mary) to daughter Elizabeth, ux. Aron Pengry,

Dec. 8. Ingleby, Sir Wm., Ripley. Will to Lady Margaret Ingleby and Sir John Ingleby, bart. Also Tuition of children, Sir John, Margt., and Anne I., to said Lady Margt., their mother.

Dec. 1. Clarke, Hy., Thorpe Grange, par. Ampleford. Will to son Ralph C.

Dec. 4. Batty, Francis, esq., Wadworth. Will to widow Martha.

Dec. 15. White, John, Ampleford. Adm. to dau. Elizabeth W. (daus. Mary and Margery W. renouncing.)

Dec. 16. Corbett, Sarah, viscountess, Linslade. Adm. to Sir Chas. Lee, knt., her husband.

Dec. 29. Wood, John, Ampleford. Adm. to mother Elizth. W., to use of Elizth., Mary, and Anne W., infant daughters of deceased.

1682. Dec. 28. Cunningham, Geo., Robert Land in Sotland. Adm. of a Bond dated 23rd March, 1649, taken in the name of deceased, and entered into by Sir John Fenwicke, of Walkington, co. Northumberland, knt., and Geo. Fenwicke, esq., his son, in £4640, (not yet adm. by Richd. Cunningham, late of Kilmarch in Scotland, deceased), granted to Richard Cunningham, junr., next of kin to said Geo. C. deceased.

Dec. 7. Robson, Wm., Old Towne. Will to widow Margt.

Dec. 7. Waineman, Richd, Hexham. Will to widow Elizth.

Dec. 7. Kell, John, Wall, [co. Northumberland]. Adm. to mother Barbara K., widow.

Dec. 7. Heron, John, Hexham. Adm. to widow Anne.

Jan. 4. Westray, John, Beckbanke. Will to widow Elizth.

Jan. 16. Sayner, Richard, Selby. Adm. with Will to Michael Barstow and Robert Sayner, to use of Thos. and Robert S., infant sons of deceased, (Elizabeth S., widow of deceased, renouncing.)

Jan. 25. Fort, Anne, daughter of Wm. F., Twiston. Tuition to Gabriel Wilkinson.

Jan. 26. Sheppeard, Thos., Newcastle-on-Tyne. Adm. to daughter Margt. S.

Jan. 29. Inman, Thos., York. Will to widow Hester.

Jan. 31. Cooke, Nathan, York. Will to brother Marmaduke Cooke, S. T. P.

Jan. .... Brounsell, John, Haddingham. Will to wid. Elizth.

Jan. 8. Kingston-upon-Hull, Robert, earl of, Holme Pierrepointe, co. Notts. Adm. to Wm. now earl of Kingston-upon-Hull.

Jan. 13. Woolfe, Benjn. Will. (*Vide* Buckrose).

Feb. 21. Laurence, John, York. Ad. with Will to son Thos. L.

Feb. 2. Baines, Jacobus, York. Will to widow Elizth.

Feb. 6. Aislabie, Mary, York. Will to Wm. Robinson and Arthur Ingram, esq.

Feb. 7. Waddington, Frances, York. Will to Thos. Lee, notary public.

Feb. 14. Colebye, John, Heaning. Adm. to son Alex. C.

Feb. 22. Hardistie, Thos., Shereburne. Adm. to son Peter H.

March 1. Warde, Geo., Pickering. Adm. with Will to John Francke, (Alice Ward, the widow renouncing.)

1682. March 7. Hobman, Wm., Newport, gent. Adm. to widow Jane.

March 7. Watson, Cuthbert, Heigh. Adm. to widow Margt.

March 12. Watson, Anne, Beedall. Will to son John W.

March 20. Caley, Roger, York. Will to Thos. Waite, senr., esq., and Elizth. Smith, widow.

March 20. Pilkington, Rosamund, daughter of Thomas P. of Dawgreene, co. York, gent., and niece of Lady Mary Beaumount, late of York, decd. Tuition to Rd. P., gent., brother of the infant.

1683. March 28. Agar, John, Stockton. Will to son Thomas Agar.

April 2. Norfolk, Thomas, duke of, London. Adm. to brother Henry, duke of Norfolk.

April 3. Howard, Francis, London, esq. Adm. to brother Henry, duke of Norfolk.

April 18. Clayton, Wm., Ribchester. Adm. to sister Anne, ux. John Hide.

April 20. Leake, Clifton, Newark, but dying at Overlevens, co. Westmoreland. Will to nephew [nepos] Drewell Leake.

April 21. Etherington, Geo., Heslington. Adm. with Will to John Tennant, guardian of Mary E. the extrix.

April 23. Tatham, Wm., Lincoln's Inn. Will to John Browne.

April 24. Wright, Rebecca, Chester. Adm. to son John W.

May 3. Robinson, Stephen, Catherick. Adm. to nephews [nepotes] Leonard R. and Leonard R.

May 7. Clarkson, Samuel, Snaith. Adm. to cousin [consanguineus] Samuel Hoyle.

May 7. Baldwin, Christ., Stonedge. Adm. with Will to widow Margt. (Nich. Stephenson, the exor. renouncing.)

May 11. Heape, William, Finney Foote. Will to widow Margt.

May 11. Gamble, Robert, Farmanby. Will to wid. Elizth.

May 12. Boseman, Geo., Trafford Hill. Will to son Robt. B.

May 26. Scott, Jacobus, Lowther. Will to Susanna Allen.

May 18. Seamer, Christ., Brettanby Mill. Will to widow Alice.

May 18. Dove, John, Welton, gent. Adm. to widow Anne.

1683. May 25. Currey, Wm., Woodall Mill. Will to daughter Dorothy C.

May 25. Spaine, Rd., Acomb. Will to daughter Mary S.

May 25. Jenkinson, Frances, Thockington. Will to daughter Mercy J.

May 25. Stappert, Thos., Hexham. Adm. to cousin [consang'] Edward Nicholson.

May 25. Dunn, Thomas, Bingfield. Adm. to widow Ursula.

May 25. Dixon *als*. Myers, Anne, Nether Mire House. Adm. to brother Henry D.

May 25. Coxon, Jane, Hexham. Adm. to son Michael C.

May 25. Curry, Matthew, Margt. and Susanna, children of Wm. C. of Woodhall Mill, decd. Tuition to their sister Dorothy C.

May 25. Dunn, Thos., John and Mary, children of Thos. D., of Bingfield, decd. Tuition to their mother Ursula D.

June 6. Bell, Phyllis, Nether Silton. Adm. to mother Anne, ux. Cuthbert Wilson.

June 9. Hollyday, Thos., Ecclesfield. Will to widow Anne.

June 11. Danby, Christ., Thorpe Parse, esq. Adm. to mother Margt. D., widow.

June 12. Andrews, Wm., Oxton. Adm. to widow Amy A., widow.

Sept. 14. Smith, Geo., Hemingbrough. Adm. to widow Lenox.

Sept. 12. Nicholson, Geo., Orton *als*. Overton. Will to Chr. Atkinson.

Sept. 13. Wilkinson, Thos., York. Adm. to brother Wm. W.

Oct. 10. Bulcock, Mary, Rough Lee. Will to father Robt. B.

Oct. 11. Dugdill, Eliazer, Harwood, co. Lanc. Will to John Hartley.

Oct. 11. Perkin, Rd., Ricknell Grainge, Durham diocese. Will to widow Jane.

Oct. 20. Thompson, Richd., St. Robert's Convent, near Knaresbro'. Will to Anne, ux. Wm. Inman; Jane, ux. Henry Pulleine, and Isabella Thompson.

Oct. 22. Craven, Elizth. Snainton. Will to son Wm. C.

Oct. 25. Reynard, Wm., Newton, par. Ripley. Will to son Wm. R. (widow Ellena R. and son Robt. R. renouncing.)

1683. Oct 25. Tong, Ellenora, York. Will to Sara, ux. John Bradley, clerk.

Nov. 10. Bell, Geo., Selby. Will to Wm. B.

Nov. 23. Shuttleworth, Rd., Forcett, esq. Will to Rd. S. (Former Probate 25th May, 1681.)

Nov. 28. Smagghe, John, Waughen. Adm. to John S.

Nov. 16. Best, Henry, Westminster. Adm. to Edward Goddard to use of his wife Cath. Goddard, *als.* Best, sister of decd.

Dec. 27. Hutton, Rd., Goldsbrough, esq. Adm. to widow Mary.

Jan. 9. Starkie, Alice, Bolton. Adm. to son John S.

Jan. 21. Dawney, Thos., Selby. Will to widow Elizth.

Jan. 31. Thompson, Wm., son of Wm. T., of Readness, decd. Curation to Thos. T.

Jan. 17. Tillitson, John, St. Gregory, London. Adm. with Will to Elsena Mitton to use of Isabella T. daughter of decd. (Former grant, June 1681.)

Feb. 2. Rowell, Thos., Woodhead. Will to Thos. Welton. Also Tuition of Margt. R. daughter of decd.

Feb. 2. Frailer, Margt., Knocksheile. Will to daughter Elizth. F.

Feb. 2. Forster, Wm., St. John Lees. Adm. to father Wm. F.

Feb. 2. Stephenson, Adam, Hexham. Adm. to widow Cath.

Feb. 2. Blacklock, John, Cross House, par. Allandale. Adm. to " afini " Roger B.

Feb. 2. Chickin, John, Anick. Adm. to John Carthingley.

Feb. 6. Poole, Nehemiah, Manchester. Adm. to sister Mary ux. Ralph Ridgway.

Feb. 7. Morley, Rd., Darlington. Adm. to brother Thos. M. to use of Elizth. and Barbara M. nieces of decd.

Feb. 11. Shuttleworth, Edmund, Manchester. Will to Edmund S.

Feb. 13. Whitelock, Geo., Rainton. Will to Robt. Browne.

Feb. 13. Knight, Wm. Lincoln. As to a statute merchant dated 9th April, 19 Jac. entered by Thos. Lewis of Marr, decd., to said Wm. K., decd. Adm. (by Decree) to Anne ux. Bernard Greenvile.

Feb. 26. Norfolk,......Duke of. Will to Chas. Mawson.

1683. March 5. Burton, Francis and Tabitha, children of Francis B., of Shereburne. Tuition to said Francis B.

March 5. Baldwin, Anthony, Bridgend in Hatergham Eaves. Adm. to widow Margt.

March 6. Evat, Edward, Kellins, co. Flint, esq. Adm. with Will to John Daniell, (the exors renouncing.)

March 19. Bosvile, Mary, Susanna and Charles, children of Chas. B., of Selby, decd. Tuition to Debora, ux. Christ. Bales. Also curation of decd's. son, Wm. B., to said Christ.

March 19. Hartley, Roger, Reedimore. Will to wid. Elizth.

March 19. Sagar, Oates, Colne. Adm. to widow Jane.

March 20. Atkinson, Thos., Northallerton. Will to brother Stephen A.

March 24. Scaife, John, Winton. Adm. to mother Mary S.

March 26. Pooley, Rd., Wray, par. Mellin. Will to Rd. P. *als.* Marshall, and Ellen P. widow of decd.

March 26. Crew, John, Crew Hall, esq. Will to wid. Lucy.

April 2. Hartley, Christ., Whitley booth. Will to Elizth. H.

April 3. Nisbett, Susanna, York. Will to Susanna, ux. Jacobi Althrop, and Elizabeth, ux. Sam. Potter.

April 9. Cole, Gervase, Rampton. Will to Eliz. C. and Thos. C.

April 15. Dobbs, Mary, ux. John D., St. Margt's., Westminster. Adm. to daughter Lady Frances St. Leger, *als.* London.

1684. April 15. Forster, Catherine, Trough head. Will (by Decree) to Hy. F.

April 16. Nicholson, Geo., Ulleskelf. Will to wid. Susanna.

April 17. King, Edward, All Saints, London, but dying at Hull. Will to John Eaton.

April 30. Beane, Wm. Killinghall. Adm. to widow Frances.

May 5. Bowes, Elizth., Penrith. Will to Thomas Webster.

May. 14. Shawter, John, Stainthropp. Adm. to grandmother Thomasin Wrangham.

May 9. Hutton, Rd., Goldsbrough, esq. Adm. (as to goods left unadministered by widow Helen) to Philip Wharton, esq., to use of his daughter Mary W., niece of decd.

May 22. Towneley, Nicholas, Royle. Will to widow Margt. and son Rd. T.

SOME WILLS FROM THE RICHMOND REGISTRY.*

Arch. Richmond.
Sir Thomas Aubrowe, priest.

"I Sir Thomas Anbrowe, prest, of Reithe, in the parishe of Grynton. I commende my soule to God Allmightie my maiker and redeamer, and my bodye to be buryed in the Churche of Grynton. To every house in Reithe ij^d, and to the poor of the parish x^s. To the beuyldinge of Grynton Brige x^s, and to the mendinge of Reithe Brige xx^d."

To Cuthbert Typladye ij^s. To my uncle Willam Dawson xx^s, whereof he hath x^s in his hands which I lent him when he married his daughter Kateren. To my brother Leonarde Symson, 1 cow and calf and vij shepe, to ye use of Xpofer Symson; and I give to my sister Margete Symson, the said Leonarde's wife, 1 cow and a calf for her life, to remain to the said Cristofer Symson, and I give to my said sister Margarete my best gowne. I give to the said Leonarde my shorte marbyll cloke. To my said sister Margarete all my implements of howeseholde and all my beddinge, saveinge onely my feather bedde, the wiche I give to her said sonne Cristover. I give to every one of my said uncle William Dawson's daughters, and to Felys Scotte xij^d each. To Sir Jameis Place a reade chalmeyt dubleyd, a worsteite typeid, and a cappe. Item I geve to the vicar of Grinton a cappe. To Sir Matthewe Charder a marbyll gowne, a clothe typeid, and a cappe. To Doctor Sygiswyke my best cappe. To Doctor Carter a velveite neightcappe, and to the parson of Kyrtlynton a sallen neightcappe. To my aunte Dawson my thrussynge bedstockes, the wiche I had lent to her. The residue of my goods I give to the said Cristover Symson, my sister's son, whom I make my exor.

I will that the said Christover Symson have the goodwill and tenantright of my fermolde at Reithe, and the yearly rent of viij^s, with the licence of the lord and of the steward. I will that the said Margaret, my sister, have the third-part of the said fermolde, the

* Continued from page 112.

wiche her father William Benshawe had in occupation, during her life. I make George Pettye, Jhan Dawson, and Jhan Duglas, my supervisors, and I will that they put the said Christover to an occupation, they having the occupation of the said fermolde until the said Christover come to twenty years of age. I make Master George Catter my chief supervisor. Witness, Matthewe Charder, prest, George Atkynson, Jameis Hutcheson. Dat. ult. Feb. 1564. (No probate clause). Endorsed—Richmond. Sir Thomas Aubrowe testament, pish of Grynton, pb^{er} parochialis, anno xpi, 1565.

Arch. Richmond.
RICHARD CROPPER.

Richard Cropper, clerke, vicar of Pulton. "I gyve and bequethe my sawle to almightie God. And my body to be buryed w'in the pysshe churche of Pulton, in the hyghest chansell nere unto the table."

To Heghe Byllynche, of Lathum, and Richard Cropper the elder of the same town, and to their heirs for ever, all my right, title, &c., of all my lands in Burstkow and Lathum, and most specially the lands which I put in trust to be purchased with my goods by Hughe Raynforthe, of Aygheton, decd. for me in my name. Jenet Mason my sister; John Cropper, son of James Cropper, of Lathum; Jenet Dwarrchowsse, my servant; Custand, wife of George Walker; Richard Mason, son of the said Jenet; James Cropper, yonger; Ellyn and Margeret Walker, daus. of George Walker. To the said George Walker, one close of land now in my tenure, pcell of the tenement of Richard Tayler and the late wyfe of Thoms Tayler, for the term of two years. Richard Cropper, son of Thoms. Cropper; the children of Henry Cropper; the wife of Symon Smythe. To Margeret Walker, one-half close now in my tenure, parcel of the tent. of William Wylkocke. To Ellyn Walker, the half of a meadow called "the Carre medowe," parcel of the tent. of George Heye for 13 years. To George Walker, one acre of ground now in my tenure and occupation, and parcel of the tent. of Thoms Bocher for 5 years; and also one meadow and two closes, parcel of the tent. of William Awards, for 6 years; and also a parcel of land, parcel of the tent. of the late wife of Thoms Tayler.

I give to Richard Cropper, of Pulton, the wiche I have brought up in my howsse, a parcel of ground in my tenure, parcel of the tent. of Willm Thomason and Willm Patson, for a term of 4 years; and a parcel of ground in my tenure, parcel of the tent. of Wyllm Whitsyde, of Carlton, for the term of 5 years; and one parcel of land for the term of 4 years, parcel of the tent. of Robt. and Richard Tayler, &c., &c., and I give him one-half the debts due to me from Henry Leyn, Henry Tayler, and Richard Chantrell; the other half of which I give to Richard Cropper the elder. To Richard Cropper, of Pulton, I give all the rest of my goods, and I make him my exor.; the said Hughe Byllynges and Richard Cropper the elder being my overseers and rulers of the aforesaid Richard. Dat. 2 Oct., 1565. No witness. (A long schedule of debts and credits follows.)

Arch. Richmond.

Andrew Steward.

"M[d] that upon Saint Mathewe day [*sic.*] being the xxiiij[th] daye of Februarie, ano. dni. 1570, Sir Andrewe Steward, curat of Askarthe, maide rehearse of his last Will and Testamente by worde of mouthe as foloweth, viz. :—That the said Sir Andrewe did give and bequithe all his goods to Custance Metcalfe, the wiffe of Oswoulde Metcalfe." Bond dat. ... 13th, 1571, by which Oswald Metcalff, of Wodhall, co. York, chirurgeon, is bound to administer the goods of Sir Andrew Steward, decd. Witness, Thomas Talor, Willm. Danbye, Richard Langdaell. Signed, Oswold Metcalf. Sealed, O.M.

Arch. Richmond.

John Emerson.

John Em[r]sson, curate of Eryholme. "First, I comend my soule into hands of my Lord God." I will that Richard Ward have the half oxgang of land that John Dobson let to me during the lease, to helpe to bryng him up at ye scole, his porcion, and a sylver spone and y[e] hole oxgang of John Ward's land duryng y[t] lease, if his bretheren and systers be content. Agnes Ward shall have my best chyst, a sylver spone, and my best hatt. And I will that Laurence Ward, Jane Ward, Edward Ward, and Marye Ward, have each a sylver spone. Residue to Laurence, Jane, Agnes, Edwarde, Mary, and Richarde Ward, my exors. No witness. Dat. 11 April, 1571.

Debts owing to me from Robert Emmersonn, Henry Emmerson, Richard Northe, the wives of Johnson the elder, and Johnson the younger, William Burton, Thomas Foxcrotte, of Brandon. Debts that I owe to my systers children, that is to say—Edward, Jane, Agnes, Mary, and Richard Ward, xxvij^{li}. Debts owing to Willm Burnet and Cuthbert Wytham. Proved 21 Nov., 1571, by Laurence Ward. Power reserved. Inventory made 10 June, 1571, of the goods of Sir John Emerson, decd., by Robert Emerson, John Dobson, Roberte Myddelton, and Anthonie Elge. Summa clara, xvij^{li} x^s ij^d.

Arch. Richmond.

RYCHERDE SOVLLE.

Rycherde Sovlle, curate of the pishe of picall in the county of Yorke. "First, I comend my soule to Almyghty God, my savioure and redemer, and my body to be buried wthin the pishe chirche yearde of picll." To my sister Margret, towe kye and a wresete slevles jacket fased wth fore, and a dublett of wresete, and my best shorte gowne, and a payre of hoose of halfe thiked clothe, and the worste of my longe gownes. To Rycherd Willson her son, my best hose jacket. To the said Margret, I give one sylke girdell. To Isabell Willson, dowter to the sayde Margret, my worst shorte goweine. Itm to Annes my sister, I give my best long gowene and best hatt and a payre of blakke hoose, and to Ellen her daughter, a long frise gowne. To my sister Annes, one white pettekoote; and to Willyam Willson her son, my worste frese jacket and an owlde fustchane dublet, and a payre of white cottome stockexs, and a waste koote of hardne, and my worste hatt, a payre of browne briches. To my sister Margret, towe chayres, thre quisines, and a payre of bolles, and a salt pye, and sertayne salte, and a long table, a longe forme, &c., &c. To the poure peple regestred in the pishe booke, ij^d a peyse. Willyam Robyson, Firmyne Lakine's wife. Residue to my sisters Agnes and Margarett, my extrices. Witnesses, Willyam Grantt, John Browene, John Raper the elder, John Raper the younger, Christopher Newsteyd. Dat. 9 July, 16 Eliz. Inventory made .... by Willm. Graunt the elder, Xpofer Whittling, John Raper, Robt. Lumbley. Sum of goods vj^{li} xiij^s vj^d.

Arch. Richmond.
WILLIAM CARTER.

I Sir Wyllyam Carter, prest, late of Hunton within y₀ pyshe of Patterycke Brunton. "I gyve and bequieth my soulle unto Almyghty God, my Creator and Redemer, and my body to be buryed within the pyshe churche of Pattericke Brunton afore sayd." Unto my nephew Frances Carter's children, all my beddynge after my dyscease, at y₀ dyscretion of their parents, and I give them all my apparel. Unto my nephew Syr Thomas Carter, my best longe gowne, if he be favorable and agreable with his brother Frances Carter. Residue to my cousin Frances Carter and his wife, my exors. he giving my cousin George Bell's children, my blew gowne. Witnesses, Richard Roweth, Lancelot Roweth, George Bancke. Dat. 28 Jan., 1577. Proved, 16 Nov., 1578, by exor. Inventory Dat. 14 Nov., 1578, made by George Bell and Lancelot Askwith. Sum of goods xx^s viij^d.

Arch. Richmond.
THOMAS TAYLER.

I, Thomas Tayler, pson of Lanketon in the county of York. First, I geve and bequithe my sowle to Allmyghtye God, my Creator Redemer and Sanctifier, and my bodye to be buried under an oulde tombe or monyment wthin the Chaunsell of Lanketon Church. Ite. I geve to Xpofer Danbye, Thomas Danbye, Robertt Danbye, Susanna Danbye, and Marye Danbye, ev^{r}ye of theym iij^{li} vj^s viij^d. Ite. I geve to Magdalen Langestafe, to Raphe Danbye, Martyne Danbye, and Grace Danbye, everye of theym x^s, and to be paed to every of the above named nyne children now unmarid, wthin ten dayes after there severall mariges, or at 21 years.

Xpofer and Margrett Wivell, children of Samson Wivell, decd., and Marmaduke Wivell their brother. To Mr. Edward Huton, Batchelor in the Lawes, all my bookes, and to Anness his sister x^s. Ite. I geve to the worshipfull and my app'ved good Mr. Mr. Methome, of Kyrbye, an oulde angell, and to his good wife an oulde ryall. To the worshipfull and my verye good Mr. Mr. Nicholas Girdlingeton, of Hacforde, an oulde angell, and to my good Mrs. his wife, an oulde riall, and to his sonne John Girdlington x^s. Mr. George Pudsey and Faith his wife; my neighbour Mr. Gilbert Ootes, vicar of Flethom; Christopher Newstead; Mr. Seale; Rychard Tayler, of Richemounte; Richard Tayler the elder, of Askey, and Richard Tayler the younger;

Thomas Tayler, of Northallerton; Giles Person; Raphe Hoton; Willyam Stevnson, of Exelbye; John Tayler, brother to Thos. Tayler, of Scorton; Thomas Tayler, of Fletehome; Willyam Tayler, of Scorton; Robertt Stevenson, of Bedall, and his elder dau.; Mr. George Pudsey's children; Marmaduke Symson's wife; Xpofer Thorneton, of Brokemore; John Denney, of Hunton; Margrett Tayler; Thomas Procter; Raphe Hodshon; my cousin Thomas Tayler's servants; Robertt Swan's wife, of Thrintofte; Robert Mershall; Xpofer Moyses; Poor of Lanketon, Fencottes, Flethome, Scorton, Bowton, Ellerton, and Kypline; Poor of Danbye and Yafforde; Steven Whelpden, of Brockamoure; Widow Thorneton.

To Thomas Rychmounde ... for openynge and enclosynge of my tombe, x^s. Residue to Thomas Tayler, of Scorton, exor. Mr. Geo. Pudsey and Mr. Edwarde Huton, supervisors. Witnesses, Edward Hutton, Xpofer Newton, Richard Tailor, John Tailor. Dat. 27 Sep., 1585. Proved, 26 Sep., 1586, by exor. Inventory made 7 Nov., 1585, of goods of Thomas Tailor, late parson of Langton, decd., by Willm Danbie, Christofer Danbie, Giles Pearson, and John Pearson. Sum of goods xlj^{li} ij^d. Owing by deceased to his cosen Thomas Tailor, of Scorton x^{li}.

Arch. Richmond.

Roger Thomlinson.

Roger Thomlinson, clerke. "First, I give and bequeath my soule to Almightie God, my maker and redemer, and my bodie to be buried in the churchyard of Wensleye." And whereas Willm Bennet, clerke, p'son of Wensley, my maister, oweth and is indepted unto me the day of the dait hereof the some of vj^{li} xix^s for my service to him done in the curatshipp at the chapellrie of Richmond within the said pish; my will is that my debts be paid therewith, prayinge my said Mr. to pay the same thankfullie ... which I trust he will do without further trouble, consideringe that I have no other goods for payment thereof. To my sister Agnes, wife to James Coulton viij^s. Residue to Matthewe Pearson, *als.* Robinson, my exor. Friend Thomas Tailor, of Richmond, supervisor. Debts owing: to Richard Pearson, *als.* Robinson, myne host, xlvj^s viij^d for his diete; to Mathew Pearson, *als.* Robinson, his sonne in borowed money, xxx^s; to the wiffe of Robert Kidde, xxij^d. Witness, W. Barker, Willm. Sewel, Thomas Tailor, Jo. Barker. Dat. 2 July 1587. By me, Roger Thomlinson. (No probate clause.)

GIVENDALE REGISTER TRANSCRIPTS.

The Register commences in 1710.

1699. Staveley, Jane, dau. of Wm., bapt. March 22.
1700. Staveley, Wm. and Abigail Berry, married May 1.
(No burials.)
     (Signed) Edw. Dunning, *Vicar.*
          Chas. Nellis, *Churchwarden.*

1702. No transcript.
1703. Flint, Thomas, son of Robt., bapt. June 26.
Richardson, Thos., and Eliz. Pinkney, married Nov. 20.
Burley, John, and Mary Johnson, married Nov. 20.
Staveley, Mary, ux. Rd., buried April 25.
Etty, John, of Great Givendale, buried Jan. 10.
Berry, Ann, dau. of Mary, buried Jan. 26.
     (Signed) Edw. Dunning, *Vicar.*
         Thos. Richardson, *Churchwarden.*

1704. Nothing but a note of Service of Citation upon Wm. Dawson, and payment of 1/- fee.
1705. No christenings, marriages, or burials.
     (Signed) Edw. Dunning, *Vicar.*
         Robt. Quarton, *Churchwarden.*

1706. Walgate, James, and Anna Staveley, married May 10.
Walgate, Anna, dau. of James, bapt. Jan. 25.
Smith, Edward, buried Nov. 10.
     (Signed) Robt. Quarton, *Churchwarden.*

1707. Richardson, Mary, dau. of Thos., bapt. Jan. 6.
(No marriages or burials.)
     (Signed) Edw. Dunning, *Vicar.*
         Robt. Quarton, *Churchwarden.*

1708. Walgate, James, son of James, bapt. Jan. 10, 1707.
Quarton, Eliz., ux. Robt. buried Nov. 10, 1708.
(No marriages.)
     (Signed) Edw. Dunning, *Vicar*.
         Robt. Quarton, *Churchwarden*.

1709. Richardson, Grace, dau. of Thos., bapt. Feb. 6.
Kirby, Edmond, son of Jane, buried, Feb. 16.
Dunning, Mr. Edward, minister, buried, March 11.
     (Signed) Geo. Richardson, *Churchwarden*.

1710. Staveley, Mary, dau. of William and Abigel, bapt. (*sic.*)
Waugate, Mary, dau. of James and Ann, bapt.
Jepson, Robt., and Sarah Fell, of Kilwick, maried.
(No burials.)
     (Signed) J. Drake, *Curate*.
         Geo. Heardson, *Churchwarden*.

AN ANALYTICAL CALENDAR OF LINCOLNSHIRE WILLS,*

Proved in the Prerogative Court of Canterbury.

By Major-General W. H. Smith.

REGISTER "SHEFFELDE." Anno 1568-69.

Flyntham, Richard, St. Mary Torksey, yeo. John Jarvis, William Darwyn, and Leonard Banister exors. [Fo. 1.]

Chester, John, Boston, "keleman." Wife Margaret and brother Nicholas Chester, exors. [Fo. 1.]

Grandorge, Humfry, Donynton in Holland, gent. Sons Charles, eldest, Nicholas, Willm. and George. [Fo. 2.]

Dysney, Thomas, Carlton-in-Moreland, gent. Sons Edward, eldest, Thos, 4th son. Anthony Dysney brother, exor. [Fo. 5.]

Marshall, Jane, Holme, widow. To be buried in Bottesford church. Late husband Edmond Marshall; cousin William Dallison, of Laughton. [Fo. 8.]

Clerke, John, Market Deepinge, mercer. Wife Mary, sole extrix. [Fo. 10.]

Gote, William, "Burne," yeo. Son Thomas Gote, exor. (Bourn). [Fo. 10.)

Kelle, John, Revesby, yeo. Sons Robt. and Thomas Keylle, exors. [Fo. 11.]

Curteys, William, Welton-by-Louth. Sons Willm. exor., and Robt. Curteys; daus. Agnes Taylor, Margery Barker, and Cristen Cardon. [Fo. 12.]

Castle, Robert, "Moltone" [Moulton], yeo. Wife Kathrine, extrix. Church bridge named. [Fo. 14.]

Adam, William, Tydd St. Mary, pts. Holland. Wife Margt. Sons Henry and Thomas, exors. [Fo. 15.]

Cooke, John, Louthe. Wife Jennyt and son John Cooke, exors. Mr. John Dyon, of Louth, esq., supervisor. [Fo. 16.]

* Continued from page 198 of Vol. for 1896.

Porter, Helen, [Belton], widow. Lands in Belton. Sons John, Edmund, and Willm. Porter. Poor man's box in Syeston, iii^s iiii^d. Son-in-law Thomas Disney, son-in-law Rowland Sharrard. [Fo. 19.]

Thorold, William, Marston, esq. Sons Anthony, eldest and exor., Robt., Edmond, William, and Richd.; dau. Alice Porter; nieces Alice, Jennie, and Rose Harrington; Phillipp Northroppe; Thos. son of Anthony Thorold; wife, not named; my capital messuage in Blanckney purchased of Thos. Wymbyshe; son John Riggs and his children. [Fo. 23.]

[25 Folios in Sheffelde.]

REGISTER "LYON." Anno 1569-70.

Wymberley, Christopher, Bychefield. Son Thomas, exor. Thomas and Richard Coney, named. [Fo. 5.]

Manne, John, Bollingbrook, esq. Wife Audrey, extrix.; brother Thos. Ogle, esq. [Fo. 6.]

Smyth, John, Crowland. Wife Elizth.; sons Richard and Thomas, both minors; sisters Alice Bowthe and Agnes Robinson, and their children. To Elizth. my wife, my swanne marke called "The Surgines." Thos. Ffairechilde, curate. [Fo. 8.]

Goate, William, Borne, yeo. Wife Elizth; son Thos. Goate, exor. [Fo. 11.]

Walpole, Robert, Stamford. Exors. Adelard Welby, Edmund Hall, Leonard Irbye, &c. [Fo. 13.]

Ryndge, Thomas, Sutton-in-Holland. Wife Johan, and brother Nicholas R., exor. Mother Dey. [Fo. 14.]

Stowe, John, Newton-by-Trent. Wife Edithe; sons John, Alexander and Hugh S. [Fo. 15.]

Wormell, George, Long Benington. Wife Margret; son Oliver, sole exor. [Fo. 21.]

Poplewell, James, Belton, I. of Axholme, yeo. Wife Jane; son Francis and Dorothy his wife, son David P.; daurs. Kathren Glewe, Isabel Pynder, and Elizth. Thornton; son-in-law Willm. Glewe. [Fo. 29.]

Richardson, Henry, Watterton, co. Lincoln. Wife Anne; sons Robt., Willm., and Thos. R. [Fo. 30.]

Taylor, Henry, Haxey, I. of Axeholme. Wife Margt.; son Gregory
T., Samuel son of Michael T.; Richard Barnard, of Belton,
his children. [Fo. 30.]

Butler, Anthony, Cotts, next Stowe, esq. Wife Margt. (Long Will.)
[Fo. 31.]

[39 Folios in Lyon.]

REGISTER "HOLNEY." Anno 1570-71.

Phillippe, David, Holbiche. Wife Maryon extrix. [Fo. 10.]

Thompson, John, Prebendary, Coll. of Windesore. Wife Alice sole
extrix.; brother Hewghe Cooke, of Winterton, and my sister
Jane his wife; brother Thomas Bryse, of Kirton Linesey;
brother John Cooper and my sister Isabell his wife, of Alder-
kirke in Holland; cousin Thos. Brumbie and Elizth. his wife;
cousin Margt. Thompson and her husband, of Kirton in
Lyndsey. [Fo. 19.]

Asheton, Lewis, Spawlding. Brother Nichs. Wooldriche, and Mr.
Adelard Welby, of Gedney, supervisors. [Fo. 19.]

Swane, Thomas, clerk, Person of Sutton. Wife Susan sole extrix.
[Fo. 21.]

Welbye, Adlarde, the elder, Gedney, esq. Wife Cassander extrix.
Willm. Newland, vicar of Gednay; (in margin) Henry Welbye
and Adlard Welby sons of deceased. (Will 18 lines.) [Fo. 29.]

Johnson, David, Kaister. Wife Jenett; son James; daur. Alice.
Goods at Brigge and Keilbie. Matthew Marshall, clerk.
(Will 20 lines.) [Fo. 29.]

Dale, Thomas, Alford, gent. Wife Anne; sons Edward and Fras.
D.; daurs. Jane D. and Elizth. Weslehead. Dorcas Wesle-
hed. My parsonage of Carleton. John Hamby, of London,
esq., supervisor. [Fo. 29.]

Balie, William, Fotherbie, gent. Brother Xpofer. Balie; kinsman
Jeffrey Balie; Robt. Shake, of Horncastle; Sir Robt. Dough-
tie, vicar of Louth; brother Xpofer. Baylie, and Richard
Brighte, of Louth, exors. [Fo. 31.]

Rathebye, Lyan, Sotbye, gent. Daur. Barbarae Ydle; son John R.
all my lands in Sotby; John Weste, of Hawneleye; nephew
Robert, son to Willm. Rathebye. Mr. Geo. Hennage, of
Sixhills, esq., supervisor. Alice, wife of Allin Creede. [Fo. 31.]

Jackson, William, Staynton, husbn. Wife Alice; brothers Richard and Lawrence Jackson; son-in-law Willm. Smyth and Robt. S. his brother; Anne and Lucy Smyth; Helene Barthilmew my wife's daur.; Robt. Hassarde my son. Thos. Scyntpole, my best horse. [Fo. 32.]

Arnolde, Thomas, St. James' Deeping. Wife Agnes; sons Jefferye, Thomas, Willm., and Roger; daurs. Agnes A. and Elizth. Burne. Kinswoman, Johan Arnolde. Sir Thos. Thompson, vicar. [Fo. 37.]

Lanain, Johd, Boston, alderman. Wife Dorothy and son Rd., exors. [Fo. 39.]

Irbye, Leonard, Boston, esq. Wife Anne; my mother Alice Irbye; Kelham, son of my brother John Irbye, sole heir after wife's death. [Fo. 42.]

Skipwith, William, Utterby, gent. Wife not named but with child; brother Thos. S.; brother-in-law Ffrancis Carscy; mother Elenor Skipwith; sister Mabell Skipwith. Lyon Skipwith, esq. named. Nicholas Missendine named. [Fo. 45.]

[49 Folios in Holney.]

REGISTER "DAPER." Anno 1571.

Madison, John, Marshe Chappell, gent. Son Thos. M. and brother Thos. M., exors. [Fo. 1.]

Madison, Thomas, Grimsby. Wife Margt., extrix. (Will 2 pages.) [Fo. 1.]

Spalding, John, Louth, yeo. Brothers Stephen and Richard Spalding, exors. [Fo. 4.]

Brokilsby, Richard, Kirton Linsey. Wife Eme; sons Edward, Richard, and Robert B. [Fo. 5.]

Hewicke, William, Louth, showmaker. Kinsman, Anthy. Hewicke, exor. [Fo. 11.]

Wiles, Nicholas, Stamford, draper. Sons Nicholas, Thobie, Henry, Chas., Willm., and Arthur Wiles. [Fo. 12.]

Woulbie, Richard, Crofte. Wife Marie, and John Mawer, exors. Vincent Wraye, witness. [Fo. 13.]

Jellowe, Henry, Holbiche, yeo. Wife Margt. extrix. [Fo. 14.]

Colthirste, John, Awnsbie, gent. Wife Mary, extrix. Sons Edmd. and Thos. C. [Fo. 19.]

Baston, Sir Henry, Louth, clerk. Robert Doughtie, and Brian Yarborough, exors. [Fo. 19.]

Lockett, Thomas, Spalding. Wife Edythe, extrix. [Fo. 21.]

Salmon, Richard, Pickworth, yeo. Wife Jane; Willm. and Mychael sons, exors. [Fo. 32.]

Wardall, Thomas, Lowthe, tanner. Wife Margt. and son John, exors. [Fo. 32.]

Hynman, Johan, Northwitham, widow. Sons Roland, John, and Edward H., exors. [Fo. 33.]

Deynes, John, Sutton St. James, Pts. Holland. Wife Agnes, extrix. [Fo. 44.]

[Folios in Daper.]

REGISTER "PETER." Anno 1572-73.

Warde, Roger, Manthorpe, parish Witham [on the Hill]. Wife Margt.; sons Edmund and Arthur; daurs. Elizth., Jane, Dorothye, and Isabell W. [Fo. 2.]

Chapman, Robert, Lowthe, tanner. Son John; Ellen and Jane Jackson my daughter's children. Thos. Jackson, of Louth, exor. [Fo. 5.]

Clarke, Sir William, Louth, priste. Willm. Clarke son of my cosen John C., decd., and Gartred C. his sister; cosen Willm. Symcotts, of Louth; Nicholas son of my cosen John Clarke, decd. Lands in Swaby, Saltfleetby, Awthorpe, and Carleton. [Fo. 6.]

Richardson, William, Louth, weaver. Brother-in-law Richard Awncell, Glentham. A number of bequests to town charities. [Fo. 7.]

Holdernes, Thomas, Lowthe. Wife Ales; sons Richard and Allen; daur. Joan Holdernes. [Fo. 7.]

Townend, Edward, Glamford Brigges, draper. Wife Margery; son John T.; uncle Richard T., decd.; Anthony Gilliot's wife, of Appleby; Thomas son of my brother Gilbert Townend; Richard son of Christopher Townend; daur. Margaret T. [Fo. 7.]

Cooke, Tristram, Flixbrugh. Children of Isabell Wood; children of my brother John Cooke; sister Agnes Kirkland; sister Bennett Kyte's children; sister Margaret Beadame; brother Thos. Cooke; sister Isabell C., late wife of my brother Rd. Cooke (? wife of late brother); Ralf, eldest son of brother Rd. Cooke, of Scawbie; Tristram, youngest son and Elizabeth, dau. of my brother Richard Cooke, of Scawby; wife Margaret; Geo. Smith, of Hull; Bartholemew Beck, vicar of Roxby. "Thirteen greate sylver spoones called 'The Apostles.'" [Fo. 8.]

Walpoole, Dorothey, Stamford, widow. Sons John W. eldest, Erasmus W. youngest; Alice W. daur.; Arthur W. my husband's son; daur. Houghton, daur. Mary W., daur. Anne Hall; Mrs. Suzan Walpoole; Elizth. wife of son John; daur. Joane Sodoe, daur. Suzane; son Erasmus W. sole exor. (Vide Genealogist, Vol I., pp. 6—12, 193.) [Fo. 10.]

Cocke, Richard, citizen and fishmonger, London. Son of Wm. Cocke, of Spalding; wife Elizabeth. Brothers Xpofer. and Thomas C., of Spalding. [Fo. 11.]

Gibson, Robert, St. Maryeted in Holland (Tyd St. Mary), gent. Wife Isabell; Sons Willm., Gilbert, and John; my Manor of Tylney; William Downam and John Deanes my sisters' children; daurs. Dorothie, Elizth., Margt., and Sara G. To Mary Pye, one heckfurthe. [Fo. 11.]

Tompson, Edward, Gedney, Pts. Holland, gent. Wife Awdry; mother Margt. Tompson; father Willm. T., decd.; brother Robt. Tompson; brother Richard Welby. [Fo. 12.]

Parker, Richard, Wrauby. Wife Jane; sons Richard, Phillip, Edward, and Roger; daurs. Annie and Alice; Willm. Rudde, of Barrow; Jno. Thompson, vicar of Wrauby; Sir Robt. Tirwhit, and Mr. William Tirwhit, supervisors. Poor of Barton, Barrow, Goxhill, Kirmington, Brigg, and Wrauby, xx^s each. [Fo. 14.]

Wormsley, Thomas, Frampton, yeo. Wife Katheryn; sons Willm. and Francis; daur. Margt.; John Tonarde, son of Richard T., of Frampton. [Fo. 15.]

Thomas, Richard, Holbich. Thomas Harriman my sister's son; sister Dorothey Leeke, wife of Willm. L.; sisters children and John and Johan Milner, residue. [Fo. 21.]

WAIFS AND STRAYS.

Blackburne. 1748. Thomas Blackburne, of Marylebone, London, and Mary Whitehead, of Boroughbridge, married by licence, Oct. 16. [Aldbrough parish register.]

Carr, Colonel, of Bradford in Yorkshire, mariner, and Mary Sweet, of Sidwell, spinster. Marriage Licence at Exeter, Oct. 6, 1760.

Cartwright, John, of Nottingham, hosier, and Mary Churchill, of Exeter, spinster, a minor. Marriage licence at Exeter, May 30, 1774.

Delattre. 1760. Stephen Delattre of this parish, late of Dunkirk, now a Prisoner upon Parole, gent., and Mary Hauge of this parish, spinster, married by licence, Feb. 19. [St. John, Micklegate, York.]

Farrier. 1752. James, son of James Farrier, of Bamff, in the shire of Bamff, Scotland, buried March 26. [Aldbro' parish register.]

Griffith. 1757. Edward Griffith, of Wirksworth, co. Derby, and Ann Ardron, of this parish, married by licence, May 9. [St. Laurence, York.]

Hailstone. 1757. John Hailstone, of St. George's in the East, co. Middlesex, gent., and Elizth. Whitaker, of this parish, spinster, married by licence, Sept. 5. [St. John, Micklegate, York.]

Harrison. 1763. March 29, Thomas, son of Thomas and Elizth. Harrison, of Lazonby, near Carlisle, in Cumberland, bapt. [Parish register of Southover, in Lewes, co. Sussex.]

Hepworth. 1735. April 24, Thomas, son of Thomas and Easter Hepworth, of the parish of Pontefract, in Yorkshire (a soldier), bapt. [Ibid.]

Jackson. 1759. Thos. Jackson, of Newmarket, co. Suffolk, and Ann Clark, of this parish, married by licence, July 9. [St. Martin, Coney Street, York.]

Lumb. 1758. John Lumb, of Barwick in Elmet, and Ann Burnett, of this parish, married by banns, April 10. [St. Mary Bishophill, junr., York.]

Marsingale, Antony, of Hull, in Yorkshire, mariner, and Mary Williams, of Falmouth, spinster. Marriage licence at Exeter, Oct. 5, 1749.

Nicholson. 1756. John N., of Appleby, co. Westmoreland, and Mary Robinson, of this parish, married by licence, April 20. [St. Sampson, York.]

Otter. 1761. William Otter, of Ouston, Lincolnshire, and Margt. Corringham, married March 10. [Misterton parish register.]

Parkinson. 1761. John P., of Bodsford (Bottesford), Lincolnshire, and Alice Parr, married Feb. 4. [Misterton parish register.]

Stone. 1757. Charles Stone, from London, gent., buried Sept. 9. [St. Laurence, York.]

Tonstall. 1742. Bryan Tonstall, a reputed Roman Priest, buried June 2. [St. Michael Belfry parish register, York.]

Upton. 1709. Jan. 5, William Upton, of Great Drayton, co. Nott., yeoman, 26, and Jane Norfolk, of same, 26. Surety, John Upton, of South Leverton, yeoman. [Marriage Bond, Dean and Chapter of York.]

Wansell. 1745. Edmund Wansell, Lieutenant in General Oglethorp's regiment, buried March 19. [St. Martin, Coney Street, York, parish register.]

Weston, Charles, of Somerby, co. Lincoln, clerk, and Anne Weston, of Dawlish, spinster. Marriage licence at Exeter, Nov. 15, 1759.

Willett. 1750. Mrs. Mary Willett, servant to Mrs. Margaret Willet, spinster, who was borne in the land of St. Christopher in America, who died in ye parish of St. John's, and was buried in ye side chancell in the parish of St. Martin's, Coney Street, ye 8th of April. [St. Martin's parish register.]

PARISH REGISTER OF CLAY COTON,
Northants.*

(Transcribed by the Rev. Gordon H. Poole.)

Clement Codsbrook and Agnes Barford were mar. the xxii. of Maye.

Thomas Reeve and Margaret Murcote weare mar. the viith of Julye.

John Sutton, the sone of John Sutton, was bap. the xxiith of Aprill.

Francis Killingley, the sonne of Barthollemew Killingley, was bap. the iiiith of Julye.

Elizabeth Williams, the dau. of Willia. Williams, was bap. the xxvith of October.

Katherine Heward, the dau. of John Heward, was bap. the viith of March.

Katherine Heward, the dau. of Thomas, was bap. the viith of Februarye.

Obadia Williams, the sone of Willia. Williams, was bap. the xviith daye of Februarie.

Mathewe Brian, the sone of Willia. Bryan, was bap. the xxviii. daye of Februarie.

Anno domini 1597.

Richard Reeve, the sonne of Thomas Reeve, was bap. the xth day of Julye.

Robert Sutton, the sonne of John Sutton, was bap. the ii. daye of October.

Richard Stafford and Joane Burnam weare mar. the vth daye of November.

Roger Wood and Marie Brewesse weare mar. the xiiith daye of November.

Thomas Hutchins and Agnes Reeve weare mar. the xxiiiith daye of November.

Richard Hulley was bur. the xxvth of Aprill.

John Hulley was bur. the xxviiith of Aprill.

Nicholas Marche was bur. the xxviii. of January.

* Continued from page 95.

Anno domini 1598.

Per me Robertum Cleye, *ministrum ibidem*.

Thomas Reeve } *Churchwardens.*
John Mariat

Barsabe Richardson, the dau. of Richard Richardson, was bap. the xiii. of January.
John Croyley was bur. the xviii. day of Januarie.
Nicholas Marche was bur. the xxviiith of Januarie.
Humfrey Killingley was bur. the xviii. of Januarie.
Richard Richardson, the sonne of Richard, was bur. the xxxth daye of Januarie.
Margret Force was bur. the first of Februarie.
Henry Ballard, the sone of John Ballard, was bap. the vi. daye of Februarye.
Alice Wood, the dau. of Agnes Wood, was bur. the ixth daye of Feb.
Richard Ballard was bur. the xiiith day of Februarie.
Michaell West, the sonne of Henrye West, bap. the xvii. daye of Februarie.
Elizabeth Ballard, the wife of John Ballard, was bur. the vth daye of Marche.
Marie Killingley, the dau. of Bartholomew Killingley, was bap. the viii. of September.
Thomas Heward was bur. the xx. daye of September.
Alice West, widow, was bur. the xth daye of Feb.
Elizabeth Packe was bur. the xxiiii. day of Januarie.

Anno domini 1599.

Margret Wood, the dau. of Roger Wood, was bap. the xxth day of Maye. The same Margret was bur. the ii. day of June.
Richard Dabs and Agnes West weare mar. the xiiii. daye of Julye.
Bartholomew Killingley was bur. the xxth daye of Julye, anno p'dicto.

Written by me, Robert Cleye, *Minister.*

Thomas Reeve } *Churchwardens.*
John Mariat

Elizabeth Ballard, the dau. of Thomas Ballard, was bap. the ii. daye of Marche.

Willia. Sutton, the sonne of John Sutton, was bap. the xi. daye of
Marche.

Anno domini 1600.

Grace Murcote, dau. of John Murcote, was bap. the 2 daye of
August.

Valentine Wood, sonne of Roger Wood, was bap. the 22 of August.

John Ballarde and Prudence March were mar. the xxixth daie of
October.

Richarde Reeve was bur. the xxiiiith daie of November.

Elizabethe Reeve, dau. of Thomas Reeve, was bap. the 3 daye of
Januarie.

Anno domini 1601.

Grace Bende, dau. of Willia. Bend, was bap. 28° of June.

Roger Weste, sonne of Henrie West, was bap. the 5° of Julie.

John Heward, sonne of Christopher Heward, was bapt. the 9° of
August.

Richarde Richardson was bur. the 29th daie of November.

Elizabethe Hawforde was bur. the 13th daie of Januarye.

Michaell Webster was bur. the 3° daie of Marche.

Edwarde Killingly was bur. the 6° daie of Marche.

Edwarde Astell, *Minister there*.

William Bende }
William Hulley } *Churchwardens*.

Anno domini 1602.

Jone Ballard, dau. of John Ballarde, was bap. the 14 daie of June.

Alice Reeve, dau. of William Reeve, was bap. the 27 daie of June.

Thomas Joliffe and Agnes Richardson were mar. the 24 daie of
Aprill.

Nicholas Webbe and Isabell Hulley were mar. the 7° daie of Aug.

Valentine Wood, sonne of Rodger, was bur. the 30 daie of Aprill.

Agnes Smithe, dau. of Henrie Smithe, was bur. the 22 daie of Maye.

Katherine West, dau. of Richarde West, was bur. the 12° of Sept.

John Joliffe, sonne of Thomas Joliffe, was bap. the 14th daye of
November.

Lambert Sutton, the sonne of John Sutton, was bap. the 6th daie of
Januarie.

Marie Wood, dau. of Rodger Wood, was bap. the 12th of Januarye.

John Bende, the sonne of William Bende, was bap. the 27th of Feb.

Anno domini 1603.

Margaret Marche, dau. of Edwarde Marche, was bur. the xxiith daye of Aprill.

Richarde Moore, and Isabell Murcote were mar. the xvith daye of July.

Nathanaell Reeve, the sonne of Robert Reeve, was bap. the 1st daye of November.

Dorothie West, dau. of Henrye West, was bur. the xxvth daye of December.

Jone Yerpe was bur. the the seconde of Januarye.

Nicholas Heward was buried the 4th of Januarye.

Richarde Webster and Elizabeth Paulmer were mar. the xvith of Januarye.

By me, Edwarde Astell, *Minister there.*

William Bend } *Churchwardens.*
Robert Webster

Anno domini 1604.

Edwarde Moore, sonne of Richarde Moore, was bap. the 18th of Aprill.

Anne Hewarde, dau. of Marie Hewarde, was bur. the xxiiiith of Aprill.

Alice Reeve, dau. of Thomas Reeve, was bap. the vith of Maye.

Isabell Hulley, dau. of William Hulley, was bap. the xxth of Maye.

Robert Bende, sonne of William Bend, was bap. the seconde daye of September.

Agnes Reave, daughter of William Reave, was bap. the iiiith of Oct.

Marie Webster, dau. of Robert Webster, was bap. the 8th of October.

William Burgesse, sonne of John Burgesse, was bur. the Fourthe of November.

Stephen Joliffe, sonne of Thomas Joliffe, was bap. the xith of November.

Henrie Ballarde, sonne of John Ballarde, was bap. the xviiith of November.

Richarde Harrison and Katherine Murcote were mar. the 8th of Maye.

John West, sonne of Henrie West, was bap. the 17th of Februarie.

CUMBERLAND WILLS.*

Henry Fletcher Partis, of Tallentire Hall, co. Cumberland, esq. 23 March, 1775. Kinsman, Hendry Hopper, of Durham, attorney at law, all my manor of Tallentire, co. Cumberland, and lands there or elsewhere, subject to payment of £30 a year for life to my natural daur. Frances, now living with Catherine Thompson, of Cockermouth, schoolmistress. Friend Christr. Fawcett, of Newcastle-on-Tyne, esq., £500. My steward John Evening, of Scale in Embleton, co. Cumberland, yeo., £100. Cousin Rd. Partis, £20. Friends Peter Brougham, of Cockermouth, esq.; Benjamin Wilson, of same place, surgeon; and John Rudd, of same place, attorney at law, £20 each. All my personal estate to said Hendry Hopper, exor. Witnesses, John Bacon, John Cockton, John Pearson. Proved at York, April, 1777. [cxxi., 507.]

John Langton, of Cockermouth, co. Cumberland, esq., 19 Dec., 1776. Son Gawen Wren Langton, all my lands at Fold, co. Westmoreland, and at Carnhow in Brackenthwaite, co. Cumberland, except my free and customary rents at Fold which belong to my estate at High Close, co. Westmoreland, subject to payment of £400 to my son Thos. Langton. Wm. Tatham, late of Askham, co. Westmoreland, esq., decd., owed me divers moneys with long arrears of interest; I give same to my three sons John Langton, Gawen Wren L., and Thomas L., equally. Servant John Hetherington, £10. Servant Sarah Watson, £5. Residue to son John L., exor. Witnesses, John Meals, John Dixon, Ro. Baynes. Proved at York, 12 March, 1777. [cxxi., 366.]

Mary Grayburne, of Whitehaven, co. Cumberland, widow, 18 Sep., 1794. To John King, of London, attorney at law, the husband of Ann King, late Ann Simmonds, all my leaseholds in Dublin. Joshua, William, and Rd. Dixon, sons of Dr. Joshua Dixon, of Whitehaven, M.D., £10 each. Mrs. Senhouse, wife of Humphrey S., of White-

* Continued from page 62.

haven, esq., my silver coffee pot and stand, &c. Servant Isabella Hamilton, £10. Residue to said Dr. Dixon, exor. Proved May, 1795.

Deposition (as to want of execution) of Peter How, junr., of Whitehaven, co. Cumberland, attorney at law, and notary public, æt. 37, a witness on behalf of Dr. Dixon, against Mary Robbins, aunt and only next-of-kin of decd.

John Dodgson, of Tallentire, parish of Bridekirk, co. Cumberland, yeoman, 13 Dec., 1778. Wife Eleanor, all my household goods. Son Lancaster Dodgson, £5. Daur. Eleanor, ux. Matt. Fearon, £200. Granddaughter Isabella Fearon, £100. Daughter Anne Dodgson, £500. Residue to wife Eleanor, son John Dodgson, and son-in-law Matt. Fearon, exors. Witnesses, John Bacon and Sarah Aken. Proved at York, June 1779. [cxxiii., 278.]

Thomas Irwen, of Aldston, co. Cumberland, merchant, 12 Feb., 1778. Wife Jane, the house I live in, during her widowhood, and then to my son John, he paying his brother Thomas, £40. Son John, the stock on hand of Irish linen. Residue to wife, extrix. Witnesses, John Reay, and Henry Proud. Proved at York, June, 1779. [cxxiii., 293.]

SIR ROGER SALVIN, 1420.

In the nam off Gode, I, Sr Roger Salwayn, knygch, ye xxvj. day off Octobr in the yer off our lord mccccxx. makys my testament in this maner. First I wyle my soule to gode almythty, to our lady seynt Mary, and to all ye seinttes off hewin, and my bones to be beriede in ye grey frerres atte Yorke. Also I will that ther where my bones shall be beryde be a flat ston off marbill ewyn wt the grounde. Also I will yt ye forsaid freres have all my gounes of cloth off gold, and off sylke, wt outyn ye furres. Also I will yt ye same frers have xl^{li} for to synge and pray for me. Also I will yt ilken off ye other thre orders in Yorke have x. marc. Also I will yt my wyffe have all my housholde holy wt vc^{li} that is in hir handes. Also I will yt ther be ordeine for byynge off lande for John Salwayn my son, cccc^{li}, also for ye mariage off Alison my daughter cccc marc, also for ye mariage of Isabel my daughter ccc marc. Also I will yt my fader dettis and my moder be paide off my goodez that is in the coillors or in ye fermors handes off my rent, and if any tennt be so pour yt he may nought for pov'tee pay his ferme that is owing, I will yt ther be nought reseyued off hym but yt he may resonably pay and yt ye remennt be for yeffyn. Also I will yt som goode man be ordeine to goo for me to Jhrusalem in pilgremage, and as far as it cost is lese than c^{li} in comyng and goyng yt hit be gewyn for my soule to poure men wher most allmose is. Also I will yt Richard Chace have v. marc off monee and a bay hors yt was Gerard my son; William Lister, xx^{li}; Thomas Fairchild, xl. marc; Acris Mersk, xx^{li}; litill Petir liard Manley and x. marc; and yt Acris Mersk have ye grey geldyng Gerard, and John my brothir liard Botiller, and a sorede horse yt was bought off Hamden, and yt Gerard my brothir Chese. Also I will yt Gerard my brodir have xl^{li} and Thomas my brothir a place in Duffelde, termyn off his liue yt I purchased off John Fulthorpe, and after the desese off hym to turn agayn to ye reght haiers of me. Also I will yt Sr Robt. Shottesbroke, knyught, have ye sorde hors, and litill Hans ye hoby and xl^s aboven his hir. Also I will that that Frost Mores and litill Robyn ilken off them have xl^s. Also I will yt Pomfretth Skynnr, of Yorke, be paied of v.

or vi^li whedir yt hit be for furres yt my lady my moder knowes off. Also I will yt William Tropmell, taillor, of London, and Hunt Crouderere, be paied of their billes for makyng off a liverey of myn. Also I will yt Henry Lound have a blake goun furred vt funes and a habirgon of Mylen opyn befor yt Richard Stell haves in hys kepyng. Also I will yt giff any servaunt of myn have labord for me in my countree sen my fader died yt they be resonably rewardid after the service yt they have don. Also gif any man can aske any dete off me other be evidence, or yt they be credibill p'sones, I will yt they be paied. Also I will that Elyn Saluayn, my brothir Gerard daur., xl. marc for hir mariage. Also I will yt Gerard my brothir have a new fure of murtirs and j harbirgon of millen. Also I will yt Johan my brothir have j habirgon of gesseran. Also I will yt ye none yt kepid me in my sicknes have ij. nobl, and yt ther be gif in to the hous yt she wonnes in xx˚ for to syng and pray for me. Also I will yt Thomas Fairchild have as mych monee as he may purches hym xl˚ be yer. Also I will yt all all ye furrurs yt I have be sould and doon for my soule. Also I will yt Chase have a habirion of myn executors of my testament. I will and ordeine Piers de la Hay, Gerard Saluayn, Robt. Rodeston, Sr Nichol Dixon clerk, Robt. Cawode, Robt. Dry, Richard Chace, and Thomas Fairchild, to whom I giff and wit ye residue ofi all ye good and catell yt I have yt they ordeine and dispoce hit in sich wys as may be most meritory for my soule, as they will aunswer befor gode on dredfullday of doom. And the surveiors of my testament I will and ordeine Wm. Kylwolmerssh clerke, and my wyfe. Wyttenesyng, William Philipe chivaler, Richard Wodevill, William Lister, and other. Also I will yt Wm. Lister have as mych of monee as the sorde hors is worth yt Shottesbroke haves. Proved 7 March, 1422, by Richard Chace and Thos. Fairchyld.

NOTES ON SOME OF THE TERMS IN THE WILL, &c.

Jazerine-Jesseraunt. A light armour composed of splints or small plates of metal rivetted to each other, or to a lining of some stout material. Sir R. Salvayn (the Will now printed) in his Will 1420, bequeaths his " Habirgen of gesseran." (Fairholt costume in England, Ed. 3, by H. A. Dillon, ii. p. 260.)

Habergeon-Haburion. A coat of mail or breastplate, the diminutive of hauberk, being shorter and lighter ...... in 1420, Sir Roger

Salvayn bequeaths a " Habirgen of gesseran," another of " Mylen open befor," and another " Habirjoun of millon." [Ibid.]

Sir Roger Salvayn was son of Sir Gerard Salvayn, of Herswell and North Duffield, co. York, by Alice his wife, daughter of .... (Surtees Hist. Durh., iv. p. 118.)

He was one of the Knights of the body of King Henry V., who left him in his Will, dated 1415, £100 in gold. (Rymer Fœdera, iv. pt. 2, p. 139.)

He was present at the Battle of Agincourt in the retinue of the King, and was made a Knight of the Bath at the Feast of St. George at Caen. 6 Hen. V., 23 April, 1419. (Battle of Agincourt, by Sir N. H. Nicolas, p. 383. Surtees Hist. Durh., ut supra.)

He married Matilda, daughter of Sir Robert Hilton, of Swine in Holderness. She survived him and was living a widow in 1429, when her daughter Isabel made her Will.

Of the persons mentioned in Sir Roger's Will, Sir Gerard Salvayn his father was born in 1358. Served in Scotland 1383 and 1385. Gave evidence in favour of Sir Richard Scrope in the Scrope and Grosvenor controversy. (Scrope and Grosvenor Roll, by Sir N. H. Nicolas, ii. p. 340.) He took an Oath of Allegiance in 1403, to King Henry IV., to hold no communication with Henry, Earl of Northumberland. (Rymer Fœdera, iv. pt. 1, p. 52.)

He died before 26 Oct., 1420, when his son Sir Roger made his Will, and was buried in the church of the Grey Friars, York. (Collect. Topogr. et Geneal., iv. p. 78.) Administration of his goods was granted to Lady Alice his widow, 9 May, 1423. (Vacancy Reg. of Dean and Chap. of York, fol. 330.)

Thomas (brother of Sir Roger) was probably the soldier of that name who was present at the Battle of Agincourt in the retinue of Sir John Grey. (Battle of Agincourt, by Sir N. H. Nicolas. p. 346.) Sir John was brother of Sir Thomas Grey, of Heton, who was beheaded at Southampton, 5 Aug., 1415, whose daughter Johanna married Sir John Salvayn, of Newbiggin. (Graves' Hist. of Cleveland, p. 289.)

John (brother of Sir Roger). Sir John Salvayn's name is included in the list of persons entitled to the ransom of French prisoners between 1415 and 1430. (Battle of Agincourt, app. No. xv., p. 61.)

In 1416-17, safe conduct was granted to Rodricus de St. Andre, prisoner of Sir John Salvayn. (Carter's French Gascon Rolls, p. 234.) Sir John was with the Earl of Salisbury at the siege and capture of Yory, and at the subsequent battle, 1425, and was also probably at Agincourt. (Hall's Chronicle, Ed. 1809, p. 121.)

He married Johanna ...... and died before 1432, when administration of his goods was granted at York. He was buried in the church of the Grey Friars, at York. (Coll. Topogr. et Geneal., iv. p. 78.)

Gerard (brother of Sir Roger) married Agnes de Whalton, heiress of Croxdale, and was the ancestor of the Salvins, of Croxdale, co. Durham, of the present time. (Surtees Hist. Durh. iv. p. 118.) He had livery of his wife's lands in Croxdale and Queryngdon, co. Durham, 1st Oct., 1402. His Will is dated 4 May, 1422, and was proved 6 Dec. following. It is in the Principal Registry of the Court of Probate.

John (son of Sir Roger) became Bailiff of Rouen during the English occupation, 1431-1432. He married Eleanor, 4th daughter of Sir John Willoughby, but died without issue in 1441. His seal attached to one of the charters shews a Fleur de lys between the Mullets of the usual shield of Salvayn, and two wolves or dogs as supporters. (Brit. Mus. Add. Charters, Nos. 1421, 1431, 3723, 3724, 3695, 3697, 3798. Coll. Topogr. et Geneal., vii. p. 155.)

Gerard (son of Sir Roger) was probably Sir Gerard Salvayn who left a daughter and heir Margaret married to ...... Clervaux. She died in 1478, and in the inq. p. m. lands are mentioned as her portion which were formerly in the possession of her great grandfather Sir Gerard Salvayn.

Alison or Alice (daughter of Sir Roger) married Henry Wilton, and their son John Wilton, *als*. Salvin, became heir to his uncle Sir John Salvayn, Bailiff of Rouen, aged 16 years, 1443. Another son Henry was under age at that date. (Surtees Hist. Durh., iv. p. 118.)

Isabel (daughter of Sir Roger) died in 1429, unmarried. Her Will is printed at length (Test. Ebor, i., p. 418) in which many members of her family are mentioned. She was buried in the quire of the Convent at Swine in Holderness. (Burton Monas. Ebor, p. 255.)

OSBERT SALVIN.

STARTFORTH PARISH REGISTER,

CO. YORK.*

Transcribed by Mark W. Bullen, Esq., by kind permission of the Rev. Hartley Jennings, the Vicar.

7b.   1697.

Benjamin Garnet and Dorothy Shepherd were married the 28 of July.
John Hambie and Frances Barton were married February the 14th.

Burials.

Tho. Jamson buried March 7th.
Anne Jamson buried March 13th.
Thomosine Brench buried March 14th.

1698.

Jane, the wife of Rich. Kelley, buried April 9°.
Thomas Alkins buried April 15th.
Elizth., daughter of Vincent Coates, buried May 25th.
Jane, the daughter of Jam. Scot, buried May 30th.
Ralph, the son of Rob. Laidman, deceased, was buried June 3rd.
James Richardson buried June the 14th.
A daughter of Geo. Harker buried Oct. 12.
Rowland Cheesebrough buried Nov. 15th.
Matth. Scott buried November 30th.
Mary Laidman, widow, buried the same day.
Mrs. Katherine Fielding buried December 19th.
Mrs. Dorothy Romaine, widow, buried Jan. 19th.
Bridget Morgan buried Feb. 22nd.
Isabel, the wife of John Simpson, buried Feb. 25th.

8.

1698.   Baptism'.

Ane, the daughter of Charl. Birckbeck, was bapt. March 25th.
Phillis, the daughter of Joshua Clarkson, bapt. March 27th.

* Concluded from page 108.

Mary, the daughter of James Clifton, bapt. June the 19th.
Susannah, the daughter of Benj. Garnet, bapt. July the 29th.
Mary, the daughter of Will. Clarkson, bapt. Sept. 4th.
Hannah, the daughter of Senie Morgan, bapt. Sept. 6th.
Samuel, the son of Robt. Barnes, bapt. Oct. 16th.
James, the son of Matthew Dent, bapt. Oct. 22nd.
Elizabeth, the daughter of Geo. Harker, bapt. Nov. 13.

Marriages, 1698.

James Brown and Anne Hambie married May the 4th.
John Simpson and Isabel Clarkson married May 5th.
Rich. Richardson and Margery Hodgson married May 12th.
James Stout and Anne Jackson married June 19th.
Will. Jamson, of Bolron, and Elianor Robinson, of Barnard Castle, married 27th October.

Baptism'.

Michael, the son of Tho. Clarkson, bapt. Decemb. 11th.
Isabell, the daughter of Tho. Garstell, bapt. the same day.
Jane, the daughter of Rich. Richardson, bapt. the same day.

8b.

Burials, 1699.

Joseph, the son of Tho. Newton, of Bolron, buried 20° Aprilis.
Cicily Birckbeck, of Egleston Abbey, buried May 7th.
Margaret, the wife of Geo. Procter, buried July the 4th.
Franc. Jefferson buried July 26th.
Elizabeth, the daughter of James Bowes, deceased, was buried Sept. 13.
Tho., a child of Tho. Garstell, buried Sept. 19th.
Isabell, the daughter of Thomas Garstell, buried Oct. 3.
Mary, the daughter of W. Grainger, buried Oct. 1st.
Franc. Grainger buried October 28th.
Eliz. Pearson buried Nov. 18th.
Robert Naitbie buried Nov. 29th,
Gillian Carter buried Dec. 7th.
Phillis Clarkson buried January the 2nd.
Will. Jamson buried Jan. 18th.
Brian and Anne Jamson buried January 19th.
Mary Jamson buried Jan. 20th.

Tho. Brench buried Jan. 21st.
Will. Hanbie buried Jan. 23rd.
Anne Soulbie buried Jan. 24th.
Isabel Birckbeck buried Feb. 5th.
Will. Jamson buried Feb. 9th.
Anne Richardson buried Feb. 24th.

Baptisms, 1699.

Will., the son of Jo. Jamson, bapt. Aug. 6th.
Jane, the daughter of John Hanbie, bapt. Aug. 24th.
Mary, the daughter of Will. Grainger, bapt. Sept. 22nd.
John, the son of Jo. Peircy, bapt. Nov. 13th.
Margaret, the daughter of Rich. Coates, bapt. Dec. the 10th day.
Will., the son of Tho. Morgan, bapt. Dec. 28th.
Christian, the daughter of Will. Hanbie, bapt. Jan. 1st.
Jane, the daughter of Benj. Garnett, bapt. March 21st.

Baptisms, 1700.

Elizabeth, daughter of Wm. Wood, bapt. Aprill the 21st.
Benj., the son of Anth. Brunskell, bapt. June 16th.
Tho. the son of Robt. Kipling, bapt. July 24.
Thomas, the son of John Thompson, bapt. Septemb. first.
Rachael, the daughter of Tho. Kipling, bapt. Octob. 6th.
Thos., the son of Wm. Grainger, bapt. the 27 of October.
Katharine (?), the daughter of Tho. Richardson, bapt. the ......

9.

Marriages, 1699.

Francis Grainger and Ann Canon married May 11th.
Will. Proctor and Elizabeth Telburne married June 6th.
Geo. Procter and Isabell Dent married Nov. 5th.
Anth. Brunskill and Jenet Cheesebrough married Nov. 6th.

Burials, 1700.

Elizabeth, the wife of Wm. Procter, buried March the 26.
Richard Brunskell buried Aprill the 5th.
Mary Taylor buried Aprill the 19th.
Susannah, the daughter of Benjamin Garnett, buried the 8th of May.
Michael Clarkson buried July 6th.
Eliz. Audd buried May 27th.

Jane Langstaff buried May 28th.
James Clarkson buried July 6th.
Annie Thompson buried August 18th.
William Richardson buried August 20th.
Thomas Jameson buried the 16th of October.
Elianor Thompson buried the 25th of Dec., wife of Mr. Thompson, the younger, of Bowron.
Lionell Mitshell, of Bowron, buried the 18th of December.
Robert Tilburne buried the 23rd of December.
Ann Thompson, of Bowron, buried the 25th of December.
Wm. Thompson, of Bowron, the 13th of January.
Anne, the wife of George Harker, of Bowron, the 16th of November.
Susannah Feilding, wife of William Feilding, buried the 23 of January.

9b.

Marriages, 1700.

.... Crampton and Hannah Jackson married the 29th of April.
............es Clarkeson and Mary Blakelock married the 1st of May.
Christo. Finley and Jane Wardell married August the 26th.
Ambros Waller, of Stenton, and Ruth Banks, of this parish, married the 13th of February.

MARRIAGE BONDS

OF THE

DEAN AND CHAPTER OF YORK.*

By T. B. Whytehead, Esq., Chapter Registrar.

"SEDE VACANTE."

1686. May 15. John Arnett, of Rocliff, butcher, aged 33, and Dorothy Clearland, spinster, aged 34. [St. Olave's.]
May 31. Joshua Turner, of York, and Bridgett Buckle, spr.
June 4. Joshua Seller, of Bulmer, blacksmith, and Alice Wilson.
June 5. Peter Bedell, of Humbleton, yeoman, aged 26, and Judith Wray, of Humbleton, aged 30, spinster.
[Drypool, Hessle, or St. Mary's, Hull.]
April 19. Edmund Dring, junr., of New Malton, grocer, and Mary Maddocks, spinster.
April 21. Wm. Browne, of Calvertree, Warwick, gent., and Mary Townsend.
April 26. Thomas Agar, of York, woollen draper, and Elizth. Beaumont.
May 6. Nicholas Fenay, of Wakefield, gent., and Jane Thornton, spinster.
April 29. Philip Snowdon, of York, plumber, aged 21, and Barbara Anneson, of New Malton, spinster, aged 21.
[Holy Trinity, Goodramgate.]
April 28. Thos. Ballan, of New Malton, cooper, and Naomi Atkinson, spinster.
May 9. Thomas Lownsdaile, of Maltby, gent., aged 23, and Jane Ingoldesby, of Guisbro', spinster. [Guisbro'.]
April 26. Thomas Brayshaw, of Giggleswick, yeoman, and Mary Harrison, spinster.

* Continued from page 101.

1686. April 19. Rd. Waine, of Lower Heaton, husbandman, and Hannah Harding.

April 14. John Clarke, of Pannall, yeoman, and Deborah Webster.

April 17. Richard Mancklins, of York, stationer, and Francis Denkin, spinster.

April 15. Abraham Hall, of Spofforth, felmonger, and Elizth. Pullaine.

April 20. John Bickars, of Settrington, butcher, and Jane Moorde, spinster.

1687. Sept. 13. Amos Raw, of Hexham, Northumberland, merchant, and Anne Williamstone, spinster.

May 30. Robert Fairbridge, of Hackfoord, Northumberland, gent., and Ann Swinburn, spinster.

April 25. Nicholas Carr, of Dathan, Northumberland, gent., and Isabell Swallwell, widow.

April 26. John Beckwith, of Nether Poppleton, gent., and Mary Smithson, spinster.

April 30. John Smith, of York, (St. Michael, Ouse brigg), goldsmith, aged 30, and Elizth. Wilson, (St. Denis), spinster, aged 22. [Bishopthorpe.]

April 23. John Greene, of Bramley, yeoman, and Mary Wood, spinster.

April 30. Christr. Darby, of Helperby, yeoman, aged 21, and Anne Slater, of Easingwold, spinster, aged 21. [Brafferton.]

Nov. 8. Thos. Lee, of West Acomb, Northumberland, gent., and Alice Helmsley, spinster.

Sept. 17. Henry Dacre, of Hexham, Northumberland, gent., and Elianor Jopling, spinster.

1688. May 7. John Kitching, of Skipton, gent., and Elizabeth Patefield.

May 8. George Wood, of Aberforth, carrier, and Dorothy Langdale.

1757. May 14. Christr. Thompson, of South Kilvington, farmer, aged 25, bachelor, and Mary Huggon, of Upsal, aged 25, spinster. [South Kilvington.]

May 18. Wm. Cass, of Scarbro', yeoman, aged 24, bachelor, and Margaret Johnson, of Cayton, Seamer, aged 22, spinster. [Seamer.]

1757. May 13. Robert Hardcastle, of Leeds, butcher, aged 23, bachelor, and Sarah Thackray, of Sawley, Ripon, aged 23, spinster. [Ripon.]

May 7. Wm. Wrather, of Pannall, schoolmeister, aged 23, bachelor, and Elizth. Tiplady, of Blubberhouses, Fewstone, aged 42, widow. [Pannall.]

May 10. Nathaniel Wilson, of Featherston, yeoman, aged 33, bachelor, and Elizth. Littlewood, of Wakefield, aged 22, spinster. [Wakefield.]

May 12. Edward Plumpton, clerk, Rector of Everingham, aged 25, bachelor, and Ann Brigham, of Wyton, Swine, aged 24, spinster.

May 12. Wm. Newstead, of St. Martin, Micklegate, yeoman, aged 25, bachelor, and Mary Thompson, of same, aged 25, spinster. [St. Martin's.]

May 21. Jas. Oliver, of Heslington, yeoman, aged 26, bach., and Ann Harrison, of Wheldrake, aged 22, spinster. [Wheldrake.]

May 20. Butler Burton, of St. Helen's, Stonegate, grocer, aged 25, bachelor, and Mary Wells, of St. Martin, Coney Street, aged 22, spinster. [St. Martin.]

1776. Dec. 11. Henry Creed, of Leeds, esq., aged 21, bachelor, and Hannah Read, of Leeds, spinster, aged 21. [Leeds.]

Dec. 11. William Lee, of Hull, book-keeper, aged 27, bach., and Mary Dring, of Hull, widow, aged 25. [St. Mary's.]

Dec. 12. Thomas Johnson, of Stillington, farmer, aged 22, bachelor, and Elizabeth Milburn, of Huby, Sutton, aged 22, spinster. [Sutton.]

Dec. 13. Thomas Suttell, of St. Mary Bishophill Senior, wine merchant, aged 46, bachelor, and Elizabeth Agar, of same, widow, aged 34. [St. Mary Bishophill Senior.]

Dec. 14. John Cade, of Bishop Burton, jockey, aged 25, bachelor, and Mary Wright, of St. Mary's Beverley, aged 20, spinster, daughter of Sarah Spenceley. [St. Mary's.]

Dec. 14. James Campbell, of Huddersfield, shop-keeper, aged 23, bachelor, and Hannah Noble, of same parish, aged 21, spinster. [Huddersfield.]

Dec. 14. Thomas Bellwood, of Whitby, saddler, aged 23, bachelor, and Rachael Clark, of same, spinster. [Whitby.]

1776. Dec. 14. Robert Thompson, of Whitby, joiner, aged 23, bachelor, and Elizabeth Bailey, of same, spinster, aged 17, daughter of Wm. Bailey. [Whitby.]

Dec. 14. Richard Tyas, of Rotherham, grocer, aged 21, bachelor, and Mary Whittaker, of Bolton-on-Deane, aged 21, spinster. [Bolton-on-Derne.]

Dec. 15. Thomas Holgate, of Hole House, Long Preston, aged 31, bachelor, and Mary Geldard, of Rathmell, Giggleswick, aged 27, spinster. [Long Preston.]

Dec. 15. John Burgon, of Wentworth, Wath, tailor, aged 30, bachelor, and Ann Smith, of Wentworth, aged 23, spinster. [Wath.]

Dec. 16. William Starnwhite, of Wakefield, husbandman, aged 25, bachelor, and Mary Wilkes, of Wakefield, aged 25, widow. [Wakefield.]

Dec. 16. George March, of Sutton, farmer, aged 30, bach., and Mary Gray, of same, aged 21, spinster. [Sutton.]

Dec. 16. William Baker, of Holy Trinity, Hull, aged 21, bachelor, and Ann Wood, of St. John's, Beverley, aged 22, spinster. [St. John's, Beverley.]

Dec. 16. Paul Jubb, of Micklebring, Braithwell, yeoman, aged 38, bachelor, and Rebekah Wright, of Wickersley, aged 26, spinster. [Wickersley.]

Dec. 16. Saml. Turner, of South Milford, Sherburn, farmer, aged 30, bachelor, and Ann Hibberd, of Ecclesfield, aged 26, spinster. [Ecclesfield.]

Dec. 17. Thomas Barker, of Rawcliff, Snaith, aged 35, widower, and Mary Airey, of Hatfield, aged 25, widow. [Hatfield.]

Dec. 17. Cham. Hadfield, of Doncaster, mercer, aged 25, bachelor, and Martha Knowles, of Pontefract, aged 25, spinster. [Doncaster.]

Dec. 17. William Highmore Forster, of Otley, fellmonger, aged 23, bachelor, and Isabella Guyer, of Storithes, Bolton, Skipton, aged 18, spinster, daughter of John Guyer.

Dec. 17. Soloman Robinson, of Ripon, clerk, aged 30, widower, and Elizabeth Bramley, of Bedale (Chester Dio.), aged 29, spinster. [Ripon.]

1776. Dec. 17. Edmund Slaughter, of St. Clement Danes, London, cheesemonger, aged 24, bachelor, and Susannah Keld, of Bishop Burton, aged 25, spinster. [Bishop Burton.]

Dec. 18. Robert Carr, of Tankersley, farmer, aged 30, widower, and Sarah Firth, of same, widow, aged 30. [Tankersley.]

Dec. 18. John Harrison, of Sheffield, coach-painter, aged 27, bachelor, and Margaret Whitehead, of Todwick, aged 27, spinster. [Todwick.]

Dec. 18. William Pape, of Sewerby, Bridlington, servant, aged 21, bachelor, and Ann Gourry, of Atwick, aged 26, spinster. [Atwick.]

Dec. 18. Thomas Stork, of Flamborough, fisherman, aged 25, bachelor, and Elizabeth Staveley, of same, aged 22, spinster. [Flambro'.]

Dec. 19. Thomas Elgie, of St. Leonard, New Malton, gent., aged 21, bachelor, and Cicely Hickes, of St. Martin's Micklegate, York, aged 21, spinster. [St. Martin's.]

Dec 19. Henry Robson, of Kirbymoorside, labourer, aged 29, bachelor, and Sarah Horsley, of Appleton, Lastingham, aged 22, spinster. [Kirbymoorside.]

Dec. 19. Wm. Clarkson, of Topcliffe, farmer, aged 24, bach., and Mary Pick, of same, aged 24, spinster. [Topcliffe.]

Dec. 19. James Flintoff, of Stokesley, yeoman, aged 30, bachelor, and Mary Metcalfe, of Kirby, aged 30, spinster. [Kirby.]

Dec. 19. John Bond, of Scarboro', mariner, aged 27, bach., and Ann Burton, of same, aged 27, spinster. [Scarbro']

Dec. 20. Will. Booth, of Warmfield, aged 23, bachelor, and Jane Goodair, of Wragby, aged 16, spinster, dau. of Jane Marshall. [Warmfield.]

Dec. 20. Thomas Kemp, of Leeds, painter, aged 25, bach., and Patience Bolland, of Morley, Batley, aged 25, spinster. [Leeds.]

Dec. 21. Matthew Johnson, of Whitby, mariner, aged 22, bachelor, and Jane Jackson, of same, aged 19, spinster, daughter of Elizabeth Jackson, widow. [Whitby.]

Dec. 21. Henry Atkinson, of Leeds, gent., aged 40, bachelor, and Katherine Brooke, of same, aged 25, spr. [Leeds.]

1776. Dec. 21. William Thompson, of Thorne, mariner, aged 40, widower, and Ann Cornet, of same, aged 34, spinster.
[Thorne.]

Dec. 21. Thomas Bradley, of Halifax, joiner, aged 24, bach., and Jane Appleyard, of Skircoat, Halifax, aged 23, spinster.
[Halifax.]

Dec. 21. Samuel Mell, of Holy Trinity, Hull, labourer, aged 23, bachelor, and Ann Ellerdice, of Hull, widow.
[Holy Trinity, Hull.]

Dec. 21. Christopher Craven, of Whitby, mariner, aged 31, bachelor, and Mary Barry, of same, aged 23, spinster.
[Whitby.]

Dec. 22. Samuel Lee, of Wakefield, farmer, aged 26, bach., and Susanna Rushworth, of Halifax, aged 26, spinster.
[Halifax.]

Dec. 22. Robert Nicholson, of Wakefield, aged 30, bachelor, and Mary Walker, of Crofton, aged 30, spinster.
[Crofton.]

Dec. 22. Richard Carr, of Harbottom, Kettlewell, aged 30, widower, and Mary Beckwith, of same, aged 30, spinster.
[Kettlewell.]

Dec. 23. Francis Sledge, of Stillingfleet, blacksmith, aged 23, bachelor, and Mary Slater, of same, widow, aged 38.
[Stillingfleet.]

Dec. 23. Richard Kay, of Doncaster, cordwainer, aged 25, bachelor, and Mary Goodinson, of Barmby Dunn, aged 25, spinster. [Barmby Dunn.]

Dec. 23. Michael Sever, of Emsall, Little Driffield, husbn., aged 26, bachelor, and Sarah Sugden, of Skerne, aged 25, spinster. [Skerne.]

Dec. 24. William Hawkswell, of Armley, Leeds, tailor, aged 30, bachelor, and Mary Kirkby, of same, spinster, aged 24.
[Leeds.]

Dec. 24. Thomas Wollin, of Shire Green, Ecclesfield, husbn., and Ann Lister, of Wincobank, aged 22, spinster.
[Ecclesfield.]

Dec. 24. Michael Pilmoor, of Lastingham, servant, aged 24, bachelor, and Elizabeth Leife, of Harom, Helmsley Blakamoor, aged 24, spinster. [Helmsley.]

SANDAL MAGNA PARISH REGISTERS.

The existing Parish Registers commence in 1652, but the Archbishop has Transcripts for the following years, and probably for several others between 1631 and 1642 :—1598, 1600, 1601, 1602, 1603, 1604, 1608, 1626, 1627, 1628, 1629, 1630, 1631.

1598 May 10 to 1599 April 24.

Thos. Warde and Susanna Wood, married 20 May.
Edward Robinson, son of Henry, bapt. 22 May.
Edward Robinson, the elder, buried 4 June.
Esay Pigergill, son of Thomas, bapt. 6 June.
Edward Robinson, son of Edward, buried 8 June.
John Goodyeare, son of John, bapt. 9 June.
Anne Medlay, daughter of Wm. M., junr., bapt. 14 June.
Wm. Oxelay, son of Richard, bapt. 3 July.
Wm. Sparke, son of Wm., buried 10 July.
John Robert, son of John, bapt. 31 July.
A child without name of Wm. Marshals, buried 6 August.
Edward Styance, son of Wm., bapt. 20 August.
Cuthbert Haighe, son of Rauphe, bapt. 27 August.
Thomas Lockewood and Margrett Scolaye, married 8 September.
Anthony Sunderland, son of Wm., bapt. 10 October.
Anthony Tayler, son of John, bapt. 20 November.
Luke Carter, buried 16 December.
Emott Tayler, buried 27 December.
Paull Browneld, son of Robert, bapt. 25 January.
Mary Oxelay, daughter of Robert, bapt. 26 January.
Elizabeth Poule, daughter of Xproffer, bapt. 26 February.
Josias Davison and Henry Davison, sons of Thomas, bapt. 26 Feb., beinge twynes.
Periwall More and Johan Hirst, widow, married 26 February.
Samuell Poule, son of Thomas, bapt. 6 March.
John Baull, son of Robert, bapt. 8 March.
John Gomersall, son of Richard, bapt. 12 March.

Henry Pruston, son of Thomas, bapt. 12 March.
William Kaye, son of John, bapt. 10 April.

Per me, Phillippum Leighe, *Vicarium.*
John Lambart, George Watson, Robert Carter } *Churchwardens.*
Thomas Williamson, John Waid, Robert Oxelaye

1600 Ladyday to 1601 Ladyday.

Richard Pruston, son of Richard, bapt. 29 March.
Thomas Johnson and Ane Wattertoun, married 6 April.
Suzana Pruston, daughter of Thomas, buried 10 April.
George Truelove and Alice Haighe, married 8 May.
Izabell Bery, buried 17 May.
Martha Dicconson, daughter of Wm., bapt. 29 May.
John Beatsoun, son of John, bapt. 11 June.
Richard Abbott and Beatrix Robinsoun, married 23 June.
Rose Watson, buried 13 July.
Thomas Raunslay, son of Thomas, bapt. 3 August.
Martha Oxelay, bapt. 8 August.
Elizabeth Browneld, daughter of George, bapt. 12 August.
Cornelius Senior, son of Brian, bapt. 16 August.
Jeffray Bordman and Elizth. Couldocke married 7 Sept.
Jeffray Haighe, son of Rauphe, bapt. 30 September.
Martha Wright, daughter of Robert, bapt. 9 October.
Faith Rooke, daughter of Francis, bapt. 16 October.
Richard Shawe and Jenett Carter, married 17 October.
Richard Boyne, son of Thomas, bapt. 18 December.
Beatrix Robinson, daughter of Thomas, bapt. 13 January.
Robert Browne and Anne Scholay, married 4 February.
Gervise Coward and Elizabeth Couper, married 6 February.
Anthony Arnold and Izabell Benkes, married 7 February.
Edmund Nelson, buried 9 February.
William Brooke, son of Wm., buried 16 February.
Henry Killingbecke and Anne Haighe, married 16 February.
Grace Pruston, ux. Thomas, buried 18 February.
Roger Allott, son of Roger, bapt. 24 February.
John Kay, son of Alice Kay and of the people, bapt. 10 March.

Francys Wood, Briann Senior, Thomas Wright } *Churchwardens.*
Wm. Browneld, Richard Arnold, Robert Bratton

1601.

Thomas Hall, buried 6 April.
Robert Haukett and Izabell Hirst, married 10 May.
Edward Wayd, son of John, bapt. 6 June.
Vidua Wayd, buried 17 July.
A child without name of Wm. Arundell, buried 10 August.
Thomas Longlay and Elizabeth Hall, married 8 August.
Rauphe Ball, son of Robert, bapt. 8 September.
Faith Stiance, bapt. 12 October.
John Hitchon and Izabell Couper, married 18 October.
Henry Smythe and Mercy Norton, married 17 October.
Wm. Bynnes and Elizabeth Norton, married 18 October.
Elizabeth Clarke, buried 2 January.
Anthony Tayler, son of John, bapt. 7 February.
Thomas Arnold, son of Anthony, bapt. 6 March.
Henry Burdett, buried 7 March.
Agnes Thornton, buried 8 March.
Wm. Stringer, buried 10 March.
Richard Read, son of Wm., bapt. 12 March.
Wm. Davison, son of Thomas, bapt. 13 March.
John Nelson, buried 17 March.
Izabell Wright, daughter of Thomas, bapt. 6 March.
Frauncys Blacker, buried 16 March.
Jane Thompson, daughter of John, bapt. 13 March.
Rebecca Blacker, buried 20 March.
George Norton, son of Anthony, bapt. 8 April, 1602.
John Johnson, buried 10 March.
Thomas Radcliff, buried 31 March, 1602.

> William Baxter, John Sykes, Robert Johnsonn } *Churchwardens.*
> Thos. Bayne, Thos. Lockewood, Henry Mooke }

1602.

George Norton, son of Anthony, bapt. 8 April.
Alice Leache, daughter of Thomas, bapt. 2 May.
Ane Arnold, buried 4 May.
Richard Dishfurth and Alice Arundell, married 9 May.
Thomas Fell, buried 9 May.
George Pearson, buried 12 May.

George Stringer, buried 13 May.
Suzanna Browneld, daughter of Robert, bapt. 16 May.
John Hitchon, buried 20 May.
Thomas Bilcliffe, buried 29 May.
Edward Bordman, son of Geffray, bapt. 30 May.
Thomas Ure, buried 2 June.
Edward Allott, son of Edward, bapt. 4 June.
Thomas Sprigonell, buried 8 June.
Johannett Fletchar, buried 16 June.
Margret Tayler, buried 5 July.
Beatrix Copplay, ux. Richard, buried 20 September.
Izabell Bywater, buried 22 October.
John Clarke, buried 3 November.
Richard Pruston, buried 26 October.
Thomas Leake and Dyonese Ure, married 28 October.
Christ. Roboucke, buried 6 November.
Mathewe Newton and Xprabell Scholeye, married 8 November.
George Downes and Agnes Hawkesworth, married 16 November.
Margery Burdett, buried 18 November.
John Cutlar, buried 7 January.
David Parker and Elizabeth Brooke, married 17 January.
Elizabeth Haigh, daughter of Rauphe, bapt. 6 February.
Johannett Haighe, buried 20 February.
Thomas Copplay, buried 6 March.
Samuell Pruston, son of Richard, bapt. 7 March.
Richard Jewett, son of Robert, bapt. 7 March.
Elizabeth Sprigonell, buried 8 April, 1603.
Elizabeth Dishfurth, buried 10 April.
Izabell Hitchon, bapt. 12 April.
Agnes Watson, buried 16 April.

1603.

Edward Allott, son of Edward, bapt. 24 April.
John Burnand and Elizabeth Pruston, married 28 April.
Edward Robinson and Beatrix Thornton, married 6 May.
Thomas Walker, buried 10 June.
John Bedfford and Anne Ingle, married 20 August.
John Kay and Izabell Bradffeld, married 30 August.

Margret Leighe, buried 10 September.
Josephe Oxelay, bapt. 20 October.
Dyonese Thompson, buried 20 October.
Roger Bettsonn and Anne Dey, married 20 November.
Richard Robinson, son of Thomas, bapt. 10 December.
Elizabeth Ashburne, bapt. 8 January.
Robert Webster and Elixabeth Bouth, married 28 February.
Henry Beamonde, son of Richard, bapt. last of February.
Henry Amer and Elizabeth A., children of Thomas, bapt. 2 March.
Izabell Oxelay, buried 4 March.
Thomas Raunselay, buried 8 March.
Henry Goodyeare, bapt. 8 March.
John Wightman and Izabell Hitchon, married 9 March.
Frances Watterton, daughter of Thomas, bapt. 4 February.
Suzanna Rooe, daughter of John, bapt. 24 February.
John Scholey, son of Richard, bapt. 6 March.
Wm. Battes and Jane Slater, married 26 February.
Dorathie Wayd, daughter of John, bapt. 16 April, 1604.
John Bacon and Dorathie Shawe, married 22 April, 1604.

   Per me, Philippum Leighe, *vicarium ibidem*.

1604.

Wm. Pearson, buried 27 March.
John Wood and Agnes Bouth, married 30 April.
Georye Scholey and Susannah Bolland, married 4 May.
William Lee, bapt. 10 May.
Robert Webster, son of Robert, bapt. 17 May.
John Brokebanncke and Frances Beamond, married 27 May.
Elizabeth Webster, buried 8 June.
Luke Bretton and Mary Pullan, married 18 June.
George Pearson, buried 6 July.
William Carter, son of Robert, bapt. 10 July.
Johannett Beamond, buried 24 August.
Francis Brokebannke, buried 2 September.
Elizabeth Poolle, ux. William, buried same day.
William Bines, son of William, bapt. 4 August.
Thomas Norton, son of Anthony, bapt. 6 August.
Thomas Arundell, buried 8 August.

Robert Townend, buried 10 August.
Francis Sourby and Mary Poule, married 11 August.
William Oxley and Margret Blacker, married 12 August.
Margret Dishworth, buried 13 August.
Mary Robinson, buried 20 September.
Ane Wayd, buried 20 September.
Robert Jowett, buried 22 September.
Richard Shay, buried 23 September.
Two children of Robert Tayler, buried 25 September.
Alex. Remington, buried same day.
Elizabeth Allott, bapt. 26 September.
Thomas Poole, buried same day.
Roger Poole, buried 28 September.
Thomas Norton, buried 29 September.
A child of said Thomas, buried last of September.
Uxon Willan, buried 2 October.
Thomas Robucke, buried 6 October.
George Norton, buried 15 October.
Dorathie Leach, bapt. 16 October.
Elizabeth Watson, bapt. 16 October.
Richard More and Margret Hirst, married 18 October.
Izabell Wightman, buried 20 October.
Adam Burdett, buried 21 October.
Emor Burdett, buried 23 October.
Alice Kay, buried 24 October.
Suzanna Burdet, buried 25 October.
Izabell Couper, buried 26 October.
Izabell Baron and William Lee, buried 27 October.
John Locke[s]ley, buried 27 October.
Margret Robucke, buried 2 November.
Edmund Garffurth a child of his and a child of Thomas Winkes, buried 10 November.
Margret Burdett, buried 12 November.
Margret Rooe, buried 13 November.
Gervis Wightman, buried 13 November.
Elizabeth Fozard, buried 15 November.
Rauphe and Thomas Fozard, buried 18 November.
Rauphe Stringer, buried 20 November.
Thomas Thornton and Isabell Wilkinson, married 25 November.

Izabell Watt, buried 27 November.
Anthony Noton.
William Blagburne, buried 1 January.
Richard Stringer and Mary Arnold, married 26 January.
John Burnand, bapt. 20 February.
Beatrix Steavenson, bapt. 7 February.
Benjamin Goodyeare, bapt. 23 February.
Elizabeth Walker, daughter of Mathewe, bapt. 9 March.
Josephe Lister, son of Richard, bapt. 25 March.
Edmund Hutchenson and Jane Lee, married 7 April, 1605.
Josephe Oxelay, son of Richard, bapt. 7 April.
Richard Grise, son of Henry, esq., bapt. 6 April.
Gervis Newton, bapt. 9 April.
Robert Browneld, buried 8 April.

   Per me, Philippum Leighe, *Vicarium*.

 Rauphe Oxelay, Richard Norton, Robert Wright } *Churchwardens*.
 David Parker, Thomas Bouth, Francis Grene }

1608.

Mary Waterton, daughter of Thomas W., esq., bapt. 18 Feb., 1607.
Vidna Boythroyd, buried 26 February.
Edward Gryce, bapt. 16 March.
Edyth Lister, daughter of Richard, bapt. 22 March.
William Lockwood and Suzanna Poule, married 6 April, 1608.
James Micklethwayte and Izabell Kaye, married 28 April.
Elizabeth Clayton, daughter of Daniell, bapt. 6 May.
Dorathye Clayton, ux. Daniell, buried 15 May.
Robert Towler and Elizabeth Austen, married 22 May.
Richard Dickson, buried 26 June.
Elizabeth Roger, buried 31 July.
Robert Beisbye and Alice Barber, married 6 August.
Michaell Fysher and Helen Burdett, married 14 August.
Anne Norton, daughter of Richard, bapt. 18 August.
Samuell Tompson, bapt. 22 August.
James Roboucke, buried 20 September.
Jane Boyne, bapt. 26 September.
Rauphe Smythe, bapt. 30 September.
Anthony Stringer, bapt. 5 October.

Steaven Townend and Johannett Shawe, married 12 October.
Thomas Davison, son of Thomas, bapt. 15 October.
Robert Jubb and Anne Lollye, married 23 October.
William Waud, son of John, bapt. 28 November.
Samuell Oxelay, son of Rauphe, buried 30 November.
John Rogers and Sarah Pell, married 29 November.
Francis Poule and Dorathy Chrawshey, married 3 December.
Samuell Lockwood, son of William, bapt. 20 January.
Thomas Steavenson, son of Richard, bapt. 21 January.
John Nelson and Alice Crawsheye, married 15 February.
Elizabeth Norton, ux. Richard, buried 25 February.
Edward Arnold and Alice Poolle, married 27 February.
Samuell Oxelay, son of William, bapt. 28 March, 1609.
Richard Roger, buried 16 April.
Elizabethe Hanson, bapt. 30 April.
Judith Blacker, daughter of George, bapt. 1 May.

1626. (no dates.)

Mary, daughter of John Smithe, bapt.
Elizabeth, daughter of Jos. .... bapt.
Mary, daughter of George Ff.........d, bapt.
Hester, daughter of Ffrancis Bla[cke]r, bapt.
John Spence and Ellen Austwicke, married.
Anthony, son of Anthony Hirst, bapt.
Francis Armitage, buried.
William Senior and Elizabeth Benkes, married.
Mary, daughter of William Lambert, bapt.
Robert Cooke, buried.
Isabell, daughter of Peter Kay, buried.
Lionell Raynor and Elizabeth Walker, married.
Anne, daughter of William Barber, bapt.
William Stringer, buried.
John, son of John Oxeley, bapt.
Thomas, son of Gervase Hirst, buried.
Mary, daughter of William Preestley, bapt.
John Hill and Frances Oxeley, married.
Thomas, son of William Savage, bapt.
Mary, daughter of Robert Dickenson, bapt.
Thomas Robinson and Mary Scorer, married.

Susannathe, daughter of Thomas Pollard, bapt.
Isabell, daughter of Peter Kay, bapt.   Ralphe Haigh, buried.
Anne, daughter of John Clarke, bapt.
Elizabeth, daughter of William Sikes, bapt.
Mary, daughter of Francis Taylor, bapt.
Susanna, daughter of John Hill, bapt.
Elizabeth, daughter of Richard Preston, bapt.
Rebeccah, daughter of George Flower, bapt.
Robert Smith and Mary Tine, married.
Isabell, daughter of Richard Bedford, bapt.
John Jawett, buried.
William Taylor and Jane Cratchley, married.
Robert, son of Phillip Lee, bapt.
Martin, son of Edward Arnold, bapt.
Gervase Hanson and Anne Audeslay, married.
Robert Pearson, buried.
William, son of John Pollard, bapt.
Widdowe Hinchcliffe, buried.
William, son of John Pollard, buried.
Anne, daughter of Thomas White, bapt.
Mary, daughter of Michaell Oates, bapt.
Widdowe Lambert, buried.
Widdowe Thomson, buried.
Francis, son of Richard Jepson, bapt.
Richard, son of Gervase Norton, buried.
Widdowe Pearson, buried.   Richard Arnold, buried.
Thomas, son of Thomas Norton, bapt.   Arthure Lee, buried.
John, son of William Dobson, bapt.
John, son of John Speche, bapt.
Elizabeth, daughter of Edward Johnson, bapt.
Anne, daughter of Thomas Norton, bapt.
Sybell, daughter of Brian Barbar, bapt.
Alice, daughter of Thomas Waterton, buried.
Anne, daughter of Thomas Billcliffe, bapt.
Jennet, ux. John Pollard, buried.
Anne, daughter of Francis Norfolke, buried.

John Stocke, *Vicar*.

Thomas Bryce, Anthony Arnoll, John Lee, *Churchwardens*.

Date.	Name.	Residence.	Document.	Reference.
1610	Fawcett, Leonard.	Easthauxwell.	I.A.	—
1557	,, Martin.	Aysgarth.	W.I.	—
1583	,, Miles.	Nidd.	W.I.	F. 131.
1606	,, Nicholas.	Rocliffe.	I.A.	—
1554	,, Ninian.	Kidstones.	W.I.	—
1560	,, Richard.	Gayle.	W.I.	—
1562	,, Robert.	Sedbergh.	W.I.	—
1537	,, Thomas.	Dent.‡	W.	+ 142.
1556	,, ,,	Haulbanke.	W.	—
1557	,, ,,	Bishopdale.	W.I.	—
1598	,, William.	Birtell.	W.I.	—
	Feilden, see Fielden.			
1562-3	Fell, Brian.	Penington.*	W.I.	—
1478	,, Richard.	,, *	W.	+ 24.
1542	,, Leonard.	Ulverston.*	W.I.	—
1602	Fellowes, William.	Easby.	W.	—
1580	Fernam. Richard.	Thornton Wallis.	W.I.	—
1573	Feriman, Thomas.	Whixley.	W.I.	—
1590	Fetham, George.	Dalton.	W.I.	—
1573	,, John.	Melsambe.	A.	D. 3.
1592	,, Thomas.	Aldbrough.	W.I.	—
1541	Fetherstonhaw, John.	Hornby.	W.	+ 206.
1553	Fielden (Feilden), Robert, clerk.	Garstang.	W.	C. 21.
1604	Fidler, Francis.	East Witton.	W.I.	—
1535	,, John.	,,	W.	+ 135.
1575	Firby, Anne.	Cartrop.	W.	—
1582	,, Jennett.	Burneston.	W.I.	—
1558	,, John.	,,	W.I.	—
1573	,, Laurence.	Chaythopp.	W.	—
1606	,, Robert.	Burneston.	W.I.	—
1558	,, John.	,,	W.I.	—
1553	Finch, John.	Wensley.	I.	—
1556	Firbank, Christopher.	Disforth.	W.I.	—
1591	,, ,,	Sutton.	W.I.†	—
1564	,, Helen.	Disforth.	W.I.	B. 6.
1601	,, Edmond.	Melsonby.	A.I.	—

* In Furness. † Also a libel seven years later. ‡ In Lonsdale.

F

Date.	Name.	Residence.	Document.	Reference
1538	Firbank, James.	Kirklington.	W.	+ 163.
1573	,, John.	Melsonby.	W.I.	D. 42.
1552	Fishborne, William.	Eppleby.	W.I.	C. 5.
1583	Fishwick, John.	Gosnargh.*	W.	—
1557	Fishe, George, clerk.	Vicar of Kirkby-on-Moors.		C. 50.
1564	Fisher, Edward.	Kendall.	W.	—
1582	,, Edward.	Bilton.	A.	F. 115.
1577	,, Elizabeth.	Disforth.	A.I.	F. 56.
1552	,, John.	Mawnby.	W.I.	C. 10.
1560	,, Thomas.	Cockeram.*	W.I.	—
1558	,, John.	Hutton Conyers.	W.I.	—
1576	,, Richard.	Newby Wisk.	W.I.	D. 117.
1587	,, Robert.	Snape.	W.I.	—
1575	,, William.	Disforth.	W.	—
1598	,, ,,	Manby.	W.I.	—
1477‡	Fitzrandolph, Thos. esq.	Pikall.	W.	+ 24.
1602	Fitling, Roger.	Whixley.	W.I.	—
1573	Fleming, Roger.	Burneston.	W.	—
1602	Fletcher, Edmund.	Burton Leonard.	W.I.	—
1553	,, William.	Usborne Magna.	W.I.	—
1576	Fletham, Margaret.	Knaresborough.	A.	—
	Flint, see Flynt.			
1557	Flour, John.	East Cowton.	W.	C. 46.
1544	Flynt, Christopher.	Whyxley.	W.I.	—
1571	,, Edmund.	,,	W.I.	—
1556	,, Edward.	Farnham.	W.	—
1610	,, ,,	Knaresbro'.	W.I.	—
1583	,, Henry.	Asenby.	A.I.	F. 130.
1566	,, Janet.	Marton.	W.I.	B. 23.
1570	,, John.	,,	W.I.	—
1576	,, ,,	Whyxley.	W.I.	—
1554	,, Margaret.	,,	W.	—
1608	,, ,,	Pontsbury.	I.A.	—
1606	,, Richard.	Rockliffe.	A.I.	—
1605	,, Robert.	Burrobridge.	I.	—
1573	,, Thomas.	Aldborough.	W.I.	B. 93.

* Co. Lancaster. ‡ Will of Sir Ralph Fyz-Randall, Kt., 1457 (to be buried at Spenythorne), printed *Surtees So.* for 1853, and in Clarkson's Richmond Appx., xxxii., p. c.

Date.	Name.	Residence.	Document.	Reference.
1607	Flynt, Thomas.	Farnham.	A.I.	—
1534	,, William.	Whixley.	W.	+ 141.
1597	Foggathwaite, John.	Ravensworth.	W.I.	—
1561	Forde, John.	Cundall.	W.I.	—
1568	Ford, John.	,,	A.	—
1587	,, Thomas.	,,	W.I.	—
1598	,, William.	,,	W.	—
1599	Forest, George.	East Witton.	W.	—
1571	,, Richard.	Osborne.	W.I.	—
1531	,, Thomas.	Brignall.	W.	+ 91.
1584	Fosse, Ralph.	Laborne.	W.	—
1574	Foster, Brian.	Gilling.	W.I.	D. 66.
1574	,, Christopher.	Ravensworth.	W.	D. 56.
1574	,, James.	[No place]	A.	D. 63.
1560	,, John, gent.	Laborne.	W.	—
1594	,, John.	Hutton Conyers.	W.I.	—
1541	,, Lancelot.	Topcliffe.	W.I.	—
1605	,, Margarie.	Forcet.	W.I.	—
1600	,, Nicholas.	Little Fencoat.	I.	—
1603	,, ,,	West Scrafton.	W.	—
1605	,, Sir Rawfe.*	Richmond.	W.	+ 61.
1559	,, Richard.	Ainderby.	W.I.	—
1544	,, Robert.	Ravensworth.	W.I.	—
1560	,, ,,	,,	W.I.	—
1471	,, William.	Exilby.	W.	+ 21.
1537	,, ,,	,,	W.	+ 150.
1574	,, ,,	[No place]	A.	D. 63.
1586	,, ,,	Gamarskell.	W.I.	—
1609	,, ,,	,,	W.I.	—
1593	Fothergill, Lawrence.	Bedale.	W.I.	—
1575	,, Matthew.	Grinton.	W.I.	D. 104.
1563	,, Vincent.	Barforth.	W.	C. 103.
1610	Fox, Anthony.	Milling.†	W.	—
1535	,, Christopher.	Kendal.	W.	+ 132.
1610	,, Richard.	London.	A.I.	—
1563	,, Robert.	Cockeram.†	W.I.	—
1546	Foxton, John.	Richmond.	W.I.	—

* Chantry Priest of St. Thomas of Canterbury.   † In co. Lancaster.

Date.	Name.	Residence.	Document.	Reference.
1602	Franck, Ann.	Disforth.	W.I.	—
1580	,, Alice.	Kneton.	W.I.	—
1608	,, George, esq.	,,	W.I.	—
1531	,, Henry.	Tanfield.	W.B.	+ 78.
1593	,, ,, esq.	Kneeton.	A.	—
1563	,, John.	Middleton Tyas.	W.I.	C. 106.
1563	Frank, Marmaduke.	Kneeton.	A.	C. 102.
1584	,, William.	[No place]	Account	—
1525	Frankland, Alyson.	Little St. Peter, York.	W.	—
1529	Freman, Thomas.	Farnham.	W.	+ 95.
1570	,, ,,	,,	W.I.	B. 53.
1577	Frere, Brian.	Bishopdale.	W.I.	D. 126.
1573	,, George.	Patrick Brompton.*	W.I.	D. 48.
1610	,, ,,	Bishopdale.	W.I.	—
1543	,, Henry.	Barningham.	W.I.	—
1589	,, Isabel.	Eryholme.	W.I.	—
1573	,, James.	Barningham.	W.	D. 30.
1575	,, ,,	Eryholme.	B.	D. 72.
1597	,, John.	Melbecks.	W.I.	—
1596	,, ,,	Law Rowe.	W.I.	—
1601	,, ,,	Hypiswell.	W.	—
1559	,, Margaret.	Caterick.	W.I.	—
1591	,, als. Thomson, Mary.	Marrick.	W.	—
1557	,, Michael.	Newhouse.	W.I.	—
1557	,, Richard.	Whixley.	W.	—
1572	,, ,,	Usborne.	W.	—
1583	,, Robert.	Barningham.	W.I.	—
1605	Fridgeley, Humfrey.	Snape.	W.I.	—
1576	Frogg, Richard.	W. Tanfield.	W.I.	—
1580	Fuesdale, Brian.	K. Hamerton.	W.I.	—
1580	,, Elizabeth.	,,	P.	—
1599	,, John.	Burton Leonard.	W.I.	—
1568	,, Richard.	Grenehamerton.	W.I.	B. 37.
1541	Fultrop, Alice.	Caterick.	W.	+ 198.
1531	,, Christopher, esq.	,,	W.	+ 73.
1566	,, Jane.	Hipwell.	W.I.	—
1574?	,, John, esq.	,,	W.	—

* Also of Eryholme.

Date.	Name.	Residence.	Document.	Reference.
1577	Fultrop, Simon.	Longmores.	W.	D. 128.
1558	Furnes, Robert.	Hunburton.	W.I.	—
1589	Galloway, Cicilie.	Bellerbie.	W.I.	—
1582	,, Raulph.	Helay.	W.I.	—
1539	Ganfurth, Agnes.	Topclif.	W.	+ 164.
1536	Garbere, John.	Richmond.	W.	+ 145.
1537	Gardener, Nichs., gent.	Tatham.	W.	+ 142.
1609	Gargrave, Lucy.	Fingall.	W.I.	—
1536	Gargill, John.	Richmond.	W.	+ 128.
1577	Garlick, Stephen.	Knaresbro'.	A.	F. 46.
1560-70	,, William.	Pulton.*	W.I.	—
1593	Garnet, John.	K. Ravensworth.	W.	—
1557	,, Margery.	Ravensworth.	W.	C. 57.
1591	Garsdell (Garstell), Brian.	Romaldkirk.	W.I.	—
1575	,, Lawrence.	Fremyngton.	A.	D. 95.
1603	,, Margaret.	Romaldkirk.	W.I.	—
1575	,, Nicholas.	,,	A.	D 106-8.
	Garstell, *see* Garsdell.			
1547	Garthe, John.	Estlaton.	W.	—
1553	,, ,,	Startforth.	W.	—
1595	,, ,,	Estlaton.	W.I.	—
1601	Garthwaite, Robert.	Hipswell.	W.I.	—
1605	Gascoigne, Jane.	Sedbury.	W.I.	—
1475	,, Margaret.	Nonmonkton.	W.	+ 16.
1603	,, Richard, esq.	Sedbury.	W.	—
1560	Gaskell, Edward.	———†	W.I.	—
1587	Gawthrope, Elizabeth.	Askrigg.	W.I.	—
1561	,, Richard.	Knaresboro'.	W.I.	—
1557	Gayle, Isabell.	Gatenby.	W.I.	C. 49.
1558	,, Isabell.	Ainderby.	W.I.	—
1562-6	,, Janet.	Burneston.	W.I.	—
1552	,, John.	,,	W.	—
1565	,, Lancelot.	Scroton.	W.I.	—
1571	,, Leonard.	Burneston.	W.I.	—
1609	,, Ninian.	Scruton.	W.I.	—
1576	,, Rauf.	,,	W.I.	—

* Co. Lancaster.   † No place given but (?) co. Lancaster.

Date.	Name.	Residence.	Document.	Reference.
1587	Gayle, Rychard.	Burneston.	W.I.	—
1530	,, William.	,,	W.	+ 75.
1557	,, ,,	Scruton.	W.	C. 41.
1602	Gaynes, Jean.	Richmond.	W.	—
1565	,, Robert.	P. Brompton.	W.I.	—
	Gaynforth, see Ganfurth.			
1595	Gaytell, Jacob.	Usburne.	W.I.	—
1553	,, Robert.	,,	W.I.	—
1555	Gaytynby, als.			
	Thomson, John.	Bedale.	W.	—
1610	,, John.	Exilby.	W.I.	—
1593	,, Robert.	Snape.	W.	—
1536	,, William.	Burneston.	W.	+ 140.
1558	,, ,, gent.	Gatenby.	W.	—
1572	,, ,,	Kirklington.	W.	—
1579	Gaytord (Gatard), Mich.	Thrintoft.	W.I.	—
1586	,, (Gaytherd), Robt.	Diderston Grange.	W.I.T.	—
1558	,, (Gaterd), Wm.	Melsamby.	W.I.	C. 73.
1601	Geldert, Agnes.	Watlass.	W.I.	—
1582	,, Anthony.	,,	W.I.	—
1558	,, James.	,,	W.I.	—
1583	,, ,,	West Scrafton.	W.I.	—
1597	,, John.	Carleton.	W.I.	—
1602	,, ,,	Burrell.	W.I.	—
1607	,, Lionel.	West Bolton.	W.I.	—
1564	,, Richard.	Coverham.	W.I.	—
1565	,, Thomas.	,,	W.I.	—
1541	Gennyng, George.	Knaresbro'.	W.	—
1578	Gibbon, Henry.	Whashton.	W.	D. 141.
1577	,, William.	Uckerbie.	A.	D. 137.
1548	Gibson, Alison.	Cliffe.	W.I.	—
1574	,, George.	Eplebie.	W.I.	D. 70.
1578	,, Henry.	K. Ravensworth.	W.I.	—
1603	,, James.	Richmond.	W.I.	—
1597	,, Janett.	,,	W.	—
1480	,, Sir John.	Chap. of S. Oswald.	W.	+ 29.
1592	,, John.	Tunstall.	W.I.	—
1595	,, Mary.	Richmond.	W.I.	—

Date.	Name.	Residence.	Document.	Reference.
1554	Gibson, Richard.	Ingleton.	W.	—
1576	,, ,,	Romaldkirk.	W.	D. 113.
1542	,, Robert.	Kirkby Lonsdale.	W.	+ 207.
1540	,, ,,	,,	W.	+ 207.
1541	,, Robert.	Copgrave.	W.	+ 183.
1566	,, Sir Robert.	Rector of Staveley.	W.I.	B. 28.
1558	,, Stephen.	Usborne.	W.I.	—
1579	,, Thomas.	Burton Leonard.	W.	—
1600	,, † ,,	Aldbrough.	W.I.	—
1585	Gilbertson, Richard.	Rocliffe.	W.	—
1575	Gill, Annes.	West Tanfeld.	W.I.	—
1608	,, Christopher.	Canswick Park.	W.	—
1550	,, James.	Watlass.	W.I.	—
1601	,, Richard.	Bronton.	A.	—
1542	,, Annes.	Topcliffe.	W.I.	—
1541	Gilling, Thomas.	Rocliff or Topcliffe.	W.I.	—
1529	Gilpin, Ewan.	?Kendal.	W.	+ 63.
1541	Girlington, Henry, esq.	Wycliff.	W.	+ 184.
1587	,, Nicholas, esq.	Hackforth.	W.	—
1475	Girsington, William.	Wathe.	W.	+ 13.
1578	Goldesborough, Geo.	Goldisborough.	W.I.	—
1581	,, Helen.	,,	I.	F. 110.
1566	,, Thomas, esq.	,,	W.	B. 26.
1562	Goose, Henry.	Corney.‡	W.I.	—
1599	,, John.	Sawicke.*	W.	—
1587	Gouldthwait, Agnes.	Goldthwayt.	W.I.	—
1567	Gower, Rauf, esq.	——	W.I.	—
1593	Gowerley (Gorlay), Wm.	Wensley.	W.I.	—
1551	Gowland (Golland), John.	Melbie.	W.I.	—
1583	,, John.	,,	W.I.	—
1559	,, Rawf.	Langthorp.	W.I.	—
1558	,, William.	Burton.	W.I.	—
1539	Gowthwhat, Robert.	Monkton.	W.	+ 175.
1558	Grange, William.	Smeton.	W.	C. 74.
1586	Grante, Thomas.	Synderby.	W.I.	—
1596	,, William.	Roxby.	W.	—
1607	Graues, William.	Knaresboro'.	W.I.	—

* Co. Lancaster.   † Possibly Gilson.   ‡ ? Co. Cumberland.

Date.	Name.	Residence.	Document.	Reference.
1582	Gray, Oswald.	Wilstropp.	W.	F. 113.
1558	,, Patrick.	Monkton.	W.	—
1576	,, William, clk.	Vicar of Kirkby.	W.I.	—
1549	Grayson, John.	Caterick.	W.	—
1578	Grayson, Margaret.	Brearton.	A.	—
1560	,, Thomas.	Gilling.	W.	—
1582	,, ,,	Monkton.	W.I.	—
1588	,, William.	Melmerby.	W.	—
1598	,, ,,	Gilling.	A.	—
1561	Graystock, Thomas.	Garstang.*	W.	—
1579	Greathead, Agnes.	Hipswell.	W.I.	—
1564	,, Connaunde.	Bedale.	W.	—
1541	,, George.	Richmond.	W.	+ 206.
1582	,, als. Bower, Jas.	Hipswell.	W.I.	—
1559	,, John.	Brompton-on-Swale.	W.I.	—
1566	,, ,,	Caterick.	W.I.	—
1599	,, Marmaduke.	Richmond.	W.	—
1610	,, Robert.	Easthauxwell.	W.I.	—
1566	,, Thomas.	Scotton.	W.I.	—
1594	Gregge, Jenet.	Knaresborough.	W.I.	—
1577	Gregret, Richard.	Cleasby.	A.	D. 126.
1573	Gregson, Janet.	Preston.*	W.	—
1592	,, Richard.	Staneley.	W.I.	—
1540	,, Thomas.	Plompton.	W.	+ 180.
1561	Grenall, John.	Gosenarghe.*	W.I.	—
1564	Grenburie, Wm.	Anderby.	W.I.	—
1558	Grene, Henry, esq.	Newbie.	W.	C. 63.
1540-50	,, John.	Knaresbro'.	I.	—
1557	,, ,,	Marske.	W.I.	C. 58.
1564	,, ,,	Danby.	W.I.	C. 114.
1597	,, ,,	Richmond.	W.I.	—
1563	,, William.	Alston in Ribchester.*	W.	—
1569	Grindall, Robert.	S. Bees.	W.	—
1606	Gristhawite, Elizth.	Woodhall.	W.I.	—
1558	,, James.	Skebye.	W.	C. 68.
1574	,, John.	—	I.	—
1581	,, ,,	Askrig.	W.	—

* In co. Lancaster.

www.ingramcontent.com/pod-product-compliance
Lightning Source LLC
Chambersburg PA
CBHW020923230426
43666CB00008B/1547